CONFEDERATE OUTLAW

CONFLICTING WORLDS:
NEW DIMENSIONS OF THE AMERICAN CIVIL WAR
T. Michael Parrish, Series Editor

CONFEDERATE OUTLAW

CHAMP FERGUSON AND THE CIVIL WAR IN APPALACHIA

BRIAN D. McKNIGHT

Louisiana State University Press
Baton Rouge

Published by Louisiana State University Press
lsupress.org

Louisiana Paperback Edition, 2022

DESIGNER: Michelle A. Neustrom
TYPEFACE: Minion Pro

COVER PHOTOGRAPH: Champ Ferguson with his guard, from Louis E. Springsteen Collection,
Bentley Historical Library, University of Michigan.

LIBRARY OF CONGRESS CATALOGING-IN-PUBLICATION DATA

McKnight, Brian Dallas.
    Confederate outlaw : Champ Ferguson and the Civil War in Appalachia / Brian D. McKnight.
        p. cm. — (Conflicting worlds : new dimensions of the American Civil War)
    Includes bibliographical references and index.
    ISBN 978-0-8071-3769-7 (cloth : alk. paper) — ISBN 978-0-8071-3770-3 (pdf) —
        ISBN 978-0-8071-3944-8 (epub) — ISBN 978-0-8071-7820-1 (paperback)
1. Ferguson, Champ, 1821–1865. 2. Guerrillas—Confederate States of America—Biography. 3. Outlaws—Confederate States of America—Biography. 4. Tennessee—History—Civil War, 1861–1865—
Underground movements. 5. Kentucky—History—Civil War, 1861–1865—Underground movements.
6. United States—History—Civil War, 1861–1865—Underground movements. I. Title.
    E470.45.F4M4 2011
    973.7'8—dc22
    [B]
                                                                                        2010038289

For Pam and Devin, my little family

The powerful exact what they can, and the weak grant what they must.
  —THUCYDIDES, *The History of the Peloponnesian War*

We must take sides. Neutrality helps the oppressor, never the victim.
  —ELIE WIESEL, *Night*

A very thin membrane separates the sanctioned rancor of war from sheer barbarism.
  —RICK ATKINSON, *An Army at Dawn*

The guerrilla wins if he does not lose. The conventional army loses if it does not win.
  —HENRY KISSINGER

The guerrilla must move amongst the people as a fish swims in the sea.
  —MAO TSE-TUNG

CONTENTS

Illustrations follow page 106.

ACKNOWLEDGMENTS

When undertaking such a project as writing a book, one expects to incur many debts. This work has been no exception. Since I first started writing this book in the spring of 2003 and through its completion in the summer of 2005, I have met many fine people on my way to telling the story of Champ Ferguson. With their help, I have written what I hope will be a significant contribution to the study not only of one of the Confederacy's most infamous characters, but of the extremely violent side of the Civil War as it was irregularly prosecuted along what the South considered to be an international border.

Three major repositories hold much of the available material on Champ Ferguson. The Kentucky Library and Museum at Western Kentucky University possesses a transcript of the guerrilla's trial, which gave me a good start on the writing of the text; the National Archives in Washington D.C. holds the actual document, which differs minimally from the version at the Kentucky Library and Museum; and the Tennessee State Library and Archives (TSLA) has much of Military Governor Andrew Johnson's wartime correspondence. The staff at all three repositories contributed mightily to the completion of this project. Nancy Baird and Patricia Hodges deserve special mention as they worked tirelessly to make my stay as the Kentucky Library and Museum Fellow at Western Kentucky University both enjoyable and productive. The late Genella Olker of the TSLA spent most of one day excitedly helping me track down obscure references to Champ Ferguson and recounting stories of the Civil War as told to her by her parents and grandparents.

In addition to these major repositories and their staffs, it is important to thank those who clarified other, more isolated points and contributed their expertise to this project. Jack Masters of Gallatin, Tennessee, graciously provided a copy of the diary of John Weatherred; Charlie Heaberling invited me to use the collections at Lexington Theological Seminary; Jim Pritchard and Walter Bowman helped guide me through the Governor Beriah Magoffin Papers at the Kentucky Department for Libraries and Archives; Gary Robert Matthews of Lexington, Kentucky, sent more than one sheaf of copies to me; my old friend Derek Frisby of Middle Tennessee State University also sent along a few elusive and important sources; and Brandon Slone at the Kentucky Military History Museum provided access to that institution's collections. Staff of the Southern Historical Collection at the University of North Carolina at Chapel Hill, the Special Collections Library at the University of Tennessee, the Angelo and Jennette Volpe Library and Media Center at Tennessee Technological University in Cookeville, Tennessee, and the Texas State Library and Archives Commission in Austin, Texas, also worked very hard to make my research as fruitful as possible. One of the later tasks in preparing the manuscript was verifying the postwar whereabouts of Champ's wife and daughter. Phyllis Mills, a volunteer at the Independence, Kansas, Public Library, dug into various census, marriage, and death records to make sure that I had all the information necessary to accurately place Martha and Anne Ferguson after the war. Very late in the process of completing the manuscript, I found the J. D. Hale Papers at the Historical Society of Cheshire County, New Hampshire. Alan Rumrill, a Hale descendant and a dedicated historian in his own right, provided valuable assistance in researching and copying pertinent documents from that collection so that I could enhance this aspect of the study. Kim Marshall of the University of Virginia's College at Wise and Sharon Weber of Angelo State University happily gathered distant publications for my perusal.

The staff at the Louisiana State University Press must also be recognized. In particular, Rand Dotson provided unwavering support and encouragement for the project. Mike Parrish offered many important ideas and made a place for the book within his Civil War series. I am also bound to thank my personal editorial board. Bill Carter, a fine historian and great friend, read and reread every page of this manuscript, asking questions touching on everything from historical interpretation to syntax. It is unfortunate that he did not live to see any of the books that he helped shape into their final forms. My former professor and close friend Stanly Godbold still maintains a fervent interest in my work and me. His reading has always challenged me to interject more historical wisdom into my conclusions. Also, within my academic department at UVa-Wise, Brian Steel Wills and David Rouse both added significantly to the final product. Brian read the entire manuscript and pushed me to cast Ferguson in a broader light while David, a scholar of both philosophy and theology, answered my myriad questions about the Disciples of Christ and the denomination's role in the Second Great Awakening. Jim Humphreys, my old graduate school friend and UVa-Wise colleague, also read the manuscript and asked those difficult questions that invariably improve such projects.

When I finished the manuscript, I sought out Calvin Dickenson, Mike Birdwell, and Larry Whiteaker, all of Tennessee Technological University, to read the work. What these three men do not know about the history of the Upper Cumberland region is not worth knowing. All three read the manuscript and offered valuable suggestions for its improvement, often catching small geographic errors that someone not intimately familiar with the region would overlook. Thanks, gentlemen.

Outside of the office, I spend most of my time with my wife. When I travel to research, more often than not Pam is with me. She spends many of her days driving back roads, eating fast food, and reading magazines in libraries while I work in the collections. In return, she gets to see unique things such as tombstones, memorials, and obscure historic sites. I expect that over the coming years, I will have the honor of taking her on hundreds of other jaunts.

Friends Steve and Mary Drotos of Warrenton, Virginia, welcomed me on my many research trips to the Washington D.C. area. In addition, Steve's fascination with the Civil War drove us many hundreds of miles to visit battlefields and historical sites on days when I could not research. Our days at Gettysburg, Antietam, and Richmond's Hollywood Cemetery will remain with me forever. Such moments grow more valuable with the passage of time.

Finally, I must acknowledge my family's contributions to my work. My father is fascinated by history and looks forward to reading the words I write. My mother cares little for the subject, but much about me. With Pop's prodding, she may read this book. My brother Greg is as proud of me as I am of him. As I recall our childhood and youth, I conclude that no two brothers have ever had as much fun together. I expect we will spend the next several decades telling stories and laughing. Such is the nature of a family.

There is one final group to be recognized. Very often historians view teaching as the means to enjoying their hobby. In my years in the classroom, I have been fortunate to meet and know many fine students who have made the teaching aspect of the profession the most enjoyable. Folks like Brent Bailey, Matt Lawson, Sara Hurd, Sara Bailey, Amy Bugarski, Adam Malle, and Travis

Taylor have challenged me to be a good teacher. Jamie Jackson's asking me to create a course on guerrilla warfare during the Civil War forced me to look anew at many books and articles that had once been the staples of my reading, and as a result of this rereading, I found new facets of many of the central issues. I have been fortunate to teach so many fine students who graciously make me look better than I actually am. . . . To all of them, I say "thanks."

CONFEDERATE OUTLAW

INTRODUCTION

On August 12, 1858, Champ Ferguson visited a camp meeting in Fentress County, Tennessee. Whether it was coincidental or by design, several men with whom Ferguson and his Clinton County, Kentucky, neighbors had a financial dispute were also in attendance. When he noticed his adversaries together, Champ guessed that their discussion and angry glares involved him and he bolted from the gathering. Apparently, Ferguson's fear was justified, as the small band took off in pursuit. After a brief horse race, a close quarters fight broke out during which Champ killed a county constable. That day, at nearly thirty-seven years old, the rough-and-tumble farmer took his first life. Seven years later, with the United States wracked by civil war, Ferguson would find himself on trial in Nashville, Tennessee, for the murder of fifty-three persons amid rumors that he had killed dozens more during the war.[1]

Perhaps no other single participant in the Civil War could claim a bloodier career than Champ Ferguson. For a backwoodsman who, the historical record suggests, waited nearly forty years to kill a fellow human being, he grew quite accustomed to the idea during the four years of the war. What motivations pushed Ferguson toward the gallows in Nashville, Tennessee, in fall 1865? Was he a cold-blooded murderer, a product of his society, or a combination of the two? What role did the larger conflict of the Civil War play in Ferguson's development? Ultimately, what were the federal government's motivations in trying, convicting, and executing him? Despite the difficulty of examining a subject credited with such crimes, it is imperative that those interested in America's great drama address such demanding questions. While modern sensibilities may define the amount of sympathy that practitioners of guerrilla warfare receive, it is our duty to attempt to understand the nature of man, his society, his era, and how the combination of these factors shapes history.

1

As for Champ Ferguson, his complete lack of remorse exacerbates the diffi-culty of such an endeavor. He freely admitted killing more than forty men, and not only did Ferguson confess his culpability, he seemingly reveled in it.[2] Only moments before his execution, while he stood at the gallows and listened as the details of his convictions were read aloud, Ferguson callously commented about the specifics of one of the killings, "I can tell it better than that."[3] Indeed, he probably could. At a moment when timidity and repentance would be on the minds of most men, the border outlaw maintained an air of righteousness. He stood in front of the court "like a man who was about to make a speech on some leading topic."[4] For Champ Ferguson, the Civil War was personal. Just as generals and their armies fought in the great conflict, so did neighbors, brothers, and communities on a more localized level. Along the Kentucky-Tennessee border where Ferguson grew up and lived most of his life, the fight became fluid and partisan, turning men who had spent their lives as friends, neighbors, and even brothers into mortal enemies.

For Ferguson, the war was not an abstract political contest. It manifested as a daily struggle for survival against men who might come as friends, en-emies, or neutrals. During his four-year-long personal war, many pursued him, including his brother, Jim; his great adversary (and partisan in his own right) Tinker Dave Beatty; and the United States Army. With such varied (and frequently unknown) enemies, Champ, like most citizens of the mountain re-gion, grew fearful to the level of outright paranoia. For the average soldier, the rules of warfare frown upon killing sick men in their beds or unarmed minors, but to Champ Ferguson, those who were not admitted and acknowl-edged friends were dangerous enemies and subject to extermination at the earliest and most convenient opportunity. Ferguson described such actions as his taking "time by the forelock." Even President Abraham Lincoln appeared to understand the convoluted nature of partisan warfare when he wrote of a similar situation in Missouri:

> Once sincerity is questioned, and motives are assailed. Actual war coming, blood grows hot, and blood is spilled. Thought is forced from old chan-nels into confusion. Deception breeds and thrives. Confidence dies, and universal suspicion reigns. Each man feels an impulse to kill his neighbor lest he be first killed by him. Revenge and retaliation follow. And all this, as before said, may be among honest men only. But this is not all. Every foul bird comes abroad, and every dirty reptile rises up. These add crime

to confusion. Strong measures, deemed indispensable but harsh at best, such men make worse by mal-administration. Murders for old grudges, and murders for [s]elf, proceed under any cloak that will best cover for the ocasion.[5]

This very personal brand of warfare, filled with imminent threats and unknown enemies, made Ferguson, along with countless others throughout the border region, very paranoid.

A guerrilla war is also driven by opportunism. For Champ Ferguson, that opportunity came as a result of the patriotism exercised by the men of the Upper Cumberland region on both sides of the conflict. During the war, the region essentially emptied of men except for the very young, very old, and the very predatory. Ferguson and his ilk fell into the last category, and as J. D. Hale wrote, "he could roam about his old home in Clinton County, Ky" because "most of the young men . . . were in the Federal army, and a considerable force of confederates were ever in his immediate vacinity."[6] Ferguson and other guerrillas always understood the leveling effect of a local power vacuum.

When such trials and tribulations occur, religiosity grows, even among those who do not necessarily consider themselves spiritual people. Champ Ferguson was not a faithful, spiritual, or religious man, but he was a man who responded to a world in turmoil as many people do: by relying on his most basic knowledge. As an uneducated man likely devoid of real spiritual understanding, Champ fell back on the rudiments of spiritual education taught so freely during his childhood. He had grown up in southern Kentucky during the height of the Second Great Awakening and while he never offered much evidence of a personal faith, he certainly understood some basic Old Testament beliefs and lived his wartime life in accordance with these unbending rules. Life in the heavily divided and inherently dangerous region forced Ferguson to look at his world through a Manichean lens. To Champ, like the abolitionist John Brown or any variety of men throughout history who view the world in stark terms, questions and answers were clearly black and white, right or wrong, good or evil—there was no middle ground. Ferguson, however, acted not with large armies or sweeping political action, but with very personal and usually violent actions. In Ferguson's clearly divided mind, a friend would fight the good fight alongside him, and an enemy would be dealt with proactively before he could muster either strength or advantage.[7]

On its surface, the story of Champ Ferguson is an interesting tale of one man's Civil War experience; however, a deeper examination reveals much about the fluid war that wracked Appalachian Tennessee, Kentucky, and Virginia. During times of open warfare in those highly partisan regions, Ferguson excelled. Once the war began to wind down, however, he began to fail. Arrested in May 1865 for war crimes, Ferguson became a test case for the United States government in its attempt to exact revenge on a defeated enemy. Before Henry Wirz, infamous commandant of the Confederate prison at Andersonville, Georgia, would become popularly (and inaccurately) known as the only former Confederate to be executed for war crimes, America had Champ Ferguson. Just as Ferguson had taken "time by the forelock" numerous times on the Cumberland Plateau during the war, in the months that followed the end of the conflict, his enemies exacted their revenge in the same manner. They used the postwar political climate to their own advantage and vanquished their wartime enemy through legal means.

Fundamentally, Ferguson was a self-preservationist. He joined the war effort to save himself from prosecution, fought and killed in the hopes that a Confederate victory would guarantee his later freedom, and remained in the Cumberland region because it was the area he knew best and the environment that he could best exploit to his advantage. Ultimately, however, all of those things he did during the Civil War in his quest to save himself turned on him and ensured his demise. In a terrible miscalculation, Champ Ferguson's radical participation in the Civil War for the purpose of survival hastened his death rather than granted the salvation that he expected.

In the more than one hundred and forty years since the end of the Civil War, Ferguson and his legend have maintained some measure of timelessness. Numerous books, pamphlets, and articles have been written either condoning or condemning his lifestyle and manner of warfare. His story has even been translated into fictional works—sometimes unintentionally. Even during the heart of the conflict, while depredations were being committed, Ferguson's story gained national attention through the efforts of two unionists who carried on their own personal fights for the guerrilla's extermination.

Jonathan D. Hale of Overton County, Tennessee, spent the war opposing the man he felt to be the most dangerous threat to his own personal security and the progress of the broader conflict in upper-middle Tennessee. By the time hostilities broke out in 1861, Hale, who had moved south from New Hampshire several years before, had established himself as a successful businessman and a respected figure in the community. An outspoken opponent of secession, he became a marked man because of his pro-Union views. Finally overwhelmed by the fear of living among his enemies, Hale and his family loaded their things and left in the middle of the night for Champ Ferguson's former home of Albany, Kentucky, a community becoming known for its unabashed support of the Union cause. While in exile, Hale wrote several pamphlets which mainly focused on Ferguson's exploits.[8] With a pen as his preferred weapon, he helped direct Federal attention to what he considered his section's most pressing problem.

John A. Brents supplemented the pen with a sword in his fight against Ferguson. In late 1862, Brents, who had served as a major in the United States Army for several months in the early days of the war, wrote *The Patriots and Guerillas of East Tennessee and Kentucky.* His work, like that of Hale, sought to simplify the complexities of the Civil War as it was fought along the border by placing a considerable amount of blame on only a handful of perpetrators.[9] Although both men directed much of their attention toward Champ Ferguson, and rightly so in most cases, a significant portion of their stories cannot be considered reliable because of self-serving political motives and the use of rumor as a chief source.

Another major contemporary source came from the testimony offered at Ferguson's trial in Nashville, Tennessee, which stretched through two searing months of the summer of 1865. During those proceedings, numerous witnesses took the stand to tell stories of their dealings with the prisoner. Several major newspapers closely followed the daily activities of the court, with local organs publishing regular synopses of the testimony. A long stream of witnesses for the prosecution presented themselves and gave often gruesome testimony as to Ferguson's methods during the war. Interspersed were a few defense witnesses, including former Confederate General Joseph Wheeler, whose presence in Nashville angered many of the city's Federals. On the eve of his testimony, Wheeler received a personal taste of bitter vengeance when he was viciously attacked in his hotel room. Near the end of the trial, the defendant himself offered a relatively brief account in his own defense and granted a handful of interviews to newspapermen. Here too, as is the case in the works of Hale and Brents, little can be accepted at face value.

Since Ferguson's execution in October 1865, his legend has continued to grow. Unsubstantiated rumors that he cheated death competed with the growth of Lost Cause mythology to lift the guerrilla out of the obscurity of a local criminal and elevate him to a position of credit within the annals of the Southern cause. In 1942, Vanderbilt University Press published Thurman Sensing's *Champ Ferguson: Confederate Guerrilla.* Relying mainly on newspaper accounts of the trial, Sensing pieced together a complex life in a biography that remains in publication.[10]

The most recently published work on Ferguson came from Thomas D. Mays. In 1996, he wrote a doctoral dissertation eventually published in 2008 as *Cumberland Blood: Champ Ferguson's Civil War.* Mays's work seeks to understand Ferguson's violent career through the lens of the upcountry society in which he lived, placing a premium on the memory of the frontier struggles of his grandparents and beyond. As for the motivations of mountain guerrillas, Mays wrote, "The frontier culture remained strong in the isolated children and grandchildren of the original settlers." Certainly, the world in which Ferguson lived colored his outlook, but Mays's suggestion that Clinton County, Kentucky's, Champ Ferguson was deeply influenced by the region's collective experiences in the French and Indian War and the American Revolution in the Carolinas is difficult to accept without supporting evidence, which Mays does not provide.[11] Offering localism as a corollary to his multigenerational argument, Mays suggests that when war came to the mountains, "it had always been fought with local goals." In reading the litany of regional studies literature on the Civil War, examiners will find that this argument has been cast and recast with great success over the course of the past twenty years. Obviously, contested regions suffer from an inherent absence of effective civil authority and compromised military authority; therefore, a significant segment of the community will wilt under the pressure of anarchy while a small element will rise to fill the leadership void. What Mays presents as new information has actually been the foundation of dozens of nuanced works of regional history.[12] On the surface, Mays's book offers an acceptable biography of Ferguson, but it claims far too much in its attempts to construct a grand philosophy behind a relatively simple man.

The most pleasant recent addition to the study of this obscure guerrilla is Nicholas S. Miles's master's thesis. Miles opens Ferguson to the more modern interpretations of history and memory. By doing excellent research and analysis, he ties Ferguson's story to the relatively new trend of studying wartime memory and opens new avenues of exploring the motives of Ferguson's enemies, particularly through his evaluation of contemporary images.[13]

Apart from the aforementioned works, which have taken Ferguson on as their central focus, other examinations of guerrilla warfare have made excellent contributions to the broader understanding of the Civil War. Mark Grimsley's *The Hard Hand of War* partially credited the emergence of guerrilla activity with the Union's abandonment of its conciliatory policy in preference for what the author names "hard war." Clay Mountcastle's *Punitive War* follows Grimsley's lead and helps further link Confederate guerrilla activity with Union reprisals. David Williams's *A People's History of the Civil War* reaches into the depths of interpersonal conflict and devotes long passages to the intimate nature of partisan warfare and how it affected large segments of the southern and borderland populace.[14]

More recently, Robert Mackey wrote an excellent examination of guerrilla warfare in the Civil War. In *The Uncivil War,* he illustrates that irregular fighting was neither isolated nor ineffective. In reality, the Confederacy cultivated partisan activity and grew to depend on the contributions it made in the fields of intelligence, diversion, and the management of communities through fear and intimidation. Additionally, and somewhat problematically, Mackey seeks to illustrate the complex nature of irregular warfare by solidly defining *guerrillas* as small bands of unaffiliated men fighting independently of the greater conflict, *partisans* as similar to the guerrilla except drawn from uniformed forces and assigned unconventional duty, and *raiders* as conventional forces temporarily and officially acting unconventionally. In accordance with Mackey's definitions, Champ Ferguson spent significant parts of the Civil War as a member of all three groups, often switching between affiliations when another proved more beneficial to him. Although the endeavor to define guerrilla warfare is respected and appreciated, Champ Ferguson's story illustrates the futility of trying to categorize such complex and misunderstood behavior.[15]

Some of the problems with Mackey's strict categorization have been mended by Daniel Sutherland's more recent work, *A Savage Conflict,* which takes a new look at irregular warfare in the Civil War and makes a convincing argument for its centrality within the larger conflict. Correctly surmising that *guerrilla* has been used as a catch-all term for all varieties of irregular warriors, Sutherland seeks to clarify the differences between the types of irregular fighters by using more inclusive definitions and going into considerable depth into the subcategories such as the Red Legs, jayhawkers, and bushwhackers. The depth that Sutherland plumbs in his attempt to understand this underbelly of the Civil War has allowed him to produce a book that adds much social history to the story of the guerrilla. Whereas Mackey's different classifications of guerrillas appear nearly as orderly as the regular army itself, Sutherland's work leaves no doubt as to the complexity, identity, and impact of nontraditional warfare and its multifaceted practitioners.[16]

While the grand histories of the era have generally devoted themselves to conventional warfare rather than enter the slippery slope of the guerrilla ideal, regional studies have thrived by examining the irregular war that pervaded communities. Michael Fellman's *Inside War* discussed the partisan struggle in the highly fractured state of Missouri. Thomas Goodrich offered a more comprehensive treatment with his *Black Flag,* which examined the scope and nature of guerrilla warfare along the Missouri-Kansas border. Biographical works such as the *Autobiography of Samuel S. Hildebrand,* Albert Castel and Thomas Goodrich's work on Bloody Bill Anderson, and Castel's biography of William Quantrill have complemented Fellman's broad study with more specific human examples. Within the past few years, public interest in the guerrilla has grown to the point that T. J. Stiles's *Jesse James: Last Rebel of the Civil War* became a best seller, bridging the gap between recreational readers and academics.[17]

Guerrilla activity farther east has also received serious attention. Adam Rankin Johnson's standard, *The Partisan Rangers of the Confederate States Army,* remains important to anyone studying Kentucky's and Tennessee's Civil War experience, as does Phillip Shaw Paludan's riveting account of the Shelton Laurel Massacre to those interested in North Carolina. Kentucky readers will find less available, although John Sickles's short book examines the infamous duo of Sue Mundy and Samuel "One Armed" Berry. Virgil Carrington Jones's *Gray Ghosts and Rebel Raiders* and Richard Duncan's book on Winchester contribute meaningfully to the discussion, although their guerrillas were much more closely tied to the Confederacy proper than most of the western variety. Farther south along the Virginia and North Carolina coastline, Brian Steel Wills's *The War Hits Home* delves into the challenges presented within an occupied community in the form of guerrillaism.[18] The newest contribution to the historiography is Barton A. Myers's *Executing Daniel Bright,* a case study that broadly shares part of Wills's geographic area but focuses on the impact of guerrilla activity on a single community.[19]

In addition to the monographic studies, a handful of important anthologies have appeared within the past decade, written to throw light on small topics and to spur additional examination of larger phenomena. An earlier Daniel Sutherland work, *Guerrillas, Unionists, and Violence on the Confederate Home Front,* wholly focuses on extralegal wartime violence and succeeds in illustrating the tenuous duality of complexity and continuity within the various southern communities under examination. Kenneth Noe and Shannon Wilson's collection, *The Civil War in Appalachia,* brings a more varied approach to the subject and offers interpretive opportunities through the paradigm of localism. John Inscoe and Robert Kenzer utilize internal dissent to illuminate the motives behind guerrilla activity in their *Enemies of the Country.*[20] Like all works that hike already trodden ground, the present work benefits from previous studies of Ferguson, perhaps more so in that so few primary sources exist, requiring each investigator to mine the same sources for more revealing nuggets of information and new interpretations.

This work presents Champ Ferguson as a product of his place and time. Clearly he was an Appalachian figure with far more in common with eastern Kentucky and southwestern Virginia mountain farmers than with Thomas Mays's upcountry Carolinians of the previous century. Ferguson was a man driven by the circumstances that surrounded him. Certainly he was violent and willing to break the law before the war, but he did not kill out of calculated malice until the outbreak of hostilities. His 1858 murder of Jim Reed appears to have been a matter of self-defense in the face of an angry mob.

Simply claiming Ferguson to have been a product of his region and era is too basic an explanation to satisfy inquisitive minds. Within this theory lie two important elements, which, although obtuse and elusive, cannot be overlooked. In the Civil War borderland, particularly in the Appalachian region, real fear was frequently replaced by a paranoia that became a staple of many denizens' wartime experience. Coupled with rational fear, the irrational element frequently drove men and women to act in ways they could scarcely imagine before the Civil War. With this incredible level of pressure continually present, various segments of society, for manifold reasons, began acting in wholly pragmatic ways.

Throughout the Civil War, borderland warfare in the Appalachians saw frequent examples of home-front paranoia. Patsy Keel Boggs's grandfather suffered from war-induced paranoia in southwestern Virginia. Awakening one morning, he determined that a Federal deserter who visited the farm each day to beg for food was going to kill the family. When Mr. Boggs saw "Benny" walking toward the house, he sent his family away, invited the soldier in, and killed him in cold blood, a proactive murder similar in spirit to some of those committed by Ferguson.[21] Driving the paranoia was the fact that no position guaranteed safety and security. Confederate partisans nearly whipped a man to death when he refused to join the army, while Union home guards operating in the same region earned notorious reputations for their brutality.[22] The complexity of eastern Kentucky's situation drove William Tecumseh Sherman to the brink of insanity and necessitated his removal from command of the Department of the Cumberland.[23] Champ Ferguson's wartime experience was similar in that he quickly grew very paranoid as a result of the unsettled world that surrounded him.

The question of loyalty is of primary importance when one studies the Civil War in the Appalachian region. For Champ Ferguson, that loyalty was defined in stark terms. He was a Confederate, and those who were not with him were against him. While in Kentucky, he was surrounded by enemies; in fact, his entire family adhered to the Union. In Tennessee, he lived in a marginally safer climate but felt continually threatened by those whose loyalty to the southern cause was questionable or who chose not to make a statement of loyalty. In turn, he held those with whom he came into contact to an exceedingly strict interpretation of loyalty or disloyalty to his cause. No example shows this more clearly than Champ Ferguson's treatment of his longtime friend, William Frogg. When Ferguson learned that Frogg had the measles, he deduced that Frogg had joined the Union army and caught the disease in camp. Visiting the sick man at home, Ferguson was unmoved by Frogg's contention that he did go to Camp Dick Robinson, a Union recruiting depot, but had not joined the army. Unaffected by Frogg's explanation, Ferguson pulled out his revolver and killed him.[24]

Out of the intense pressures applied by the warring factions emerged men and women who came to view their position within the war as one of simple survival, and they often became intensely pragmatic in that pursuit. War turns all men into pragmatists and Ferguson was no exception. For Champ, that pragmatism manifested itself in periodic robbery and in the killing of anyone he considered to be a potential threat. Others were shocked by the war's power to turn them into self-serving beings. John McCrary wrote, "I never though[t] that I ever could have the conscience to walk up to a mans house and shoot down a hog and skin it right before his eys and the owner of them standing by and not allowed to open his mouth."[25] Throughout the contested region, theft was commonplace and sometimes grew into social revolt. In 1864, several women arrived in Abingdon, Virginia, where they robbed two stores of cotton. When asked about their motives, the women told one of the storekeepers that they lived in such poverty that they had to resort to robbery in order to make a living. The man gave them the cotton rather than pressing charges. A few days later, another group of women arrived hoping for similar treatment. After stealing two bolts of cloth, they were captured and jailed by the local authorities.[26]

The key to understanding the Appalachian Civil War, and Champ Ferguson as a part of that phenomenon, is to understand the interrelated concepts of paranoia, loyalty, and pragmatism as resultant elements of the wartime anarchy that permeated the border region. Here the suggested equation begins with a moral and ethical base built in the traditional Appalachian mold of old-style Manichaean outlook heavily influenced by the continually pressing concerns of survival. With anarchy increasing within the region, the war steadily applied pressure to these people, many of whom were desperately poor even during flush times. Eventually, many of these mountaineers grew fearful of anything outside the status quo because that had come to mean even more instability in an already unstable world. In the midst of this unhealthy situation, soldiers, partisans, politicians, neighbors, and strangers demanding a clear statement of loyalty to their cause besieged the fearful mountaineers. Understanding the level of danger associated with making such a stand, most men chose to hold their cards close, only revealing them once a winning side began to appear. In the meantime, however, they had to survive, and many Appalachians did so by behaving in uncharacteristic, but highly pragmatic, ways. What then turned a rough-and-tumble farmer into what some might legitimately call a chronic murderer?

In *Cumberland Blood,* Thomas Mays writes as if surprised by the fact that a rising farmer like Ferguson would become a partisan fighter. Citing works by Noel Fisher and Kenneth Noe, he agrees with their contentions that guerrillas came from a wide economic and social cross-section of society, but deeper analysis suggests a more interesting connection between the mountain region's successful landowners—Ferguson included—and guerrilla activity.[27] Remembering Richard Hofstadter's status anxiety thesis, modern scholars of Appalachia's Civil War can see subtle connections. Mountaineers understood that the rapid changes brought about by the Civil War would certainly have an impact on virtually all Americans, definitely including those in Appalachia who had struggled to elevate themselves in the face of the region's economic challenges. For men like these, the anarchy produced by the Civil War wielded the greatest challenge to their economic and social security and threatened to plunge them and their families into a state of abject poverty. A man like

Champ could remember his father struggling to expand the family farm in an effort to improve his fortunes. Inheriting the family holdings, Ferguson continued to work hard and increase his wealth. By the time of the Civil War, he could look back on a lifetime of continual economic improvement. When southern independence became a reality and the line between Tennessee and Kentucky an international border, Ferguson and many others in the region began to feel the mounting social, economic, and political tensions and responded by taking a stand as radical as the underlying pressures they were feeling. These borderlanders began moving through the paranoia, loyalty, and pragmatism phases out of the realization that they were suddenly surrounded by instability. The social anxiety theory that Hofstadter initially put forth and that has more recently been adopted by T. H. Breen, Altina Waller, and Pete Daniel provides a reasonable explanation of why these men, many of them landed, on the rise, and therefore pillars of stability in their neighborhoods, would take an inglorious stand and fight as guerrillas.[28]

1

THE "NATURAL MAN"

We had a scuffle, and I kept cutting him all the time, until he fell, and I stabbed him once or twice.

—CHAMP FERGUSON on his killing of a local constable in 1858

I was let out on bail, and when the war broke out, I was induced to join the army on the promise that all prosecution in the case would be abandoned. That is how I came to take up arms.

—CHAMP FERGUSON regarding his entry into the Civil War

Champ Ferguson entered the world on November 29, 1821. Born on Spring Creek near the county seat of Albany in Cumberland County, Kentucky,[1] he was the oldest of ten children who came to William R. and Zilpha Huff Ferguson.[2] A contemporary described the simplicity of William Ferguson's place as consisting of a small log house, a log stable, corn crib, and a little still-house near the creek.[3] Purportedly named after his grandfather, who carried the nickname "Champion," Ferguson probably spent his youth like other hill-country boys growing up in similar circumstances.[4] Although little is known of his childhood and teenage years, Champ likely spent the bulk of his youth performing chores around the house, at work in the fields with his father, or walking fences in search of stray livestock. When spare time presented itself, he could choose between recreation and education. The keen shooting eye and intimate knowledge of local geography and terrain that he would display in his later life suggest that recreation prevailed. Horsemanship was another important farm-grown talent that Champ cultivated. Ferguson spent a good portion of his leisure time on horseback.[5] All of these formative influences helped define the man Champ would become.

Lewis Collins's 1847 *Historical Sketches of Kentucky* described the Clinton County young Champ Ferguson knew. It held two significant towns: Albany and Seventy-Six. Although the county had borrowed the surname of DeWitt Clinton, the visionary governor of New York State and sponsor of the wildly successful Erie Canal, there was apparently no connection between the name of the county seat and New York's seat of government.[6] Collins recorded that the thriving little town of Albany "contain[ed] a court-house and other public buildings, a United Baptist church, one school, three stores, two taverns, three lawyers, two doctors, fifteen mechanics' shops, and one hundred and thirty inhabitants." Seventy-Six, presumably named after the year of American independence, was much smaller. Having only twenty-five people living in town, it also claimed "a lawyer, post office, tannery, saw and grist mill."[7]

Young men and women from the central Appalachian region have always had limited educational opportunities. Such was the case for young Champ. Near the time of his death, he recalled that he "never had much schooling," and indeed, many middling whites felt no need for education, particularly if their future would be spent in the fields. Having attended Clinton County's only school for what he estimated to have been "about three months," Champ learned to "read, write, and cipher right smart."[8] Ferguson's memory of his school days illustrates the common standard for farm boys of his era in Kentucky. Apart from the availability of a proper school, family support was also an important factor. Most parents considered an education complete when the child learned the most basic skills, expecting that a signature, limited reading skills, and a command of simple mathematics would suffice for life as an adult. However, little more is known about Ferguson's education beyond his personal reminiscences. Unfortunately, the United States census failed to record education information until 1840, a time when Ferguson was past school age, when it showed Clinton County as the home of two primary schools with forty-nine students and a single academy with twenty-five older pupils.[9] Also important is Ferguson's own estimation of his literacy skills. He considered his three months in school to have been sufficient to learn the basics of education, although he gauged his abilities as nothing "to brag on."[10]

Although Champ Ferguson's later infamy might lead one to dismiss religion as an important formative factor, it cannot be ignored. Like much of the American frontier, the region of south-central Kentucky had scant opportunities for religious education. The 1850 census provided the first record of Clinton County's churches. That year, three Baptist congregations and two Methodist churches offered the only formal religious instruction in the county. Ten

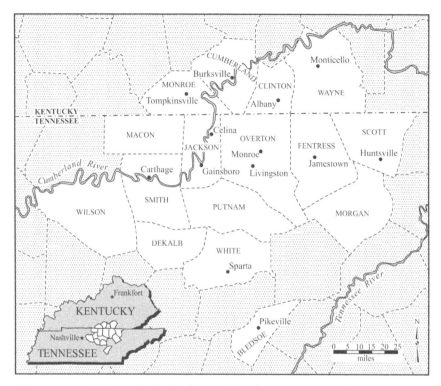

Champ Ferguson's Upper Cumberland region (Map by Mary Lee Eggart)

years later, the 1860 census noted a substantial increase to five Baptist churches, eight Methodist congregations, and a single Presbyterian church.[11] Of note is the Calvinist background of the Baptist faith. During the first decades of the nineteenth century, Calvinism and Arminianism were competing for control of the Baptists. After many failures, some Baptist churches, particularly those in the south-central part of the state, found enough common ground to unite under one roof.[12]

Ferguson grew up in this changing religious landscape of southern Kentucky. He publicly professed a belief in a higher being and attended church services. Although he never joined a specific congregation, he did, by the end of his life, announce an affinity for a group called the "Campbellites," or the Stone-Campbell Movement. Although it initially splintered into two separate groups, another group, the Disciples of Christ, maintained significant influence in the Appalachian highlands of Kentucky and Tennessee. The theology of the Disciples movement was based on a primitive form of New Testament Christianity and emphasized theological unity over denominational differences. It is likely that many mountaineers combined the basic tenets of the Disciples with more traditional and practical Old Testament teachings to build a satisfying and useful faith that could speak to God's love on the one hand and swift retribution of wrongs on the other.

The Presbyterians were another theological influence in the mountains. Like the Puritans of New England, Presbyterians brought a distinctly Calvinistic bent to their faith. As John Calvin disseminated his punitive brand of Christianity throughout Europe, the Scots received Presbyterianism as their religious link to the famous reformer. With similar behavioral standards and basic theological traditions, Presbyterians became the Puritans of the southern Appalachian region.

In the case of the Appalachian Civil War and the guerrilla tactics that dominated there, a certain style of Calvinism with particular reflection on Old Testament themes resonates. The concept of power and judgment can be seen in the behavior of the many local warlords who rose to positions of power during the war. What often seems to be a style of Old Testament tribalism appears in geographical, social, and cultural contexts and stresses the value of localism and kinship ties within the mountain region. The dual concepts of predestination and total depravity hold that man is powerless to resist his fate, and this may make it easier for him to accept the radical and illogical actions that internecine war brings about. Whatever his specific theological beliefs, Champ Ferguson interpreted religion somewhat predictably along these more fatalist and predestinarian lines. In the unforgiving world of mid-nineteenth-century Appalachia, Ferguson embraced this curious combination of love and vengeance as a way to answer the difficult questions of everyday life. As his wartime actions would later illustrate, rules were absolute and unbending; men either good or bad; and citizens either with him or against him.

Another subtle influence on Ferguson's life was political. By the time the first shots of the Civil War were fired, Kentucky's 4th district could look back on a generation of political transition. What had started with the Whig party all but dominating regional politics had evolved into open competition with the Democrats, and after the Whigs' ultimate demise, the 4th district became a Democratic stronghold until hostilities grew inevitable. With sectionalism at a crisis point, enough voters returned to their Whig roots to seek a way out of the national quandary by electing opposition, and later, Union, candidates.[13]

Conjecture puts Champ Ferguson in the Democratic Party. As a rising farmer during the 1850s, he likely sought protection for his newly acquired property and success. When secession became an issue, he allied himself with the cause of the Confederacy without hesitation. His move to Tennessee and embrace of the southern ideal during the war further bolster the suggestion of his Democratic roots. For many Kentucky Democrats, the Civil War offered hope of political influence after years of Whig near-dominance. Indeed, noted unionist and wartime nemesis J. A. Brents, in an 1863 publication, identified Ferguson as a supporter of the Democratic Party before the war.[14]

Although political and religious matters were important to the average white Kentuckian, more basic aspects of daily life proved more defining. Life in Kentucky and Tennessee during the antebellum period generally revolved around agricultural production. This was particularly true of Clinton County, in the Pennyroyal region of south-central Kentucky, along the Tennessee border. The rolling hills alternating with level and fertile bottomland and access to the navigable Cumberland River gave the county much agricultural potential. Although the Sixth Census did not record specific agricultural information, the farm dominated the nearly twenty-year-old Champ Ferguson's life. At this point, Champ shared the outside labor with his father and two younger brothers, as the family owned no slaves.[15]

Clinton County in 1840 was an anomaly. Whereas the surrounding counties of south-central Kentucky held comparatively large numbers of slaves, Clinton could only claim 188 slaves among a total population of 3,863. The holding of such a small number of slaves—less than 5 percent of the population—in the hands of the most successful men in the county embedded the idea in young minds, like Champ Ferguson's, that the ownership of slaves was the identifying factor in economic success.[16]

By the time he matured into adulthood, Champ had grown into a large and strong man. Standing a full six feet tall and weighing around 180 pounds, "without any surplus flesh," he was one of the bigger men in the community and well equipped for the physical demands of the coming war. J. A. Brents described him as having "a large foot, and [he] gives his legs a loose sling when walking, with his toes turned out—is a little stooped with his head down."[17] Combining the physical description of Ferguson with the way in which he came to prosecute the Civil War, it is easy to see him, as Daniel Sutherland sees many similar Civil War guerrillas, in the European philosophic tradition of the "natural man." Despite modern efforts, the historical record strongly indicates that Ferguson was "basic, uncomplicated, primordial," like the style of warfare he preferred.[18]

On May 12, 1844, the twenty-two-year-old Champ married Ann Eliza

Smith. It is likely that the newlyweds built a small house and remained on the family farm, which offered a subsistence living, and would one day be passed to Champ as oldest son. Shortly after, Ann gave birth to a son. Tragedy struck, however, when in 1847 both Champ's wife and young son died of unspecified causes.[19] As one would expect, the loss of his family affected him terribly.

A widower at only twenty-five, Ferguson sought to end his forced bachelorhood and on July 23, 1848, married twenty-two-year-old Martha Owens. In early 1850, the two welcomed a daughter, Ann Elizabeth, into the family.[20] Although little is known about the Ferguson women and children, the apparent naming of Martha's daughter after her husband's first wife suggests a couple of possibilities: That Martha had known and respected Ann Eliza Smith and wished to remember her husband's first wife by giving her daughter the same name, or, more likely, that Champ had not fully recovered from the death of his first wife.

Just as Champ's life began settling into a predictable pattern, he was again jolted by bad news. In 1850, his father died. That same year, the more detailed Seventh Census recorded 499 farms in Clinton County. With 29,771 improved and 55,767 unimproved acres reported, the average farm family held just under sixty acres of cleared land and nearly 112 acres still in timber or brush.[21] The size of William Ferguson's farm is unknown, but Champ probably inherited most of it along with added familial obligations. A survey done on November 1, 1855, placed 194 acres of land on Spring Creek in Champ's name, making him a larger-than-average landholder in comparison with most others in Clinton County. In addition to his own small family, he became responsible for the sustenance and care of his mother and siblings, several of whom were young children.[22]

The 1850s kept Champ busy filling his various roles and responsibilities. In the years that followed his father's death, Champ threw himself into expanding and improving the modest farm. The county census for 1860 recorded that the county's 975 families lived on 590 farms encompassing more than 41,000 acres of improved farmland, an average farm size of seventy acres.[23] By 1860, Champ owned 462 acres of land and had accumulated an estimated $2,000 in wealth. That year's census report placed Ferguson in the 13th percentile of Clinton County landowners.[24]

With his late increase in prosperity, Ferguson, like many southern farmers wishing to produce more immediate wealth and, at the same time, invest in the future, began to accumulate a few slaves. Although Clinton County's tradition of relatively small subsistence farms combined with its distance from major trade routes to make large-scale slavery largely impractical there, opportunistic farmers embraced the investment potential. In 1860, the county's white population stood at nearly 5,800, with only 258 slaves recorded.[25] Ferguson, who by the time of the Civil War could be classified as a rising farmer, owned three mulatto slaves. One, a forty-five-year-old man, assisted Champ with the myriad duties related to the farm, and two young sisters, nine-year-old Sara Eliza and her sister, Mary Jane, a year younger, helped in the home.[26] At this young age, Sara Eliza and Mary Jane provided minimal housekeeping help but remained potentially lucrative investments for the family. This small number of slaves placed Champ in the top five percent of slave owners in largely nonslaveholding Clinton County.[27] The 1860 census also notes that Marion Cowan, a twenty-one-year-old farmer, lived with the Ferguson family. Although nothing is known of Cowan or his relationship with the family, he worked for Ferguson as a farm hand. It is possible that by 1860, Champ was performing considerably less field work than before and had taken Cowan on to fill his place and supervise his older field hand.[28] Whatever the explanation, Champ was moving up economically.

Ferguson's economic status, however, did not betray what one biographer called his "cracker characteristics."[29] Long before the war and probably due in part to alcohol, he had earned a reputation as "a bully, a ruffian, and daredevil kind of fellow."[30] As an adult, he kept a still house and was widely known as a man who enjoyed drinking. His homemade whiskey and apple brandy made his property a gathering place for like characters, who often turned violent after imbibing. Gambling also played a large role in Ferguson's lowbrow recreational habits. Like many Kentuckians, he was fond of racing his own horses and spent much time at the Seven Chestnuts, Clinton County's racetrack. Race days also found numerous card games taking place near the track. The mixture of alcohol, gambling, and men with volatile tempers often resulted in explosions of violence.[31] There were also more serious questions about Champ's behavior. A contemporary claimed that the future guerrilla occupied much of his prewar time counterfeiting money and having others pass the fake bills. No evidence is offered for this assertion, but the making and passing of counterfeit notes was a popular occupation in some rural areas of the South. Ferguson likely had few qualms about breaching the law.[32]

Although there is little concrete knowledge of Ferguson's life before the outbreak of the Civil War, one defining event is well documented. Sometime in the late 1850s, probably in the spring or summer of 1857, two brothers, Floyd and Alexander Evans, from across the state border in Fentress County, Tennessee, came to Clinton County in search of hogs to purchase.[33] Many men, including Ferguson and two of his brothers, sold swine to the men on Floyd Evans's promissory note, cosigned by several upstanding citizens of Fentress. On the due date of the note, Ferguson and a few other men met Alexander Evans and some friends on their way to Albany. Expecting that Evans had returned to pay his debt, Ferguson was shocked to hear "that Floyd had ran off with all the money." Despite Alexander Evans's claims, Ferguson was sure the brothers had swindled him along with the other men from Clinton County who had sold them hogs.[34]

Collecting payment for the debt proved difficult. When approached about their responsibility for the outstanding money, the cosigners claimed Evans had forged their signatures and refused to honor the note. Ferguson and a Mr. Biter rode to Livingston, the Overton County, Tennessee, seat, and filed suit against Floyd Evans. Ferguson eventually won his case, but the probability of collecting the settlement was unlikely. Taking advantage of a Kentucky law that allowed the attachment, or confiscation, of property of nonresidents with property in the state, Ferguson and several others who had lost money to the Evans brothers began crossing into Tennessee at night and sneaking horses out of the Evanses' stable. Once back in Kentucky, the horses would either be sold outright or presented to the county sheriff for sale to help clear the debt. These nocturnal visits went on for some time before any direct conflict between Ferguson and the Evans brothers took place.[35]

Despite the apparent clarity of the Ferguson-Evans conflict, there was some question as to the legitimacy of the claim. On July 5, 1858, the Clinton County Court dismissed Ferguson's suit against the Evanses. Hoping to draw the conflict to a close, Floyd Evans gave security on the debt in return for Biter dropping his part of the suit. However, Ferguson's volatile reputation combined with his evident anger over the debt forced the Evans brothers to handle him with care. While Champ considered himself a law-abiding citizen in this case, friends of the Evans brothers in Tennessee saw the confiscation of the horses as simple thievery. An attorney advised them that they had a claim against Champ for larceny since he had stolen the horses from their places across the state line rather than legally confiscating them within the borders of Kentucky, and that if they caught Ferguson in Tennessee, a warrant could be filed for his arrest.[36]

The Ferguson-Evans feud came to a head at a camp meeting. While these gatherings were organized with pious intentions, they also served as general assembly places for the entire community. Just as some came for preaching and singing, others attended for whiskey, fights, and courting.[37] It is unclear what drew Champ Ferguson and the Evans brothers to the annual Presbyterian meeting at the Lick Creek campground in Fentress County in early August 1858, but once there, Champ learned that a warrant had been filed for his arrest in Tennessee.[38] Though he claimed ignorance of the event, a few nights earlier, Jim Ferguson and a man named Bill Jones had slipped onto the Evanses' property and taken more horses. Despite his claim of ignorance, Champ was not opposed to the confiscation because in his mind it was a legal act. Upon hearing that Ferguson was in town and convinced that he was the culprit in what they considered their recent theft, the Evans brothers called on the local justice of the peace to serve the arrest warrant. The law officer charged with placing Ferguson under arrest was James Reed, a relative of the Evanses. The friend who had traveled to the meeting with Champ warned him about the Evanses and advised Champ to leave because "he had heard them talking" and "they intended to either kill me or give me a severe thrashing." At first, Champ refused to go, but as several men gathered in support of Frank and Alexander Evans, he began to question his safety. Seeing that he was no match for what by now amounted to a small mob, Ferguson moved toward his horse.[39]

Years later, Champ remembered that as he walked toward his mount, he saw the group begin moving toward him. Probably running by the time he reached and jumped astride the mare, he recalled that through the "shower of rocks" he could hear several voices yelling "kill him." Normally a skilled rider and keeper of fine horseflesh, Ferguson had made a poor choice of mount for his trip to the camp meeting. His horse on that day was a mare in foal, and in her condition she tripped and fell, forcing Ferguson to flee on foot. It took only moments for his adversaries to catch up with him.

The first was Floyd Evans, from whom Ferguson, feinting ignorance, asked for an explanation: "Floyd what do you mean?" Without answering, Evans began throwing rocks at his quarry and Ferguson returned fire. By the time several stones had passed between the two men, Champ realized that Jim Reed, the county constable, had caught up with him. Now fully panicked, Ferguson picked up a large rock and struck Floyd Evans squarely in the stomach, doubling him over. With one man now, at least temporarily, out of the fight, Champ turned his attention to Constable Reed. Recognizing he was at a disadvantage against the larger man, Ferguson threw down his rocks and took out his "bran new" and "sharp as a razor" pocketknife. When Reed ventured too close, Champ grabbed him and began blindly slashing at the deputy. Ferguson recalled, "I kept cutting him all the time until he fell, and I stabbed him once or twice." In those brief seconds of combat, Ferguson killed Reed.[40] Without doubt, Ferguson had been efficient in his fight with the constable because the others were fast advancing. Unfortunately, later embellishment has done much to confuse this story. The unionist J. D. Hale later wrote, "either of the sixteen wounds would have proved fatal."[41] J. A. Brents, a similarly partisan unionist who was not present that day, relayed that after Reed begged Ferguson for his life, Champ "pierced his body in twenty odd places."[42] There is no doubt that Champ Ferguson killed Constable Reed, but it is unlikely that he wasted valuable time and energy sadistically slashing the dead body, as claimed by Brents and Hale, when others were still giving chase.

Abandoning his now-completed work on the constable, Champ turned his "attention to Elam Huddleston, and chased him down a hill, to a fence, which he leaped, and got away from me." Near the fence, Ferguson realized a partially recovered Floyd Evans was pursuing him. Turning on Evans, Champ drew his knife as Floyd caught up with him. Ferguson remembered, "I had my knife in my hand, but it got twisted in some way, and split my thumb clean open." Both men fought desperately for the knife, but Champ won. Ferguson "commenced sticking him" and Evans fell with his attacker astride him. Champ then "drew him up by the collar, and had my arm raised to plunge the knife in his bosom, when he looked piteously in my face." Whether out of pity or necessity, he dropped Evans and turned his attention to the other men who were now bearing down on him.[43]

Seeing an opportunity to escape, Champ began to run from the other men arriving on the scene. "I never knew how fast I could run until that time, but a man can make a big race when his life is the stake." Fortune smiled on Champ that day in the form of a farmhouse. He ran through the door, up the stairs, and found a "heavy old fashioned bed wrench." Standing at the head of the stairs, he heard the mob enter the house in search of him, asking each other, "Where is he?" Ferguson, wielding the bed wrench, answered that he was upstairs and dared them to ascend the narrow staircase. Intimidated by Champ's advantageous position and remembering one dead man and another seriously wounded, his pursuers began to argue and bluster. By this time, many women from the church meeting had arrived at the house and began to calm the men downstairs.[44]

The standoff in the house continued for two hours until the county sheriff, Jim Wright, arrived. Champ refused to surrender out of fear for his life.
After the sheriff gave him assurances that he would not be harmed, Ferguson
dropped his knife and descended the stairs.[45] Curiously, Pheroba Hale, the wife
of one of Ferguson's most fervent wartime enemies, recalled that she was at the
Lick Creek camp meeting when the fracas broke out and that Wright brought
Ferguson back to the church and tied him to a post to hold him. Remembering his face and hands covered with blood, Mrs. Hale claimed that "but for the
efforts of Reuben Woods, the excited crowd would have hung Furguson on
the grounds at once."[46] Afterward, Ferguson's hands and feet were tied and he
was transported to jail in Jamestown, Tennessee. Despite Wright's guarantees,
Champ recalled that Alexander Evans "tried hard to shoot me while I was on
the way to jail."[47]

After being examined by a local magistrate, Champ was remanded to the
Fentress county jail. At the next session of the criminal court, he was indicted
for killing Jim Reed. Most expected a second murder charge to be levied, but
Floyd Evans recovered.[48] After Champ spent two months in jail, his mother
asked three of her cousins, James, Pleasant, and William Miller, to put up
$3,000 of real estate for security. Although it was risky, the Millers consigned
their property and Champ was released on bond to await trial. In return,
Champ had to mortgage much of his Kentucky farm and his two slave girls to
"ensure his appearance in court."[49]

Fortuitously, Champ had secured a good attorney to handle his case. Willis
Scott Bledsoe, a native of Fentress County, Tennessee, was only twenty years
old when he took Ferguson's case. However, by the time of Tennessee's secession the twenty-three-year-old organized his own command, with Ferguson
as one of his first recruits, and thus began Champ's military career. After the
war ended, Bledsoe, like myriad other former Confederates, packed his family and their belongings and moved west to Texas. In Bledsoe's case, the good
Confederate settled in the newly established town of Cleburne, where he remained until his untimely death in 1877.[50]

The issue of Champ's bail cannot be lost in the violent tangle of his Civil
War years. Prior to the Civil War, the Ferguson family had been as close as any
other, but when Champ was jailed, those ties were strained. At the start of the
war the family drew closer to the Union, with Champ standing alone with the
Confederacy. By the end of his life, his relationship with his family had eroded
to the point that none of his relatives visited while he awaited execution. A

number of theories account for the schism, but the family's strong unionism in the face of Champ's pro-Confederate activities has been generally accepted as the primary reason.

While it is a logical assumption that political differences lay at the root of the familial difficulties, economic considerations cannot be dismissed. When the war started and Champ began operating alongside Confederates, it is quite likely that his mother thought her cousins, who had mortgaged a considerable amount of their holdings, would lose title to that land as a result of her son's actions. Indeed, if the Confederates had won and been able to enforce the bond, they probably would have gained the land. Additionally, Champ had put up his own property, that which had been left to him by his father, and would lose that as a result of his wartime stance. As he was her eldest son, his mother likely relied on Champ for considerable support, and his younger brothers and sisters probably resented the dual burdens of political differences and potential economic ruin their brother had placed on their mother.

The already serious sectional difficulties would continue to spiral while Ferguson waited for his day in court. Although the reasons are not recorded, the trial, initially scheduled for January 1859, was repeatedly delayed. J. A. Brents wrote, "At each succeeding term of the court, upon some pretext or another, he would obtain a continuance of the prosecution against him."[51] Probably with Scott Bledsoe's help, Ferguson's case remained unheard at the time Tennessee left the Union. The secession of Tennessee could logically make his case go away. With the impending Civil War all but begun, little time could be devoted to such relatively small matters. This theory is bolstered by a report in the *Nashville Daily Press and Times,* which, in the first days of Ferguson's trial, claimed that "the rebel elements in the State promised the criminal pardon and assistance if he would join their side." Ferguson, believing he had escaped his fate in the matter, had not gotten away as cleanly as he might have thought. Recalling his prewar situation, he claimed to have been "induced to join the army on the promise that all prosecution in that case would be abandoned."[52] This inducement probably came from his former lawyer and future commander W. Scott Bledsoe, who raised a partisan company shortly after his state voted to leave the Union.[53] Whether Champ felt indebted to Bledsoe, or his attorney manipulated him into joining his company with the promise of legal protection within the new nation, Ferguson enlisted, thus beginning what may have been the bloodiest single career of the Civil War.[54]

This version of events is bolstered by the contents of—or rather what is missing from—the Fentress County Circuit Court office minutes book. During and after the war, questionable stories circulated that Ferguson had visited Jamestown, Tennessee, in the early days of the conflict, seeking to destroy the official record of his murder charge. Those tales may have been based in truth. On one expedition, Ferguson supposedly entered the courthouse and found the minute book. Taking his knife, he cut out the pages detailing the constable's killing and the charging of the crime. Researchers who study the minute book, now on microfilm, quickly realize two things: It is indexed with the names of all entries, and the pages holding Ferguson's initial indictment are missing. While there is no proof that Champ cut those pages out, or even indications of how they were removed, it is peculiar that the book remains intact except for the pages of his indictment.[55]

If Ferguson consciously took time during the war to destroy the evidence of his 1858 murder charge, he did a poor job. The index notes five separate entries regarding *State of Tennessee v. Champion Ferguson,*[56] and only the initial indictment was removed. It is likely that Champ only visited the courtroom for the indictment proceedings and that the subsequent decisions of the court, such as setting a bond or granting a continuance, were made in his absence, causing him to assume that only a single entry held the damning information.[57]

The possible return of Ferguson to Jamestown for this purpose suggests two important points. First, if he did destroy the indictment, the conjecture that he supported the Confederacy in the hopes of clearing his prewar crime becomes stronger with the suggestion that even in war, Ferguson remained fixated on this lone event that had quite possibly driven him to take his wartime course. Second, he considered the 1858 killing of Constable Reed a more heinous crime than anything he had done since the beginning of his participation in the war. For a man with a starkly dualistic mind that drew a clear line between a killing sanctioned by wartime and one borne of a business conflict, this is a logical supposition. Reed's killing was done in peacetime when there were no official enemies; the men he had killed since had been supporters of the Union, therefore enemies to one who rode for the Confederacy. Whatever Ferguson's motives and actions in the wake of the Reed killing, there is little doubt that his participation in the war can be traced back to his killing of Reed and his resulting relationship with Scott Bledsoe.

EXILED TO TENNESSEE

We were having a sort of miscellaneous war, up there, through Fentress
county, Tennessee, and Clinton county, Kentucky, and all through that region. Every man was in danger of his life: if I hadn't kill[ed] my neighbor,
he would have killed me. Each of us had from 20 to 30 proscribed enemies,
and it was regarded as legitimate to kill them at any time, at any place,
under any circumstances.

—CHAMP FERGUSON, October 1865

he secession winter of 1860–61 brought feelings of trepidation to
all who watched the growth of the coming conflict. This uneasi-
ness was particularly pronounced along what would become the
border between the two contending nations. Although hopes for
Kentucky's secession were high, Tennessee's prospects for becoming part of
the new Confederate nation were more likely, considering its economic and
geographic relationship with the Deep South states. On the border between
the two states, Champ Ferguson, still awaiting trial for killing Constable Reed,
had a decision to make.

The question of loyalty was a difficult one. While an individual's decision
was based on many factors, in the upcountry of the Upper South the mar-
ginal importance of slavery served to relax one of the central factors tying the
more southern regions to the Confederacy. With this tenet of southern nationhood somewhat removed, the numerous secondary questions asked by all
southerners in their decision to support or oppose secession became relatively
equal in the minds of locals and fostered more diverse responses to the loyalty
question. Throughout the deeply divided Appalachian region, a pragmatic approach to Union or Confederacy was often employed, with the focus solely on

self-preservation. In such cases, the individual simply sought to appease the nearest and most threatening military force.

The presidential election of 1860 gave impetus to this turbulent time. After several years of escalating sectional tensions, the stage was set for a political showdown with slavery as the core issue. The Democrats arrived in Charleston, South Carolina, for their convention's April 23 start. Once there, southern Democrats insisted on the inclusion of a strong plank establishing a federal slave code for territories that would protect slavery and allow its expansion. Illinois senator Stephen Douglas insisted that the citizens of territories be allowed to make the decision about the institution in accordance with the doctrine of popular sovereignty, while Jefferson Davis and other southerners demanded Congress adopt the code, which would place no restrictions on what a man did with his human property. After meeting for ten days, the convention dissolved with Stephen Douglas still awaiting his expected nomination, and the Democrats scheduled another meeting for June 18 in Baltimore. There, meeting without the southern delegation, northern Democrats finally succeeded in nominating Douglas.[1]

In the meantime, the southern Democrats had left the Charleston convention and met in Richmond, Virginia, on June 11. Reconvening in Baltimore on June 28, ten days after the northern wing of the party met there and chose Douglas, the southerners gathered and nominated outgoing president James Buchanan's vice president, John C. Breckinridge, as their candidate. Placing the protection of slavery at the center of their platform, the southern Democrats wished to keep territories open to the expansion of the institution and were interested in acquiring Cuba, which could be quickly added to the Union and increase pro-slave representation.[2]

As early as 1858, conservatives from both major parties talked of forming an alternative to the Democratic and Republican parties. With the help of influential senator John J. Crittenden, an "opposition" party was formed the next year. By George Washington's birthday in 1860, this group, now known as the Constitutional Union party, was planning a national convention during which they would nominate their first presidential ticket. On May 9, in Baltimore, delegates from twenty-three states met and affirmed the Constitution as their political guide. To carry out their mandate of peace, they chose John Bell, an old and uninspiring Tennessean.[3]

Only a few days later, Republicans arrived in Chicago for their election-year meeting. The young party was preparing to nominate only its second presidential candidate, but its still-evolving political philosophy proved a difficult problem to the delegates on the floor. One thing was certain—whoever won the party's nomination would have to bring with them wide-ranging appeal in northern states and an ability to compete with John Bell in the Upper South. Despite the large number of disparate political ideas floating around the convention floor, the party, which had been seeking an identity, settled on Abraham Lincoln as its candidate. In Lincoln they had found a man who could deliver Illinois, who had a tie, however tenuous, to Kentucky, and who had adopted the very palatable stance of opposing slavery while vowing to protect it where it existed in accordance with the United States Constitution.[4]

With the Democratic Party deeply split along sectional lines and the Constitutional Unionists holding significant sway only in the states of the Upper South, the die was cast for Abraham Lincoln and the Republicans. Although the upstart party won an overwhelming electoral victory, the malady of sectionalism, which had always held some influence over political questions, had grown into an epidemic during the 1860 presidential contest. Although he failed to win a single electoral vote in a slave state and only tallied 26,388 votes of a possible 1.275 million votes in the South, Lincoln's dominance in northern states secured his victory. In free states, he earned all but three of the possible 183 electoral votes.[5]

Electorally, Champ Ferguson's world looked more like the Mississippi Delta than the small farms dotting nearby Ohio, Indiana, and Illinois. Prewar southern Kentucky was filled with Democrats and former Whigs, but few residents could stand behind the sometimes radical message of the new Republican Party, even in counties where slavery did not play a large role in daily life. Even though Lincoln was a native of Kentucky, his home state repudiated him and chose John Bell's message of union with slavery instead. After the ballots were counted, Lincoln had received less than 1 percent of votes cast in Kentucky.[6]

Almost immediately after Lincoln's victory was announced, the South began to convulse with the fear of being led by a man they considered an "abolitionist." By Christmas, the first southern state, South Carolina, had reacted to the Illinoisan's election and over the course of the six weeks that followed, other Deep South states made a steady march out of the Union. By the time the seven seceded states came together on February 9, 1861, and elected Jefferson Davis president of the new Confederacy, the debate about the future of Kentucky and Tennessee was in full swing.[7]

For the duration of the late winter and early spring 1861, the secession question festered in the Upper South. In Kentucky, the native state of the great compromisers Henry Clay and John J. Crittenden, the legislature passed a measure proclaiming the state's neutrality in the conflict. Beriah Magoffin, the Democratic governor since 1859, made his own weak and sometimes backhanded attempts to keep the state out of the conflict. An advocate of slavery and states' rights, Magoffin hoped to offer subtle support for southern nationhood by refusing to allow either army to operate within the state's borders.[8] Of course, both armies did move into Kentucky, and the governor's attempt at neutrality offered implied support for the Confederacy. For Kentucky, intellectually and geographically caught in the middle of this great struggle, neutrality was an unrealistic dream. Foreshadowing Champ Ferguson's clearly defined view of the war, Kentucky had to choose a side; there was no middle ground.

Magoffin followed the state legislature's lead by refusing to supply soldiers to either army. By declaring that he would "furnish no troops for the wicked purpose of subduing her Sister Southern States," Magoffin solidified his secessionist stance in the eyes of Kentucky unionists. Additionally, he actively lobbied for a state convention to decide upon the issue of secession. His prodding backfired as the legislature repudiated his call and gave unionists hope that the state would remain part of the United States. As a result, unionist candidates nearly swept June's statewide elections, winning nine of ten available seats. With his credibility destroyed among most Kentuckians and a completely uncooperative legislature in his future, Magoffin began to broker a deal whereby he could resign the governorship and hand the reigns of power over to another "conservative, just man."[9] Such a move was both unprecedented and unlikely.

One such man, Lieutenant Governor Linn Boyd, had died shortly after being elected to the office in 1859 and had not been replaced. Speaker of the Senate John F. Fisk was next in the line of succession, but unacceptable to Magoffin. In August 1861, a deal was finally brokered. Fisk resigned as head of the state senate and was replaced by James F. Robinson, whose political philosophy was more in tune with the governor's. Magoffin then resigned the governorship and Robinson was elevated. To close the drama, the senate returned Fisk to the speaker's chair as now-Governor Robinson's replacement.[10]

The secession crisis also played out on a local level. On April 21, 1861, a crowd descended on the Putnam County, Tennessee, courthouse in protest of new President Abraham Lincoln's response to the Fort Sumter crisis by calling for troops to put down the southern revolt. This pro-slavery, pro-secession group quickly organized itself into a body intent on publicizing to its neighbors what it considered to be a gross misuse of presidential power. Having rejected the call for a secession convention, Putnam and many of its neighbors changed course following the bombardment of Sumter.[11] Among the areas reconsidering the secession question was White County, Tennessee, where post-Sumter anxiety rose to a fever pitch. The young diarist Amanda McDowell gave evidence of the townspeople's fervor: "news is flying around that they are going to hang a man by the name of Barger tomorrow at Sparta" because "he expressed Abolition principles most too freely." Although the planned hanging was likely little more than a rumor, such talk could not be ignored. In McDowell's case, her own father became the object of suspicion. "Wm. Willhite says that they were considerable whisperings in Sparta on Saturday about Father's being an Abolitionist; whispered hints of threats, etc."[12] In May, Judge Joseph Guild gave a pro-Confederate speech at Livingston in which he declared that those men who would vote for the Union should be hanged.[13] Another unionist speaker, Senator Andrew Johnson, visited Livingston to encourage the locals to remain loyal to the Union but was ordered not to speak by a group of "rabble" and threatened by a "drunken Dr who flourished his knife."[14] On June 4, Johnson gave a speech in Huntsville, in Scott County, urging voters to reject secession. A few days later the county's voters affirmed their commitment to the Union by a margin of 521 to 19. Despite the wishes of many citizens of the Cumberland, the statewide vote made the decision to withdraw Tennessee from the Union and sent the verdict to the people for ratification on June 9. With the die having been cast, the region reversed its previous course by overwhelmingly adopting secession.[15] Despite the inevitability of secession, Scott County remained steadfast in its opposition to leaving the Union. Within weeks of Tennessee's secession, the county passed a resolution calling for the establishment of the "Free and Independent State of Scott."[16] In May 1986, Scott County was officially readmitted to the state of Tennessee.[17]

Even before the people of Tennessee confirmed the legislature's choice, the decision had already been made. In May, Confederate companies were already being formed by the county's most ardent citizens. While some of these fledgling units would become integrated into state regiments and fight as regular soldiers at places like Shiloh, Vicksburg, and Chickamauga, others would operate locally, sometimes as guerrilla units. The overwhelming affirmation of the Confederate cause by the people of Putnam County caused many of their loyal neighbors to feel unsafe in their own communities, and indeed they often were. Many unionists left home and moved north to Kentucky, where they could either live within the comfort and protection of the United States or safely join the Federal army in the hopes that they might return to Putnam County as liberators.[18]

Though Clinton County, Kentucky, would gain a reputation for its unionism, some of its neighbors fully embraced the cause of the Confederacy. The movement for disunion was particularly strong in some of the counties of Middle Tennessee, many of which bordered Clinton to the south. With the day of decision regarding Tennessee's fate scheduled for June 8, 1861, electioneering began in earnest. Despite a majority of secessionists in many Middle Tennessee counties, there were enough unionists to exert significant influence over the results of that day.

Shortly before election day, one of the state's premier unionists arrived in Livingston, Tennessee, the county seat of Overton. Horace Maynard spent the interregnum between South Carolina's secession and Tennessee's vote on the issue in early June 1861 traveling the eastern half of the state hoping to inspire its citizens to remain with the Union, sometimes being met with threats of violence by those opposed to his speeches.[19] One of his final stops before the day of decision was in Livingston, where he was scheduled to speak. By the time of Maynard's arrival, the majority of Overton County residents were ready to support the Confederacy and they opposed allowing the famous advocate of union to take the stump in Livingston. Mary Catherine Sproul, a young schoolteacher and ardent unionist herself, recalled that on the eve of Maynard's speech, she heard that southern soldiers had been sent into town with orders "riddle his hide" if he attempted to speak. The next day, several prominent secessionists agreed on a resolution that forbade Maynard from delivering his address. Realizing little could be gained from challenging the overwhelming sentiment of the town, Maynard went on to his next appointment. Although southern feeling had gotten the best of him in Livingston, seven miles away in Monroe he gave his speech without so much as an interruption and continued to speak throughout Fentress County.[20]

In regions closely divided in loyalty, both secession and union fevers quickly became epidemic. These amplified feelings turned friends against friends and separated normally close families. Even the most logical citizen became irrational due to the temper of the day. As a schoolteacher, Sproul knew nearly everyone in Livingston. After her father proudly cast the only vote for union in town, several secessionists withdrew their children from her school. She found that because of her unpopular stance, "people who had professed the warmest friendship for me, now refused to be found in my presence." Worse, her father and brother endured frequent threats, including murder and conscription.[21]

Amanda McDowell witnessed similar behavior from her home in Sparta, Tennessee. On the day following Tennessee's vote, she wrote, "I guess it [Tennessee] is voted 'out of the Union' by this time. But it would not have been had the people been allowed to vote their true sentiments." She added, "Nearly all the Union men in this neighborhood stayed at home, not wishing to get into a brawl and deeming it a hopeless cause." McDowell was correct in her assessment. "Frank Coatney voted Union, said he would do it at the risk of his life, and did it, but things got so hot that he had to leave the grounds." One of McDowell's friends informed her that a pro-secessionist party was planning to visit Coatney that very night.[22]

Soon, staying at home was not enough. Although Elijah Kogier would meet his fate at the hands of Champ Ferguson, he spent the summer months "lying out in the mountains to keep away from rebel guerrillas."[23] In nearby Scott County, Tennessee, Hiram Marcum spent the nights sleeping in his fields to avoid being caught inside his house at night by Confederate patrols. On one particular night, he was awakened by the screams of his wife and daughter, who had received a night visit by a patrol. As the Confederates left the farm, one man remained behind, hoping to perpetrate a crime against the women. Although the Confederate severely wounded one of Marcum's daughters, Hiram was able to get into the house and kill him before the attack proceeded further.[24]

On June 29, 1861, the following story appeared in the pages of the *Nashville Patriot*: "A Lincolnite in Tennessee. The Cookville *Times* of the 13th says— Report says that Dr. Hale is making up a Lincolnite company in Fentress. Said Hale is a Northern man, therefore we did not expect anything else of him. But surely the Fentress Boys do not intend to Follow him. That fellow Hale ought to be made to leave the State or stretch hemp. Treason cannot be tolerated a moment in Tennessee now."[25] The next week, Hale took his treason to a new level by publicly celebrating Independence Day inside the border of a foreign country. A native of New Hampshire who moved to northern Fentress County, Tennessee, and became a respected member of his community, Hale chose to support the Union when the question of secession was presented. During the war, he frequently returned to Overton and Fentress counties to pilot unionists through the mountains into Kentucky and served as a scout and spy for the Union army in the Upper Cumberland region. Commemorating the holiday by hoisting a United States flag over his property at Hale's Mills, as he had done for several years, Hale signified his political stand despite the message it sent to his secessionist neighbors. Joining him were an estimated one thousand Tennesseans who held similar feelings. That day, Hale's daughter sang the "Star Spangled Banner" and the patriarch read the Declaration of Independence to the crowd. With the formalities complete, the masses ate on the grounds. News of Hale's Independence Day celebration did not impress local Confederates who planned to kill Hale and the other local unionist leaders.[26] On July 7, the Hale family left their home and went to Kentucky seeking safety.[27] J. D. Hale's first duties there consisted of meeting with Judge (and future governor) Thomas Bramlette and then traveling on to Louisville, where he reported to Federal authorities on the conditions in his part of Tennessee.[28]

John Smith of Travisville, Tennessee, expected retribution for his unabashed unionism. He wrote a friend about his concerns, "I might soon be in danger as the congress of the southern confederacy will soon be in cession and it is thought that it will pass some very stringent laws in respect to those in its realm whom it does not deem loyal."[29] Another Travisville resident, C. B. Ryan, voiced comparable concerns in a letter to loyal senator Andrew Johnson. Writing, "Our whole county was thrown in to intense excitement yesterday by the arrival among us of some 300 Volunteers from East. Tenn," Ryan added that their stated purpose was to make "all the Union men leave" or swear allegiance to "the Jeff Davis Confederacy." The merchant reported that the troops had not yet made any attempt to compel loyalty to the fledgling Confederacy and, if they did, he and his loyal neighbors "are determined to defend ourselves the best we can." As all Ryan and his neighbors had for weapons were "Country rifles and shot guns," he asked Johnson for firearms and affirmed his devotion to the cause of driving out the secessionists if he could secure support.[30]

Three days later, George W. Keith relayed similar news to the senator. Keith, a Morgan County resident who had served as county clerk and county surveyor, now wrote from the relative safety of Monticello, Kentucky. He informed Johnson of "The emmergency of our Condition in Morgan Scott & Fentress Counties" and noted that those circumstances "impels me to call on you for some exertion on your part for our protection." Verifying the same Confederate presence in his home region that Andrew Hall had noted only days before, Keith assured the state's most prominent unionist that loyalty remained in that region but required the support and assistance of the full nation.[31]

By the middle of August, Benjamin Staples described the conditions in Tennessee's border counties as unbearable. "The state of things in East Tennessee is indiscribable—Many of our people are prisoners in the rebel Camps." He described a citizenry besieged by Confederate cavalry who invaded every farm, taking everything of value they found and placing men and women under arrest indiscriminately. George W. Bridges, who had traveled north to the safety of Monticello with George Keith and Benjamin Staples, had attempted to sneak back into Tennessee to visit his family when Confederate authorities arrested him.[32]

Like so many other borderland residents, Champ Ferguson was also coming to grips with the changing face of his home country. Federal soldiers, whom he would soon consider mortal enemies, were arriving within miles of his home. A strong Union man, Captain John W. Tuttle of Company H, 3rd Kentucky Volunteer Infantry (U.S.A.), arrived in Albany, Kentucky. Originally from Mill Springs in nearby Wayne County, Tuttle's path to the Union army seemed preordained. His father had grown up in Litchfield, Connecticut, and had gone to school with a young Henry Ward Beecher. John had received a standard education at a private academy in south-central Kentucky and had gone to the University of Louisville, where he earned his degree in law in 1860. Now a soldier, Tuttle put his education to work as a diarist of his corner of the conflict.[33]

To Tuttle, the Clinton county seat was also the seat of Unionism in south-central Kentucky. Upon reaching town around midmorning, he noticed "the stars and stripes gaily fluttering to the breze above the tops of the houses." High riding Union sentiment brought out "a procession with 34 ladies in front on horseback, one of whom carried a national banner followed by about 60 cavalry and 500 infantry." In all, Tuttle estimated 2,000 persons had crowded into the little town for a military parade and a speech by his commander and the county's most famous son, Thomas E. Bramlette.[34]

Bramlette was still young and vigorous at the outbreak of war. Born in 1817 in Cumberland County, Kentucky, he made the most of his common school education. After studying law, he passed the state bar in 1837 and began his professional life. Winning a seat in the Kentucky House of Representatives in 1841, the Whig served a single term and chose not to seek reelection. In 1848, new governor John J. Crittenden appointed him state attorney general, a position he held until 1850. When Crittenden resigned to become President Millard Fillmore's attorney general, Bramlette followed suit and left Frankfort behind. Returning home to south-central Kentucky, he settled in Columbia, where he waited until 1856 to reenter public life as a judge in the Sixth Judicial District. As had become his habit, Bramlette again quit his position. Resigning from the bench in 1861, he embarked on a military career by raising a company for the Union cause in Kentucky. The 3rd Kentucky Volunteer Infantry, of which Captain Tuttle was a part, resulted. As commander, he spent much of his time traveling throughout south-central Kentucky, as he was doing that day in Albany, giving speeches and doing his part to rally borderland Kentuckians around the Union cause.[35]

Following a meal, soldiers and citizens alike walked out of town to grounds that would hold them all for Bramlette's speech. For three hours, the old-line Whig beseeched his fellow citizens of south-central Kentucky to show their allegiance to the old flag by joining regiments of the Union army being enlisted in town that day. Bramlette explained that his regiment would be used "for the purpose of aiding the Union men of E. Tennessee." That day, about thirty men enlisted with Bramlette and eighty-seven cavalrymen joined a company being raised by Frank Wolford.[36]

The news that Bramlette would speak sparked the interest of the Ferguson family. During his postwar trial, Champ remembered that he and his brother—probably Jim—went to town that day to hear what Bramlette had to say. In his testimony more than four years later, Ferguson alleged that he had tried to remain neutral during the early conflict; however, this statement cannot be taken at face value. In a newspaper interview shortly before his death he stated that he was "a Union man in the beginning; I was a Union man, till after the battle of Bull Run, in 1861; I electioneered at the various polls, in Clinton County, Kentucky, at the Spring elections, for Union candidates." He went on to say that once war became a reality, "I allied myself to the interests of my section."[37] One notable problem with Champ's statement is that his section of southern Kentucky was quite strongly unionist at the time and Tennessee had not yet left the Union. In an interview published on the same day, but conducted by a different correspondent, Champ's story changed dramatically. He claimed, "I was a Southern man at the start."[38] Despite Ferguson's conflicting explanations of his early loyalty, it is quite logical that he and Jim wished to hear the remarks in order to balance either personal feelings or other influences. Champ noted that Tom Travis, a brother-in-law of Bramlette, told him "that the Judge had given the South some hard licks." If true, Ferguson's notice of Bramlette's "hard licks" suggests that Champ was particularly sensitive to anti-southern comments even while he claimed neutrality regarding the up-coming war.[39]

The success Bramlette enjoyed in Albany was indicative of the general sen-timent of the region. Captain Tuttle wrote, "The feeling for the Union here is very strong and the most intense enthusiasm prevails." Whereas the unionist Mary Catherine Sproul suffered under the heavy hand of secessionists in Fen-tress County, Tennessee, in Clinton County, Kentucky, "A Secessionist is not allowed to open his mouth." With such a committed enemy so close, the men of Clinton County were fearful that an invasion might be at hand. Tuttle noted that "They have picket guards stationed out at every pass" and that an alarm had brought men into town from all over the county the night before to guard against attack.[40]

In a 1973 article, James E. Copeland formulated a method by which the level of unionism and secessionism could be studied. In his examination of Kentucky, he found four factors to be essential in measuring the question of loyalty. Most important, he calculated the numbers and percentages of white men who joined the Union army from each of Kentucky's 109 counties. Using the results to classify the counties as class one through five, with class five counties contributing the highest percentage to the Union, he constructed a useful tool for future historical studies. From his model, Clinton County emerges as the fourth most loyal county in the state. Only the mountainous eastern Kentucky counties of Owsley (13.64 percent), Estill (12.9 percent), and Clay (12.88 percent) contributed a higher percentage of their adult, white, male populations to the Federal cause. In Clinton's case, its 690 enlistees con-stituted 12.54 percent of the county's white, male population.[41] Another part of Copeland's equation is the question of whether the county sent a delegation to the Russellville Convention, where the issue of Kentucky's secession un-derwent its most serious, high-level discussion. Though the flatter and more agricultural northern and western sections of the state were well represented, the mountainous counties of eastern and south-central Kentucky, including Clinton, boycotted the meeting.[42] The third important statistic Copeland of-fers is slaveholders as a percentage of potential voters in Kentucky in 1860. In this category, Clinton ranks twenty-fifth out of 109.[43] The final measure is more historical: How did Democrats perform in the seven presidential elec-tions from 1836 through 1860? Unlike many of their neighbors who seldom saw a victorious Democrat, Clinton County residents cast 46.75 percent of its presidential votes for the party of Jefferson and Jackson in the twenty-four years that preceded the Civil War.[44]

Like the Sproul family living in Fentress, Champ Ferguson lived among enemies in Clinton. Although questionable, Ferguson claimed that he had not started out a secessionist.[45] He recalled that in late spring 1861, the people of Clinton County cast their first vote on the secession question. Champ recalled that he voted for the Union and only two men had cast their ballots for secession. Weeks later, he changed his mind and joined twenty-six others voting for secession. In the wake of these ballots, he reportedly joined a State Guard unit under a "Captain Taylor." During his postwar trial, he remembered, "After uniforms were procured, I overheard Capt. Taylor making some angry remarks . . . he declared that he would not muster us any more." Taylor told the men, "there [are] two parties and we [had] to take sides."[46] Such stark and polarizing statements were used on both sides of the intensely partisan conflict throughout the Cumberland region and would become part of Ferguson's message to those who attempted to remain uncommitted throughout the war.

During July and August 1861, the borderland of Kentucky and Tennessee teemed with activity. Formal military organizations had been recruiting for months, and many of the most ardent secessionists and unionists had already joined their respective regiments and were in camp, oftentimes some distance from home. Into the void stepped more localized units such as Home Guard organizations and partisan bands. Citizens watched from their windows as the advancing conflict undercut their neighborhoods' relative peace and stability. Although John Smith saw that "the war dogs which barked so much, up and down, the state line have all gone," he was not complacent. Despite the fact that most of the ideologues had joined either the Confederate army or the Confederate government, he still frequently saw danger, now in the form of localized regiments who might mix military motives with personal revenge. He recalled how "a company passed with a flag on which was written in large letters 'Bull puppies,'" and added, "From what I can learn they looked like they might be man eaters, as not a man of them had touched his beard for four months."[47]

By August 1861, the pro-Union citizens of Clinton began targeting Ferguson and others who were thought to be disloyal. Early that month, the two companies of Union soldiers, including Captain Tuttle, that had been in the area for general security were called away. A group of unionist citizens bent on providing public safety organized themselves into a Home Guard. One of their first priorities was to snuff out local dissent and arrest those residents not supportive of the Union. While Ferguson sought to downplay his level of commitment to the cause of the South, he likely became very supportive of and interested in the infant Confederate army. His enemies claimed that during the summer of 1861, "he frequently visited a rebel camp in Fentress county, and conveyed to them all the information he could obtain." Champ painted his visits to the Confederate encampment more benignly.[48] He contended that when a Knoxville regiment moved into the region and camped on the Wolf River, he "went over occasionally and sometimes stopped to see them drill."[49] Whatever Ferguson's reasons for hanging out around the Confederate camp are irrelevant; his trips there clearly marked him as a secessionist living in the midst of a very unionist Clinton County.

L. W. "Bug" Duvall was one of these Home Guardsmen and had Champ Ferguson at the top of his list. Duvall remembered that one night after dark in late August 1861, he and several others were traveling south toward Jamestown, Tennessee, when they unexpectedly met Ferguson and another man on the road.[50] Needing a plan of action to take the two men, who were likely armed, Duvall's group passed and hurriedly settled on a method. Wheeling their horses, Duvall and his friends quickly caught up with Champ. Apparently not suspecting any trouble, Ferguson nervously commanded "hold on" when the men rode up to him with weapons drawn and pointed. Knowing Champ's rough reputation, his captors also felt edgy, to the point that, Bug Duvall remembered, one of his fellows "snapped" a pistol in the confusion. When Ferguson challenged Duvall's brother Van with "you had as soon shoot a man as not," Van Duvall replied, "yes, I will blow your brains out if you move." At this point, L. W. Duvall stepped in and, in an effort to defuse the situation, assured his nervous brother that Ferguson had given up and violence would not be necessary. Disarming the two men, the Duvall brothers and their fellows found Ferguson to be the lighter armed of the two, carrying only an "old 'pepperbox' six-shooter." Champ's traveling companion, "Dinton,"[51] was carrying a pistol and a large butcher's knife. With two prisoners in tow, the group turned back toward Kentucky.[52]

Duvall dropped the surprisingly docile and cooperative prisoner with friends in Clinton County. The next morning, four of the men started with Ferguson toward Camp Dick Robinson, where he would be compelled to join the Federal army. Unarmed and outnumbered, Ferguson did not force the issue, although he did look for an opportunity to escape. Although little is known about the method of his getaway, Brents noted that the prisoner seemed resigned to whatever fate awaited him and lulled his guards into complacency. After several days on the road, the opportunity came and Champ slipped away from his captors.[53]

His arrest and forced march toward the Union army at Camp Dick Robinson made a profound impression on Ferguson. Already subtly participating in the early conflict by the time of his capture, the incident apparently convinced him that he could not escape his fate as a direct participant. He immediately set about turning the tables on his captors. Alvin Piles recalled that within days of Ferguson's arrest, he saw Champ at a blacksmith's shop with one rifle, which Ferguson announced was loaded, and another under repair. He also told the smithy to make a large, double-bladed knife. Piles, a unionist who left Fentress County early in the war and moved to Indiana where he joined the 148th Indiana Volunteer Infantry, remembered that several others at the shop asked Champ what he was going to do with those weapons, to which the recently harassed Ferguson responded, he "would like them to catch him without a loaded gun these times."[54] It seems that Ferguson had by now chosen his own personal course in the war. Toward the end of his postwar trial in 1865, he claimed that after his arrest by the Home Guards, he waited a couple of months and joined Bledsoe's company in November.[55]

As part of this course, Ferguson swore to combat those he considered enemies in any way possible. The first recorded instance of his partisan activity came in middle September 1861, in Albany. Since the Union soldiers had moved out of Clinton County in early August, a crisis had been gradually escalating between unionists and secessionists. Perhaps seeking revenge for his arrest, simply wishing to financially capitalize on local instability, or both, Ferguson and a cohort met D. P. Wright on the road near Albany and proceeded to rob him. Wright, a storekeeper and outspoken advocate of the Union, had known Ferguson for what he estimated as six or seven years prior to the war, but he grew nervous when he saw that Ferguson and his partner were both armed. When Ferguson ordered Wright to stop, the storekeeper instinctively spurred his horse and fled. After a chase of approximately four miles, Ferguson turned around and went into Albany, where he proceeded to rob the man's store. When he returned to his business, Wright found that an estimated $1,500 to $2,000 worth of goods had been taken.[56]

On the afternoon of September 23, a company of two hundred partisan cavalrymen rode into Albany. In town, they visited the stores, taking whatever they wanted. They robbed individuals and stole $300 in gold from a local doctor. Several of the men took thirty-six stand of arms that had been stored in town by the Kentucky militia.[57] Although Ferguson was not specifically identified as a participant, it is unlikely that he would have let such an opportunity pass.

Clinton County Home Guards responded to this Confederate activity. The unionists spent the night rounding up and jailing suspected secessionists, expecting that their actions would destroy overt Southern sympathy in the area.[58] Confederate General Felix K. Zollicoffer estimated that "400 Lincoln men . . . made prisoners of some of our friends in the neighborhood," but Clinton County, Kentucky, historian Jack Ferguson challenged his assertion, writing that the number "seems impossibly high considering the departure of Union soldiers from the county."[59] However, Union Colonel William A. Hoskins suggested that a majority of the Home Guards, which "came to the relief of the people of this county," originated from nearby Russell County, Kentucky, explaining the large number of able-bodied unionists who converged on Albany.[60] Upon hearing of the arrests while in Tennessee, Confederate Captain W. Scott Bledsoe, Champ Ferguson's attorney, "dashed over the line to Albany" where he "routed the Union men," captured several old muskets, and freed the jailed men.[61] In Hoskins's report to his commander, George H. Thomas, he relayed that when he arrived in Albany on September 28, the town was still occupied by the unionist Home Guard.[62] On September 29, the Home Guards, with the help of Hoskins's regiment, pushed the remainder of Bledsoe's company back across the state line.[63] Although Jack Ferguson suggests that Champ was arrested by the Home Guard during this episode, no evidence supports that conclusion.[64]

Surprisingly, the polarization that the question of war fomented in Clinton County struck the Ferguson family even deeper than Champ's arrest in late August and the Home Guard roundup in September. Just as brothers had fought brothers in the American Revolution, the same would prove true in the Civil War. In Champ Ferguson's case, his family was being divided by the question of secession or union. Though he was destined to join the Confederacy, some of his siblings unabashedly supported the Union cause. One of Ferguson's younger brothers, Jim, stood as the family's most ardent and active unionist, while another, Ben, also joined the Union army. Though brothers, Champ and Jim shared little common ground and would spend a considerable part of the early war hunting for each other.[65]

John Inscoe adds to the discussion by identifying the three basic elements of divided loyalty in Appalachia. First, he sees inherent fluidity, which, in the case of Ferguson's Civil War experience, can be seen through his pragmatic movement between the categories laid out by Robert Mackey. Second, he sees localized loyalty that can divide counties, communities, and families. In Ferguson's case, he was surrounded by these realities. He found hostility to his cause in his home county in Kentucky, yet only a few miles south in Tennessee he found outright acceptance. Within his own family, the divisions were likewise clear. Third, within the divided populace, a level of concealment or deception is usually present. In this case, Ferguson departs from the equation: Simply put, he did not tolerate dissenters.[66]

On the same day that Bledsoe's band was forced back across the state line, Champ's brother Jim became involved in the war's first fight in Tennessee. At the small community of Travisville, in Fentress County, the 1st Kentucky Cavalry (U.S.A.), augmented by Clinton County Home Guards, met a substantial Confederate force.[67] In the brief fight that resulted, Union men prevailed and forced the Confederates to flee into the hills. Although few details of the affair are known, it is notable for Jim Ferguson's participation. Either during or after the fight, Ferguson, a unionist, killed James Saufley, a secessionist. Perhaps looking for vengeance, when relatives buried Saufley in the Travisville Cemetery, next to the road and overlooking the battleground, on the headstone they engraved his name and date of birth followed by "Killed by James Ferguson of 1st Ky Cav U.S.A. 29 Sept 1861."[68]

Federal forces stayed in Albany until the middle of October, when it was decided that moving northward and crossing the Cumberland River would offer a stronger defensive position. At the same time, the Union withdrawal from Clinton County would allow nearby Confederates to avenge their embarrassing expulsion from Albany. From Overton County, Tennessee, James McHenry wrote to General Albert Sidney Johnston regarding the Federal threat and urging a military movement into the area.[69] W. T. Gass urged his superior the same, writing from near Livingston, Tennessee, that since most of the Federal troops had withdrawn across the Cumberland, "There is a perfect reign of terror in Kentucky. The Southern men are greatly in fear of their lives." He offered, "My opinion is that our four companies of cavalry could do a great good by scouting in Clinton County, Kentucky."[70] For the two months that followed, small groups of Federals and Confederates occasionally competed for Albany and the surrounding area, though neither could hold it permanently.

Jim Ferguson grew into a larger man than his oldest brother. Standing an estimated six feet, two inches, and possessing remarkable strength, the younger sibling's size may have struck a nerve of intimidation in his older brother. Like Champ, Jim had a rough reputation throughout the region. J. A. Brents recorded that Jim had some experience with the law. He had been indicted for passing fake bills, although he avoided trial on the charge. His indictment could have been a result of rumors that Champ ran a counterfeiting operation, or could have contributed to the hearsay. He was also said to have been "a great litigant in court, always suing somebody, if he was not sued or prosecuted himself." His taste for alcohol proved his greatest demon. Considered a peaceful man when sober, he became rowdy and troublesome when drunk, which frequently resulted in his arrest.[71]

As the fever of secession grew, the brothers found themselves at loggerheads. Politically, the two had always differed. Champ supported the Democrats and Jim the Whigs. After the destruction of the Whig Party, Jim likely looked to the American Party and, later, the Opposition Party for political guidance. As war became inevitable, Jim grew active in the region's unionist movement. Apparently possessing a good voice, honest personality, and a convincing manner, he earned credit for "keeping several [citizens] from being carried away by the excitement into secession." When the battle lines were finally drawn, Jim went to Camp Dick Robinson and eagerly joined in the fight. Very early in the war, he enlisted in the 1st Kentucky Cavalry, but grew tired of camp life and military organization. Additionally, he found it difficult to adjust to the military bureaucracy. He apparently showed no hesitation in obeying orders given by his officers, but he could not understand how an officer from another regiment could command him. At least once he refused to follow an order from such an officer and was briefly jailed for his insubordination.[72]

Brother Jim also held the clear view of good and evil that would come to hallmark Champ Ferguson's war. J. A. Brents wrote that while Jim was in camp at Dick Robinson, he returned home on furlough where he met a man named "Beasly." When asked his position on the ongoing political question, "Beasly avowed his disunion sentiments," at which point "Ferguson told him that he must go to camp with him." Brents, who was not an eyewitness, wrote that when Beasly refused the order and attempted to draw a weapon, Jim "instantly shot him with a Sharpe's rifle." Upon his return to Camp Dick Robinson, Jim turned himself over to Federal authorities and confessed his crime. As Beasly "stood fair as a citizen," men, both unionists and secessionists, from through-out south-central Kentucky "raised a cry against Ferguson, demanding his life." Jim spent "two or three weeks" imprisoned while military authorities de-cided what to do with him. Brents explained that the initial plan had been to turn him over to the appropriate civil authorities for trial but the war had done much to disrupt the wheels of justice. Although angry locals wished Jim to be jailed and tried in their court, the system was unable to accommodate them. Not wanting to offer Jim Ferguson to a possible lynch mob and wishing to save the life of a valuable scout, the U.S. Army released him and informed civil authorities that he would be delivered to them upon their making "the proper demand, accompanied by legal authority." As the war grew more serious, Jim's case faded in importance at Camp Robinson and in Clinton County. Brents remembered, "The matter here dropped, and the case was never investigated." By November 1861, Jim had requested and secured a position as a scout, an ar-rangement that would periodically send him into his home region.[73]

Around the same time that brother Jim was earning the enmity of regional secessionists, Champ began cultivating his infamous reputation among the unionist population. On November 1, 1861, he appeared in the doorway of Mrs. Esther Frogg's one-room house. His was a familiar face to her family as she had grown up near Champ and had "known him all his life." Ferguson entered and offered her a "How d'ye." Appearing somewhat agitated, Fergu-son refused a seat when offered one by Mrs. Frogg. She offered him apples, to which he curtly responded that he had been eating apples and wanted no more. Getting to his point, Ferguson asked about William Frogg, whom Mrs. Frogg said was "in bed very sick." Seeing his longtime friend now in the darkened room with his five-month-old child lying in the cradle next to the bed, Fergu-son stepped toward him and asked, "How are you Mr. Frogg?" The sick man responded, "I am very sick. I had the measles, and have had a relapse." Unim-pressed, Ferguson answered, "I reckon you caught the measles at Camp Dick Robinson." Frogg, beginning to understand the purpose of Ferguson's visit, denied ever visiting the camp (a claim corroborated by his wife after the war was over). In no mood for excuses, regardless of their validity, Ferguson on that day began his career as a Confederate guerrilla. After silently walking to the door, then returning to the bedside, he drew out a revolver and shot Frogg. Esther Frogg remembered that she instinctively started out of the house when she heard the first gunshot and had barely crossed the threshold when the second round was fired.[74]

A. J. Mace, a fifteen-year-old boy who was visiting the Froggs at the time, bolted from his seat by the fireplace upon hearing the first report. Briefly stopping at the doorway, he turned around in time to see Frogg sitting up in bed when Ferguson fired his second shot, causing the victim to sink back into the bed. The terrified Mace then ran home, leaving Esther Frogg and her child at the house with Mr. Frogg's killer and two men who had ridden up with him but remained in the road.[75] Mrs. Frogg remembered that she stayed outside for fifteen minutes while Ferguson remained inside the house, during which time he was likely searching for weapons or valuables. When she saw Ferguson walking toward his horse, she went back inside, where she found her husband dead, shot once in the right breast and once in the right side.[76]

Ferguson's attack on William Frogg epitomizes the nature of warfare as understood by Cumberland region guerrillas. Though Ferguson had visited Confederate encampments himself and begrudged Federal harassment for his interest, he was unwilling to allow Frogg the same liberty. Despite Frogg's denial of traveling to Camp Dick Robinson, his wife testified that her husband had joined the 12th Kentucky Infantry (U.S.A.) at Albany. He had probably enlisted in August when Bramlette spoke but had "never gone with them" and "had never gone armed," probably indicating his habit of not frequently carrying weapons during his day-to-day business.[77]

Late in the postwar trial, Ferguson attempted to defend himself against the evidence offered in the Frogg incident. He contended that Frogg was an active member of the Home Guards in Clinton County and had participated in his arrest in late August. Although Frogg may have played a role in Ferguson's capture, little can be believed of his story. On Monday, September 18, 1865, Champ Ferguson took the stand in his own defense, at which time he became confused and proceeded to inflict damage to his case. He freely admitted visiting the Froggs at the time in question and recalled, "in passing near Frogg's house . . . with some men, I stopped at his place. No one was there but Frogg and his wife and child." At this point, the accused misplaced A. J. Mace, who was sitting near the fire, with Martin Hurt, a young man who testified that he had been secreted beneath another house's floorboards when Ferguson committed another murder, and claimed, "I did not see him." Concerned by the potential damage that Ferguson might do to his own case, one of his attorneys advised him to make no further statements.[78]

After all the arguments had been made and the court had decided his fate, Ferguson gave a series of candid interviews in which he discussed some of the events in question. In regard to Frogg, his story differed somewhat from the testimony given. Claiming that not only had William Frogg been an active member of the Home Guards and had "instigated my arrest while I was peaceably pursuing my avocations as a farmer," Frogg had "laid in wait on the highways to kill me" and had openly made threats to neighbors regarding Ferguson's life. He remembered arriving at Frogg's house and seeing Esther peeling apples. Ferguson did not note if any words had been spoken during the affair, just "upon seeing me, [Frogg] pulled the cover over his face." As would become common in Ferguson's defense, he concluded, "I considered myself justified in killing him."[79]

Killing a sick man confined to bed carries a suggestion of cowardice. To this, Ferguson answered that Frogg "was a stouter man than I was," and would recover and "waylay and shoot me." He went further to say that in his region, it "was our policy to take every possible advantage of our antagonist; if we did not, we would soon find ourselves in a snare." Whereas many saw Champ's actions as cowardly, he saw merit in his course. When asked if he thought Frogg would have done the same to him, Ferguson responded affirmatively and added, "I took time by the forelock, as people say . . . I thought there was nothing like being in time." Indeed, Ferguson did capitalize on all the advantages when dealing with a foe.[80] In an interview after his postwar trial, Champ, in simplistic terms, offered an explanation of the nature of war in the Upper Cumberlands. "We were having a sort of miscellaneous war, up there, through Fentress county, Tennessee, and Clinton county, Kentucky, and all through that region. Every man was in danger of his life: if I hadn't kill[ed] my neighbor, he would have killed me. Each of us had from 20 to 30 proscribed enemies, and it was regarded as legitimate to kill them at any time, at any place, under any circumstances."[81] Scarcely a month passed after the murder of William Frogg before Ferguson acted again. This time his target would nearly prove too much for him.

The second day of December began in an eventful way for Champ Ferguson. That morning in Albany, he and another man were witnessed stealing one of Daniel Kogier's horses in front of the Clinton County courthouse. The lack of civil authority along the borderland made such instances surprisingly common. Cursing loudly as he saddled the horse, Ferguson challenged the "God-damned Lincolnite" to come out so he could kill him. Either wisdom or absence kept Kogier from appearing, so Champ finished saddling the animal and rode him out of town toward the Wood farm.[82]

Prior to the war, Champ Ferguson and Reuben Wood had been good friends. Pheroba Hale even remembered Wood as saving Ferguson's life after the camp meeting incident.[83] The secession crisis, however, would irreparably damage their friendship to the point that the two were prepared to kill each other by late fall 1861. On the evening of December 2, Ferguson and two others driving hogs neared the Wood house. Reuben Wood, having just finished feeding his livestock, stepped into the road to meet them, but Ferguson ordered him out of the way. Wood, probably estimating and wishing to avoid Champ's sour mood, apparently turned and headed home. About the time Wood reached his door, Ferguson and one of the drovers galloped up to the fence and shouted for him. They repeated the question that had gotten William Frogg killed: "I suppose you have been to Camp Robinson." If the postwar trial testimony is to be believed, Ferguson responded to Wood's affirmative answer "using violent and bitter language." Reuben Wood's daughter Elizabeth recalled that Ferguson bellowed, "nobody but a damned old Lincolnite would be caught at any such place" and continued ranting for "five or ten minutes." Ferguson then drew a pistol and ordered Wood, "Don't you beg and don't you dodge." At this point, the Wood family, terrified that Champ would kill Reuben as he had killed Frogg, began begging for his life. Mother and daughter stood in the doorway pleading while Reuben Wood reminded Champ of their long friendship. He implored, "Why Champ, I have nursed you. Has there ever been any misunderstanding between us?" Ferguson's stark response followed, "No, Reuben, you have always treated me like a gentleman, but you have been to Camp Robinson, and I intend to kill you."[84]

His purpose thus stated, Ferguson "took time by the forelock" and shot Wood. Although the bullet entered above and left of the pit of his stomach, the sixty-year-old Wood remained upright. Likely surprised that his target was solidly hit and still standing, Champ fired a second time, but missed. Shot and bleeding, Reuben Wood drew his coat tight around his wound, stumbled around the corner of the house, and entered through the back door. Ferguson hopped down from his horse and started around the other side of the house, hoping to meet Wood in back. Mother and daughter now followed the path Reuben Wood took and met an incredulous Ferguson near the back door asking, "Where is he? Where is he?" Realizing Wood must have gone into the house, Champ stepped inside after his quarry. Mother and daughter heard "another shot, . . . chairs falling over and a desperate noise." Screaming, the women ran nearly a half-mile to alert neighbors.[85]

When they returned to the house moments later, Ferguson was gone and they found the wounded patriarch sitting by the fire. Fearing that if he lay down he would die, Wood insisted on telling his family his account of the fight. He recalled that, once inside the back door, he grabbed a hatchet and backed into a corner within reach of the front door, through which he mistakenly expected Champ to enter. Seeing Ferguson come in the back door, but realizing Ferguson could not see him well in the darkened house, Wood leapt at his pursuer as Champ readied for another shot. Knocking the pistol downward with the hatchet about the time Ferguson pulled the trigger, Wood saved himself from another shot. Fighting in close quarters, Wood kept knocking the revolver aside when Champ attempted to level it. The two tumbled into a bed, at which time Ferguson's grip on the gun slipped and it became lost in the quilts. With the pistol no longer a concern, Wood focused his attention on hurting Ferguson. He hit him several times with the hatchet, with the most severe blows to the side of Champ's head. Realizing the tables had turned, Ferguson got to his feet and left the house, with Wood following and inflicting more damage with his weapon. Along with Ferguson that day was Raine Philpott, an old friend who would spend much of the war years riding with Champ. Philpott came to the aid of his friend that day by shoving his pistol in Wood's face and cautioning against further pursuit of Champ. At that point, Wood staggered back to the house and went upstairs, where he could more easily defend himself, if necessary. Still holding his hatchet in one hand and a pitchfork in his right, he waited while he heard someone briefly enter the house, retrieve Ferguson's pistol, but then leave. After giving his account to his family, Wood took to the bed and never got up again. Two agonizing days later, after telling and retelling his story to all who came to visit him, Reuben Wood died.[86]

Nearly four years after the event, Elizabeth Wood took the stand in Champ Ferguson's postwar trial and testified as to his role in her father's murder. Apart from her direct testimony, she provided considerable excitement in the courtroom that day. The *Nashville Daily Press* reported that at the point she recalled her father striking Ferguson in the head with the hatchet, Miss Wood pointed at him and screamed, "There is the place the hatchet hit; you can see the scar now." The reporter watched as "The eyes of all were suddenly turned on Ferguson, and under the combined gaze, he evidently winced."[87] Indeed, Ferguson had received a serious wound that day. Numerous others around Albany remembered seeing him in the days that followed Wood's killing walking around with his head wrapped in a bandage.[88]

In his defense, Ferguson claimed he knew Wood was a member of the same company as his own brother Jim and that "I knew that he [Wood] intended killing me if he ever got a chance." Champ complained that both Jim and Reuben Wood "hunted me down, and drove me fairly to desperation." Recalling the day in question, Ferguson reversed the roles, making himself the victim. If Champ's story is to be believed, an unarmed Wood accosted three armed men on the road and "commenced on me, using the most abusive language." Ferguson finished, as would become his habit, by maintaining his unshakable air of righteousness. "I never expressed a regret for committing the act, and never will. He was in open war against me."[89]

Though Ferguson probably failed to realize it, his partisan activities were condemning him in his own home county. As Clinton County was a unionist stronghold, few citizens sympathized with Ferguson and his cause. When he killed a man, he further alienated Clinton County folks and created additional enemies to take the victim's place. Such was the case in regard to Reuben Wood. Having heard that his father had been seriously wounded, Robert Wood hurried home, finally arriving in the middle of the night several hours before the man's death. After his father's funeral, Robert, bent on revenge, began organizing a small band that he hoped could trap and kill Ferguson. He recalled that although he had always liked Champ, he began hunting him after his father's murder. Robert, along with two of his brothers, a cousin, and another man, set a trap near Ferguson's house, which stood only about a mile from the Wood place. Under the cover of darkness, the five men spread out in the woods along the road and waited, expecting to catch Ferguson leaving the house. Just after daylight, the plan started to come together. Ferguson and Philpott came down the road at a full trot, with three others following several yards behind. As Ferguson and Philpott passed the first man, he let go with both barrels of a double-barreled shotgun, with most of the charge going into the neck of Ferguson's horse. The three men following behind wheeled their horses and fled, leaving the other two to fend for themselves. Wood remembered that after the initial shock, Ferguson and Philpott lay down on their horses and rode through the gauntlet as fast as they could. Having failed in their quest and wary that a nearby Confederate company had been alerted, Wood and the other men abandoned their ambush plan.[90]

With Robert Wood's attempt at retribution, Champ Ferguson began to realize that the seeds of discord he had helped sow in Clinton County were turning against him. From that point forward, he spent a majority of his time in Tennessee, only occasionally sneaking home under the cover of darkness.[91] Not yet an official part of the Confederate cause, his recent activities irrevocably moved him outside the graces of his unionist home county. Though Clinton County officially lay behind Felix Zollicoffer's Confederate line, its faith in the Union, in part fostered by pro-Confederate guerrilla activity like Ferguson's, would remain strong.

FIGHT ON THE CUMBERLAND

Each man feels an impulse to kill his neighbor lest he be first killed by him.
—ABRAHAM LINCOLN on guerrillas

Logan's Cross Roads, Mill Springs, Beech Grove—whatever one calls the fight that took place on January 19, 1862, on the north bank of the Cumberland River, it defined the Civil War as it would progress in southern Kentucky. The war had opened in the summer of 1861 with the Confederacy facing the daunting challenge of maintaining a military line of defense along its northern border. A significant part of this responsibility fell to Brigadier General Felix K. Zollicoffer, whose undermanned and poorly prepared army struggled to hold its ground. After an opening engagement at Wildcat Mountain in October, where entrenched Federals dealt attacking Confederates a severe defeat, the defensive line that stretched across Kentucky from Cumberland Gap to the Mississippi River became even more tenuous. In January 1862, Zollicoffer's Confederates met Brigadier General George H. Thomas's Federals near Logan's Cross Roads, Kentucky. The battle that followed answered many of the questions that concerned the early days of military campaigns. It proved to the Confederacy that Lincoln's generals were serious about keeping Kentucky on the side of union. The battle gave the government in Washington its first major victory of the war. And, importantly, Thomas's nearby victory emboldened south-central Kentucky unionists while pushing many of their secessionist neighbors backward across the Tennessee border. While the broader military implications of the Battle of Mill Springs are well known, to the local community, the fight acted as a catalyst to further widen the political breach along the Kentucky-Tennessee border.

Since September 1861, Zollicoffer's Confederates had been encamped close to Cumberland Gap. Their job was to guard that important pass against a possible Federal invasion. Unionists in eastern Tennessee had spent considerable time, effort, and risk attempting to convince President Lincoln to order an invasion of their region to rescue them from their oppressors. Unwilling to allow such an incursion, the Confederate government ordered a close guard kept on this all-important passage through the mountains. For the job, the government in Richmond chose Felix Kirk Zollicoffer. A newspaper editor prior to the outbreak of war and a veteran of the Seminole War, Zollicoffer had forged a reputation for himself as one of Tennessee's leading Whigs during the 1840s and 1850s. Despite his history of poor health, he strove to remain vigorous, winning several state political offices and a term in Congress. As delegate to the Washington Peace Conference during the winter of 1860–61, he sought reconciliation rather than warfare and even declined a commission as a major general in command of all Tennessee Union troops. He realized the inevitability of the conflict in July 1861 and accepted a commission as a brigadier general charged with maintaining Confederate control over unionist eastern Tennessee. Four months later, his army had seen the elephant at Wildcat Mountain and had pulled back to a more convenient, centralized, and defensible position on the Cumberland River.[1]

On November 29, 1861, Zollicoffer, moving north through Albany, arrived at Mill Springs on the Cumberland River. There, he expected that he could cover more territory than in the mountains he had recently fled. Within days, he ordered his force across the river and had his men dig in at Beech Grove. Although much criticism has been laid at Zollicoffer's feet for placing the river at his back, the citizen-turned-soldier had learned a valuable lesson in the mountains. His movement to the north shore of the river allowed his supply train to move by water rather than overland. Additionally, the only substantial force nearby was small and fifteen miles away.[2]

The month of December opened with the Union and Confederacy headed for a showdown on the Cumberland River. To the southwest, the conflict was escalating in Clinton County. Apart from the killing of Reuben Wood, the month would prove difficult for the Ferguson family. Champ was carrying a serious head wound given him by Wood during the fight, and his brother Jim was also destined to meet fate.

By December, Jim Ferguson's 1st Kentucky Cavalry (U.S.A.) was encamped at Columbia, Kentucky, just north of the Cumberland River. With the Confederates in control of the area south of the river, Jim was sent into enemy territory on several occasions to gather intelligence from unionist citizens. After several incursions, Ferguson's luck ran out. On the night of December 18, 1861, at a house between Lancaster and Stanford, Kentucky, an unknown man called in to Jim telling him that his horse had gotten loose. He stepped outside to see about the horse when someone shot him twice with a shotgun. Despite being wounded in the stomach and thigh, Ferguson stumbled back inside, retrieved his rifle, and blindly returned fire. The seriousness of his injuries doomed him and before he died, Jim confessed that he had killed eight men during his brief military career.[3]

Another Ferguson brother, Ben, also felt the sting of war that winter. From the beginning, Ben claimed to be loyal to the Union, although he refused to join the army and stayed at home, near Albany, for the duration of the war. Apparently, his claims of loyalty were true. In the same month that Champ killed Reuben Wood and Jim was assassinated, one of Champ's closest friends and trusted allies, Raine Philpott, shot Ben in the shoulder for an unknown reason.[4] Normally, such an act perpetrated on one's relative would destroy a friendship, but Ben had abandoned Champ while Raine stood by him, causing Champ and Raine to continue to be close. While the war destroyed some bonds, it strengthened others in unlikely ways.

Raine Philpott was considerably younger than Ferguson. About twenty-four at the outbreak of the war, he was active and impetuous and became nearly inseparable from Ferguson as the war escalated. J. A. Brents noted that Philpott grew up an only child and was "of good parentage, and received an excellent education." As his father died when he was just a child, Philpott inherited a considerable amount of property when he turned twenty-one. Given to gambling and drinking, he soon wasted much of his newly received fortune. Like Ferguson, he also found himself in trouble in such surroundings. At one point while drinking, he tried to stab a man with whom he was arguing, but his adversary was quicker and more sober and stabbed Philpott first. He spent more than a month recovering from the wound, but as Brents wrote, he "was none the wiser for the lesson received." During the war, Philpott and Ferguson reportedly worked together, frequently stealing livestock and selling it to line their own purses. Stories differ about Philpott's ultimate fate. Brents relayed a rumor that Ferguson and another man killed and robbed him. Another story held that Philpott abandoned the Upper Cumberland region for the wide-open spaces of Texas.[5] Although such speculation abounds, Ferguson himself answered the question. He reported that while out on an operation, the column came to a fork in the road. Some confusion existed as to which route to take, with Philpott and another trusted lieutenant, Henry Sublett, growing loud in their argument. During the heat of the moment, both men drew their weapons and fired at the other. Philpott apparently missed his target, but Sublett's bullet found its mark.[6] While angry that he had lost a valued friend, Ferguson likely moved past the episode quickly.

As Christmas drew near, the Confederate cause in south-central Kentucky appeared strong. Now that Zollicoffer occupied the north bank of the Cumberland, the river could be used to bring in supplies; however, weather undermined his plan. A lack of rain had dropped the water level to the point that steamers could only bring supplies as far as Carthage, Tennessee, where they had to be offloaded and carried the remaining 120 miles overland.[7] During the week preceding the new year, Ferguson and Philpott were in Fentress County, Tennessee, helping guide one of Zollicoffer's wagon trains as it passed through partisan territory. Marion Johnson remembered that after dark several of the men in the column ran into himself and five others. Ferguson and Philpott ordered the men to halt. Johnson and two others dismounted and complied while the remaining three made their escape. Seeking to know the identities of those who ran off, Champ Ferguson stepped up to Johnson and asked. Probably fearing for his life, Johnson quickly supplied his captors with the names of the three who fled.[8]

While Ferguson rode off in search of the men who eluded him, Johnson, George Sandusky, and Preston Huff were forced to stay in the Confederate camp that night. The next morning came without Ferguson's return. Moving into Kentucky, the wagon train was met by several men from W. Scott Bledsoe's company, who took charge of the prisoners and delivered them to Zollicoffer's camp. At the Confederate camp, the men were turned loose, probably on the promise that they would do nothing to aid the Union or harm the Confederacy. On their way home, however, they again ran into Champ Ferguson. Likely angry that the men he had captured only days before had been released, the lone guerrilla drew his pistol and demanded that Preston Huff "get down, that he wanted that horse." Knowing Ferguson's reputation, Huff quickly dismounted and said he "could have the horse." Ferguson took the horse and told Huff that he "had a notion to kill him." Ordering him to unsaddle the animal, he asked what Huff had in his saddlebags. Huff replied that he had nothing but an empty whiskey bottle, and Ferguson, apparently carrying a bottle himself and quite possibly under its influence, then asked him if he wanted a drink, but to "touch it God-damned light."

As Ferguson was preparing to take Huff's horse, he halted two Confederate soldiers who rode up to the men. They asked what Ferguson was doing with the men and he replied that he was going to take Huff's horse. Not satisfied with his answer, the men asked why. Ferguson angrily responded, "his father is a God-damned old Lincolnite." Returning his attention to Huff, Ferguson told him if he "had anything to say to say it quick." Huff recalled that Ferguson asked him if "I did not want to go up to that little place above here they called 'New Heaven,'" explaining that "they had a new government now and had a new Heaven too" for unionists such as Huff and his friends. Huff began begging for his life, at which point Ferguson asked if Huff would go home and remain there. Inexplicably, Huff tested Ferguson's patience by replying, "it was very hard to do. A man is bound to travel about sometimes." This exchange returned Ferguson to the defining factor of his participation in the war. He told Huff that he would teach the Huff clan a set of hard lessons and then announced his intention to kill Lewis Huff, Andrew J. Huff, and Van Duvall. Apparently looking for an excuse to let Huff go and deliver his message to the family, Ferguson asked again if he "could go home and not be called away." This time Huff said he "would try it." As a final insult, Ferguson, who was still mounted, told Huff to pull the bridle of Champ's horse over its head and to place his feet in the stirrups before allowing the man to depart. Huff recalled that "he took my horse, saddle, bridle, and saddlebags with him and I never saw him anymore."[9] Indeed, few men drew such a fortunate lot when tangling with Champ Ferguson.

Many other risky characters inhabited the region, either preying on unknown victims or settling old scores. William Hull, a poor Overton County farmer, fell victim to a bushwhacker during the war. The "Yankee guerrillas" shot Hull in the face, the bullet entering between his right eye and nose and exiting out the back of his head, and they killed a man traveling with Hull. A nearby woman ran to his aid and threw her apron over Hull, screaming to the shooter, "Don't shoot again. He's dead!" Acquiescing to the woman's wishes, the men rode off. Hull would survive, however, and his son, Cordell, who grew up to become a congressman, senator, longtime secretary of state under Franklin Roosevelt, winner of the Nobel Peace Prize, and founder of the United Nations, would tell his story. Cordell wrote that his father teetered on the verge of death for quite some time but by the end of the war had significantly recovered, "although the sight of his right eye was destroyed and the wound never healed, keeping him in constant misery."[10]

Neither the end of the war nor the gunshot wound destroyed the senior Hull's memory. The war had been over for a couple of years when he learned the identity of his assailant. Cordell wrote that his father "pursued him through portions of two states, and finally ran him down, a considerable distance away in what is now Monroe County, Kentucky." When William Hull approached his attacker, the man named Stepp attempted to be friendly, greeting him with "Why, hello, Bill." Not softened, Hull shot him down. Cordell recalled that no charges were ever brought and his father never discussed it with his children. The closest he ever came to the truth was, "Now and then someone would draw him out and I would overhear a remark."[11]

Both the personal and the professional natures of the war were complex. Since October, influential Tennesseans Andrew Johnson and Horace Maynard had been hounding President Abraham Lincoln to order an invasion of East Tennessee. With near constant reports of Confederate depredations emerging from that heavily unionist part of the state, Johnson and Maynard insisted the Federal army do something to deliver their native region. Lincoln agreed, as he hoped to reach out to unionists in the seceded states, and he began to push his commanders in Kentucky to comply with his wishes.[12] Additionally, Lincoln saw the value of an invasion to cut the important Virginia and Tennessee Railroad that connected the upper Confederacy's west and east.[13]

In early October, an ill Brigadier General Robert Anderson, exhausted by his experience at Fort Sumter and Kentucky's tenuous state, left his post as commander of the Department of the Cumberland. His replacement would fare worse. Brigadier General William Tecumseh Sherman, who had served as Anderson's second-in-command for nearly six weeks when his boss stepped down, only lasted five weeks in that position. A casualty of job stress, Sherman would have to be replaced quickly. Although he knew Lincoln and hoped to exercise influence over the president through family members serving in Congress, the general was shocked at his commander in chief's insistence on an invasion of East Tennessee. Feeling that politicians were guiding a war about which they knew little, Sherman began writing all who would listen depressing letters about the state of affairs in Kentucky. He argued that Lincoln's plan to move into Tennessee was foolhardy, while the Union's situation in Kentucky remained fragile.[14] On November 13, 1861, Sherman was relieved of his duties and replaced by Brigadier General Don Carlos Buell. As his first order of business, Buell reversed his earlier position of supporting an invasion of East Tennessee in preference for a complete reorganization of his army.[15]

By New Year's Day, Zollicoffer's army occupied a strong position on the north bank of the Cumberland River. That day, Brigadier General George H. Thomas left Lebanon, Kentucky, en route to meet the Confederate army. Thomas, a Virginian by birth and 1840 graduate of the United States Military Academy at West Point, had fought in the Seminole and Mexican wars. After Mexico, he came back to the academy as an instructor of artillery and cavalry. After several years at West Point, the army sent him to serve on the western frontier in the late 1850s as part of the 2nd United States Cavalry at Fort Mason, Texas. The 2nd Cavalry was the premier frontier defense unit at that time and counted Albert Sidney Johnston, Robert E. Lee, George Stoneman, Earl Van Dorn, John Bell Hood, and William Hardee as members. Severely wounded in late 1860 when he was shot in the chin and chest by an arrow during a skirmish with the Comanche in Texas, Thomas returned home to southeastern Virginia to convalesce. Within months, however, he had recovered sufficiently to accept command in the infant Civil War.[16]

Although putting Thomas on the road toward Mill Springs appeared progressive in the eyes of many East Tennesseans, Buell's purpose was not the long-awaited invasion. Since Buell's arrival in Louisville, East Tennessee had slipped down the priority list while the maintenance of security within Kentucky's borders had risen. Buell ordered Thomas's division to combine with Brigadier General Albin Schoepf's brigade just north of Zollicoffer's position. This aggressive action against the Confederates encamped on the Cumberland would coincide with a smaller movement led by Brigadier General William "Bull" Nelson into the mountains of eastern Kentucky. Buell hoped that this small campaign would result in the Confederate army's expulsion from central and eastern Kentucky and clear a path for a future incursion into East Tennessee when his army had proven itself up to the challenge.[17]

Thomas did not know it as he left Lebanon, but his task would be made easier with the arrival of Confederate Major General George B. Crittenden at Zollicoffer's camp on January 3, 1862. Upon his arrival on the field, Crittenden was shocked to find Zollicoffer still on the north side of the river. Crittenden's concern was probably rooted in his experience at Mier, Mexico, in 1842. As a member of what was essentially a filibustering expedition into Mexico, Crittenden and others crossed the Rio Grande River and found themselves trapped with the river at their back, the Mexican army in their front, and very little internal leadership. They quickly surrendered.[18]

When Crittenden arrived at Mill Springs and found his subordinate still entrenched on the north bank with his back to the river, he surely remembered the mistake made at Mier that had cost his group so dearly. From the time he accepted his appointment, he had foreseen the danger from Knoxville and had ordered his subordinate to recross the river so as to not have his force divided or isolated with little chance for retreat. Unfortunately, Zollicoffer and fate would conspire against Crittenden's wishes. The messenger who had been given the job of delivering the order for Zollicoffer to return to Mill Springs on the south bank had supposedly been lost for several days, and by the time the message arrived, the river, which had been so low only weeks before, had reportedly risen substantially and would have made the crossing perilous. By the time the message arrived, Crittenden's arrival was imminent and Zollicoffer saw an opportunity to convince his superior that the entrenchments on the north shore, although strategically unconventional, were strong and defensible.[19]

Whatever the motives, the winter rains began to dictate the course of events. Crittenden ordered the men into the woods to cut and hew logs for flatboats, which he planned to use to pull Zollicoffer's force back across the river. Bad weather and inexperience at such work made progress slow, at best. Unable to back up, Crittenden sought to move his four thousand men forward in the face of the enemy. With Thomas's force of five thousand moving toward his position, at midnight on January 19, 1862, Crittenden ordered Zollicoffer to move away from the river to meet the incoming Thomas. By taking the initiative, Crittenden turned the weather to his advantage. With few good roads entering the region from the north, Brigadier General Albin Schoepf's command of four thousand had been following Thomas's column. That night, however, the rainfall had raised Fishing Creek sufficiently to divide Thomas's incoming force and hold Schoepf away from the battlefield. Before first light, Crittenden's pickets began sending fire into the advancing, but still distant, Union lines. By daybreak, the opposing commanders had formed their lines of battle and the field roared with activity.[20]

After more than an hour of spirited fighting, there was a lull, during which Zollicoffer became convinced that some of his men were accidentally firing on fellow Confederates. Moving forward through the drizzle, Zollicoffer, who has been described as "pathetically nearsighted," wearing a raincoat without any rank or insignia, calmly rode up to the 4th Kentucky Cavalry (U.S.A.) thinking they were his own troops. Ordering Colonel Speed Fry to halt his men's fire, Zollicoffer turned to ride away when a young Confederate appeared at his side, fired at Fry, and screamed to the general that he was in the midst of the enemy. Fry, still facing Zollicoffer and readied by the young man's shot, leveled his pistol and fired, while simultaneously ordering his men to fire on the intruder. Zollicoffer fell dead in an instant.[21]

As if on signal, the lull of battle ended with Zollicoffer's death. When Thomas restarted the fight, the confused Confederates, without a leader on the field, began to fall apart. Stunned by the disastrous results of their fight thus far, they were further shocked when Colonel Robert McCook ordered the 9th Ohio Volunteers to charge the retreating Confederates with bayonets. The Germans of the 9th cut the martyred Zollicoffer's men apart. Crittenden arrived on the field and assumed command late in the afternoon. There, he found an unsalvageable situation. By nightfall, his men were scrambling back the ten miles between the battlefield and their defensive position on the Cumberland. Thomas reformed his lines and gave a final chase, while Schoepf arrived later and began rounding up those of the enemy who had scattered. That night, Crittenden pulled his remaining men across the river and began a defeated march back to the relative safety of Tennessee.[22] By nightfall on January 19, 1862, the ascending military careers of Thomas and Buell had surpassed the destroyed careers of Crittenden and Zollicoffer and the tide of the war in south-central Kentucky had turned decidedly for the Union.

In the aftermath of Mill Springs, with the Confederacy's abandonment of Champ Ferguson's home area, southern sympathizers were again cast out into the wilderness. As for Ferguson, he was nowhere near the raging fight as the personal danger involved in such formal modes of war did not appeal to him. On the day Zollicoffer lost his life, Ferguson was near Sparta, Tennessee, the town that would later become his home.[23] In these months following Zollicoffer's death and Crittenden's professional demise, Clinton County and its surrounding area descended into full-scale guerrilla warfare.

David Beatty would become Ferguson's great nemesis. An unbending unionist, "Tinker Dave," as he was known, organized his own guerrilla company. Whereas Champ Ferguson wished to force the loyalties of the local citizens toward the Confederacy, Dave Beatty sought to point them toward the Union. He remembered that in the weeks and months that followed the Battle of Mill Springs, life in his community in Fentress County, Tennessee, became nearly unbearable. During Ferguson's postwar trial, Beatty testified that "they run in there—this man Ferguson, Bledsoe, and others, killing people and running them off and I just told the boys that before I would go away, I would turn in and fight them, and if they killed me, let them kill me." Beatty estimated that around February 1, several of Scott Bledsoe's men visited his home and stole assorted property. Suspicious of the men, Beatty remained within earshot, but out of sight, during the conversation between the visitors and his wife. They informed his wife, "I had to take sides—that I had either to leave home, or else join one side or the other." As the men rode away, Beatty, always keeping a rifle nearby, fired on the men, wounding one along with a horse. From that point forward, "they kept running in on us every few weeks and killing men off." Beatty responded to this direct threat to his safety by forming his own independent company.[24] For the remainder of the war, Tinker Dave Beatty's name would strike the same fear in secessionists as Champ Ferguson's would in unionists.

In the aftermath of Mill Springs, the Confederates, who could no longer freely operate in locations like Clinton County, began to resort to frequent raids that mainly targeted unionist citizens. Two companies of men under Scott Bledsoe and James McHenry appear primarily responsible for the outrages, riding across the state line stealing mainly horses, but also anything else of value. Champ Ferguson participated in these raids as leader of a small band and, probably, as part of Bledsoe's company. Beatty recalled that he saw Ferguson on numerous occasions during the winter of 1861–62, the latter "always with a party of armed men . . . killing and conscripting Union men, and shooting at men."[25] On one occasion, members of the 1st Kentucky Cavalry ambushed a raiding party with Ferguson at its head. After a spirited skirmish, Ferguson escaped with six stolen horses but left behind one dead man and three others mortally wounded.[26] Rufus Dowdy remembered that in the wake of Mill Springs, Ferguson and others were "running around the country. Sometimes there would be eight or ten, sometimes as high as twenty, taking stock, etc." He added, when "the Union men came back . . . and Ferguson's band increased . . . the Union men had to take to the bushes."[27]

With the small Union company encamped at Albany readying to leave shortly after the battle at Mill Springs, a potential power vacuum lurked in the region's future. Having enjoyed little protection from the Federal army, unionists began forming independent companies in an effort to maintain stability in their neighborhoods. As none of these partisan organizations existed before

Mill Springs, it is logical to assume that the removal of the 1st Kentucky Cavalry and the resultant raids acted as the impetus behind this grassroots defense movement.[28] Tinker Dave, as one of the most outspoken unionists and the organizer of one of the earliest companies, became the Confederate raider's arch nemesis.

Company C of the 1st Kentucky Cavalry no sooner arrived at Camp Negley in Casey County, Kentucky, than the men received a twenty-day furlough. As most of them had been recruited in Clinton County, many returned home to the unpredictable borderland. After the men spent a couple of weeks at home, a rumor began to spread that Champ Ferguson was planning a trip to his home near Albany. Lieutenant James E. Chilton recalled that he left a black man to watch for the Confederate raider while all the others were rounded up to make the appearance of leaving. In reality, the officers were consolidating their forces for the purpose of turning to fight Ferguson. Only gathering thirteen of the men, the small band moved in the direction of the Ferguson place. Hearing that their target was at home, but with thirty-seven men, the short column, now numbering fifteen with the addition of "a true, trusted citizen, and our colored watch," moved to within four hundred yards of the house before dismounting. Moving closer, the already outnumbered group divided into two squads, hoping to cut off escape routes. An alert picket who warned Ferguson of the skulking men destroyed the soldiers' element of surprise. Ferguson yelled for his men to get ready for a fight and they poured out of the house with their guns. Probably anticipating more men than the few who had shown up, the Confederates beat a hasty retreat from the Ferguson farm, leaving only a single casualty behind. While the small Union contingent celebrated its victory over a numerically superior force, the seventeen horses and several weapons captured after the fight made the expedition even more savory.[29]

Although much attention was focused on the activities of Scott Bledsoe and Champ Ferguson, the region of the Upper Cumberlands teemed with other partisan bands with equally bad reputations. Captain Oliver P. Hamilton led a Confederate company from Jackson County, Tennessee. A man of some means prior to the war, Hamilton had raised his own band of guerrillas at the beginning of the conflict and spent much time in Jackson and Overton counties, Tennessee, and across the state line in Monroe and Cumberland counties, Kentucky. Described by one anonymous Kentuckian as "about 35 years of age, brisk walk, and quite self important," Hamilton's motives and actions mirrored those of Ferguson. Despite being a man who talked "a great deal about

'*State rights*,'" Hamilton's activities were far more personal than political. The
writer noted that Hamilton and "a company of 9 or 10, came over to Monroe
co., Ky., on Friday last [March 28], shot James Syms, Alexander Atterberry,
and Thomas Denham." The purported reason for the killing "was, that they
were Union men." Hamilton supposedly told the mother of one of his victims,
"he '*would kill* every *union* man that he could find, and, if he could not find
the *men*, he would *kill* all the *boys* that were large enough to *plough* in that
neighborhood.'" Fearful of the repercussions of his letter, the author apparently wrestled with the question of whether to inform his addressee, Military
Governor of Tennessee Andrew Johnson, of his identity. Finally, at the end
of the letter, he relented, "You, I suppose, should know *who* I am. Well, I am
a *preacher of* the Gospel, and am a descendant of the Tiptons and Reneaus of
East Tennessee, and my own name is Isaac T. Reneau."[30] As a man who had
grown up in Tennessee, studied medicine for a time, and taught school near
Albany during the time when Ferguson would have been a young student, and
who had ultimately settled into life as a well-known and respected Disciples of
Christ minister, Reneau knew the price that would be placed on his head if his
identity was ever revealed, and he asked the governor to maintain his secret.[31]
He cautioned Johnson, "but so far as my *name* is conserned, I request you
by all that binds loyal man to loyal man, gentleman to gentleman, Christian
to Christian, *never* to let [another] human being know my name, for my *life*
would have to be sacrifised on the alter of Hamilton and Ferguson's ambition."
Apparently, Reneau's pleas were effective; Andrew Johnson's endorsement
reads "Reward to be offered for man . . . Champ Ferguson."[32]

Union Captain Jonathan Hale recalled that shortly after Nashville fell to the
Union, he and about twenty of his men were ordered to report there. Boarding
a steamer with his men, they stopped at dozens of towns and landings where
they ascertained the level of Confederate sentiment in the area. At the mouth
of the Obey River, Hale disembarked and walked to the home of a woman
known for her unionist stand. The woman, Mrs. John Stone, met him on the
porch and warned him that Confederate patrols were all around. Within minutes, one small group rode up to the house and surrounded Hale. Commanding the squad was the notorious Captain Oliver Hamilton, who recognized
Hale and drew his pistol to kill him. Just then, Mrs. Stone stepped forward and
pleaded with Hamilton to take him prisoner instead. Acquiescing, Hamilton
agreed and the escort took Hale to Hamilton's father's house where they spent
the night. That night, younger and older Hamilton discussed the war and their

involvement with Hale. Old Dr. Hamilton insisted that the prisoner deserved to be shot for distributing Andrew Johnson's unionist appeals. The next morning, with his sense of charity apparently gone, Hamilton ordered the prisoner taken away and shot, but before the deed was done, a rider came and handed the captain a note. Supposedly it was from Albert Sidney Johnston ordering the execution of all suspicious persons. Hamilton apparently ignored it intentionally and took Hale back to his father's home, and ordered a guard to escort him to Kentucky and release him with no explanation.[33]

At some point in the late winter of 1862, probably early March, representatives from Union and Confederate partisan groups met, hoping to strike a deal that would return some measure of security to their region. Meeting in Monroe, Tennessee, between the regional political poles of Livingston, Tennessee, and Albany, Kentucky, Tinker Dave Beatty and his two sons represented Fentress County, Tennessee, unionists while Clinton County, Kentuckians, James Zachary, Thomas Wood, Elijah Kogier, and others convened with Confederate representatives Winburn Goodpasture of Overton County, Tennessee, and three others. There, they hammered out the details of a deal they felt might close the state of open warfare that existed between the partisans of both sides along the Kentucky-Tennessee border.[34] An undated statement placed the impetus behind the compromise with the Confederates. It alleges that several pro-southern men "stated to the Union citizens about Monroe, that horse stealing, and raiding about, was a bad business, and proposed putting a stop to it."[35] Goodpasture recalled that both sides agreed that armed partisans would not invade the counties of Clinton, Kentucky, and Overton, Tennessee. James Beatty, the son of Tinker Dave, remembered that the "arrangement was for both parties to go home, lay down their arms, and go to work." Marion Johnson's interpretation of the compromise was equally basic: "the Home Guard was not to pester the [Confederate] soldiers, and we were to be protected, all faring alike."[36] In an attempt to get the word out to all concerned, both sides began advertising their agreement. Unfortunately, the attempt at peace fell apart quickly.[37]

With a golden opportunity for peace and stability within their grasp, Confederate guerrillas apparently broke the agreement. Confederate Captain James McHenry was aware of the brokered deal but refused to abide by its stipulations, although several of his friends had forged it. Within days, he returned to his old habits and raided Clinton County. John Capps confirmed that Confederates in the region knew about the brokered deal and added, "we got it into our head to believe that the union men hadn't went by it." His simple explanation was, "I was a rebel."[38] John Capps's admission on behalf of himself and those with whom he served illustrates man's dramatic ability to justify unacceptable actions during times of crisis. Just as Capps convinced himself that a fallacy was true, men like Ferguson justified their own radical actions through the skewed paradigm of war.

With the rapid demise of the compromise, the faith of the unionists of the region fell to an all-time low. It seemed nothing could offer security. Despite the decisive Federal victory at Mill Springs, they remained subject to raids. When the army pulled Union soldiers out of the county, the frequency of raids increased. Ultimately, not even a gentlemen's agreement could bring peace. To add insult to injury, influential politicians spent more time scheming for an invasion of East Tennessee than they invested in trying to secure the already existing borders. For the people of the Cumberland region, those who claimed to be their protectors were ignoring their plight.

During this unstable part of the war, several unionists attempted to draw Federal attention to the condition of those Kentuckians and Tennesseans who lived along the border. Major James A. Brents, an Albany resident and attorney, who had spent nearly a year in the 1st Kentucky Cavalry before resigning his commission, began compiling his experiences of life along the national border during wartime. *The Patriots and Guerillas of East Tennessee and Kentucky* offered a narrative history of the violence and depredations perpetrated by pro-Confederate guerrillas. Brents, whose book, although slanted, remains a fascinating window into a seldom-viewed place and time, hoped that such an extensive work would illuminate the plight of borderland residents for political and military leaders capable of directing aid into his region.[39]

Other important unionist tracts came from along the border. Jonathan Hale focused his attention on eliminating the most dangerous of his enemies: Champ Ferguson. During the war, he authored two pamphlets that detailed his subject's outrages: *Champ Furguson: A Sketch of the War in East Tennessee* (1862) and *Champ Furguson: The Border Rebel, the Thief, Robber and Murderer* (1864). In these tracts, Hale relayed various stories of Ferguson's brutality to what he hoped would be a sympathetic and influential audience.[40]

Hale's message reached as far as Tennessee's most prominent unionists. On December 16, 1861, he wrote loyal senator Andrew Johnson regarding the situation along the Kentucky-Tennessee border. At the time, Hale was in Somerset, Kentucky, raising a company of scouts he expected to lead back to the borderland. He reported to Tennessee's future military governor that men who arrived at his camp from Overton and Fentress counties carried with them news that "the Tories are pressing every Union man they can catch into the Service," adding that loyal citizens are "fleeing to us in considerable numbers."[41]

Although the effect of Hale's letter on Johnson is unknown, as the newly appointed military governor of Tennessee in late March 1862, Johnson immediately took a strong stand on the issue of guerrilla harassment of unionist citizens. In his first formal speech after being named governor, Johnson took time to address Tennessee's growing guerrilla problem. From the state House of Representatives, he cautioned that if "their depredations are not stopped, they shall be held to a terrible accountability."[42] Three and a half years later, Johnson would be sitting in the White House as President of the United States and Champ Ferguson, Tennessee's most notorious Confederate partisan, would be awaiting execution back in Nashville for his crimes. The day of reckoning had arrived.

Whereas Brents and Hale hoped to reach wide audiences with their horrific stories of the nature of the war along the border, others went straight to those interested persons who could affect change. On March 31, 1862, a frantic and frustrated Isaac T. Reneau wrote to Johnson on the subject of "wilful and wicked murderers" and identified Champ Ferguson as one of the most vicious of the lot.[43] Although many of the details of the crimes are inaccurate, other aspects of the letter are insightful. Four months after Ferguson killed Wood, Reneau confirmed "a scar on one side of his head," which was likely the healed wound delivered by Wood and the same scar that was pointed out during the trial more than three years later. Interestingly, he described the guerrilla, whose reputation for violence was steadily growing, as having "*blue* eyes and a *smiling* countenance, and *seems* to be friendly disposed." Reneau went further to offer examples of Ferguson's behavior. He detailed, somewhat sloppily, the killing of William Frogg and Reuben Wood and offered a recent example of Ferguson's partisan actions. He noted, "Ferguson has been engaged in horse stealing on a *large* scale ever since the great rebellion began, and, it is supposed, has stolen *thousands* of dollars' worth of property."[44] To be sure, Ferguson, like many others who operated in border regions, used the Civil War as a means to increase his personal wealth.

On April 9, Jackson County, Tennessee, attorney Leroy S. Clements wrote the governor a similar note. He began, "being a Tennessean myself having had to leave the State in the last few days on the account of several meraurdering bands of Cecessionists that are creating desperate havoc in many counties along the line." Clements, whose brother, Andrew, was at the time a sitting United States Congressman, went on to inform Johnson that "Unless there can be something done for Macon Jackson Overton Fentress in Tennessee and Wayne Clinton Cumberland Monroe and Allen in Kentucky they will be impoverished and finally ruined." He reminded the governor that "the above named Counties turned out a large number of Soldiers for the Federal Army leaving many large Families at home which must be fed and protected and that protection must come from the Army." He advised that Johnson send troops to subdue Ferguson, Scott Bledsoe, Oliver Hamilton, and James Eaton, and that cavalry would be required as "they are all mounted men and this is a hilly country." The haste of Clements's letter was mostly due to the time of the year it was written. As spring planting was just around the corner, he begged Johnson to send "a few Companies into macon, Jackson and Overton" or "it will be too late as they will get to plant nothing and thus necessarily starve." He reminded the governor, "the Rebels Say that Union men shall make nothing in all the Loyal portion of Tennessee along the line."[45]

By springtime 1862, the nature of the Civil War in the Cumberland region of Tennessee and Kentucky had changed dramatically. Although the Union army learned it could defeat an enemy on the battlefield, local residents quickly came to understand the military's limitations when their already tenuous lives were further threatened by the Confederate guerrillas. Despite attempts at compromise, partisan activity remained at a high level, putting innocent lives in constant peril. And although many men were operating in similar capacities throughout the mountain region, Champ Ferguson's name came to represent the excesses of the guerrillas. Within only months of becoming an active participant in the conflict, Ferguson had gained the worst kind of celebrity, and the name of the former Kentucky farmer rang all the way to the Tennessee state capitol.

THE TENSIONS
OF THE BORDERLAND

He was a clever man before the war, but got over it soon after the war
broke out, and arrayed himself in deadly hostility to his old friends and
neighbors.

  —FERGUSON on James Zachary

The spring campaign season of 1862 began in earnest on the banks
of the Tennessee River near Pittsburg Landing. In the first ninety
days of the year, the Federal army won impressive victories at Mill
Springs, Forts Henry and Donelson, and New Madrid and moved
into Nashville as an occupying force. In the Tennessee theater, as in Kentucky,
the Confederates were reeling. By middle April, the Confederacy suffered another defeat, its worst up to that point, and Union forces marched into Mississippi. Caught between Middle Tennessee trembling under a partial Federal
occupation and unionist East Tennessee, Ferguson and the other partisans
who occupied the Cumberland region found themselves increasingly envel-
oped by the tide of war. Realizing the fragile state of their native region, the
mountain guerrillas increased their activity and brought unprecedented violence to those citizens who had turned their backs on the cause of secession.

The compromise brokered between the partisan bands in March did not
last long. Within days of the agreement, raiders resumed their attacks on the
people of the borderland. Several years after the close of the war, John Parrott
swore a statement that he had met Ferguson and eight other men near Monroe, Tennessee, during the middle of March 1862. He recalled that Ferguson
had asked if he had been to Albany. When Parrott answered in the affirmative, Ferguson threatened to kill him if he ever went again. The men passed

and Parrott likely thought himself fortunate to escape, but the group turned around and returned, firing at the lone traveler. "I ran, but Ferguson overtook me, and demanded my money." Having none, Parrott offered the guerrillas his empty wallet, to which Ferguson responded, "Damn you and your pocket book, we are going to kill you." Unmoved by the man's pleas for his life, he shot Parrott twice and left him lying in the road, where he would be found and consequently nursed back to health.[1]

On April 1, James McHenry and Oliver Hamilton departed Livingston. Their objective was Albany, and along the way they met Ferguson, who missed few chances to raid his home county. On the road that day, the men apparently surprised a small group of armed unionists. Among them was Joseph Stover, a member of the 1st Kentucky Cavalry, upon whom Ferguson focused. Having known him before the war began, Ferguson claimed that Stover had sworn that he would kill him if given the chance. When the raiders scattered what were probably Home Guards, Stover immediately fled with Ferguson in pursuit. Firing back twice at his pursuer, Stover leveled his gun for a third attempt when he was simultaneously hit by Ferguson's and another man's shots. Surviving the brief fight, Stover was taken prisoner, although he would not remain as such very long.[2] Meanwhile, Ferguson returned to the scattered fight and found Louis Pierce running through the woods carrying a shotgun. Riding after him, Ferguson quickly caught up with his quarry and killed him. John Capps did not witness the killing of Pierce, but he saw the body afterward. His memory that the victim had been "cut in the region of the heart" suggests that Ferguson had again used his knife on an enemy.[3]

At some point after the skirmish ended, Ferguson finished Stover off with his knife. In what would become his calling card, Ferguson stabbed the man and later boldly announced that the deed had been done "after he had been taken prisoner." Ferguson, always ready with justification, remembered, "I knew him, knew he was a desperate fellow, and if he could, he would make his escape, and then . . . would guide the Federal troops through the by-roads I was hiding in." Either by paranoia or fortuitousness, Ferguson, the man who had seriously wounded and now held Stover as prisoner, stabbed him because, as he put it, "To kill him was my only chance."[4]

Ferguson's role in the killing of William Johnson is more difficult to ascertain. Although Ferguson never specified when Johnson was killed, John Capps remembered it was during the early April raid. Recalling the circumstances of that day, Ferguson stated that he and his men were in Clinton County conscripting men for the Confederate army. They visited the farm of Henry John-son, where they hoped to catch his son William and force him into the ser-vice.[5] One writer points out, however, that this statement cannot be believed, as Confederate President Jefferson Davis did not sign into law the Conscrip-tion Act until two weeks after the raid.[6] True as that is, it is not unreasonable to assume that Ferguson was attempting to force Johnson into his band and using the term *Confederate army* to lend legitimacy to his cause.

The most likely reason Ferguson and his men found themselves at the John-son farm was to recoup property. It is fairly certain that unionists in Clinton County had either legally confiscated some of Ferguson's property for nonpay-ment of a debt or by the extralegal means of raiding his farm after he relocated across the border in Tennessee. Whatever the motive and mode, Ferguson, with some cause, felt very strongly that Henry Johnson had some knowledge of the disposition of the property. Finding the older man on his place, Fergu-son rode up to him with pistols drawn and pressed Johnson to "bring back his wagon and oxen" or "he would kill him." "The old man promised to have them sent back, stating that he did not have anything to do with it," but the property had already been sold.[7]

Although the band had arrived at the Johnson farm as seekers of what Ferguson considered to be stolen property, they soon found another reason to be there. Ferguson later remembered that he and his men saw Johnson's son William, who was likely a member of a local Home Guard unit, running through the fields while they were talking with the old man and they took off after him. Before the mounted men could catch up with him, William Johnson reached the bluffs overlooking the Wolf River. "Fearing he would run down a ravine, impassible for horses," the men shot at Johnson, causing him to take his chance with the sheer drop rather than with the bullets and balls. Seriously injured from his fall, Johnson lay at the bottom of the near-cliff until Fergu-son's men climbed down to him. Ferguson, who alleged that he remained at the house while the situation played out, probably had nothing to do with the killing of William Johnson apart from urging his men to catch the fleeing man. He did, however, explain that, although he was not on site to witness the activity, one of his men stabbed the "nearly dead" Johnson "and thus ended his misery."[8]

A mysterious figure coming out of these events was a man named Robert Martin. Ferguson never mentioned Martin in any of his confessions, but he was noted during the postwar trial testimony. John Capps, without offering any details, included Martin in the group of Johnson, Pierce, and Stover as men killed on the expedition. His father, Alvin Capps, offered additional but conflicting information. Past Rome's Mill in Kentucky, Capps saw a dead man he called John Martin "shot somewhere in the head and his bosom was open and had a large gash somewhere in the breast." He finished by stating that he thought he remembered seeing "another man close to Martin who was killed."[9]

As evening neared, the column moved closer to Albany. There the men surprised Captain John A. Morrison, commander of a company of local Union soldiers. At home and not expecting trouble, Morrison attempted to saddle his horse and flee, but the raiders fired on him. Shot in the arm and mildly wounded in the back of the head, he lost his grip on his horse and ran for cover. Miraculously, Morrison slipped away in the fading light and the men continued down the road.[10]

Their next stop was at the home of Ferguson's great nemesis Jonathan Hale. Hale was away from home at the time, his wife, Pheroba, later remembered. Some of the men dismounted and "tore down our yard fence" while others came up to the house. One man approached Pheroba and asked about her husband's whereabouts; she replied he was not home, and the man walked past her into the house. She followed him into her bedroom, while at the same time Ferguson entered through the back door. He asked "if there was any ammunition, guns, or any kind of arms in the house," or "if there were any watches, gold, or silver." Spying a powder horn on the mantle, he grabbed it. Mrs. Hale asked him to leave it behind as it only had a little powder left. He took the horn and warned the lady that "we have killed four God-damned Lincolnites today" and that they intended to kill more before nightfall. Having rummaged through the house, the men exited with Ferguson crowing, "I've got two yankee coats that are worth $100 each," before the men mounted their horses and prepared to leave. Watching the proceedings, Mrs. Hale remembered that Ferguson had asked if they had seen anyone while he and the others were inside the house. One of the men replied that he had seen "only some boys going across the flat." He asked why they did not shoot them, to which they responded they did not want to shoot young boys. Now erupting with anger, he warned them, "God-damn them, take them clean as you go, you ought to have shot them."[11] With that, the band rode off into town.

They were only gone a few minutes before they returned to the Hale farm. The men immediately went to the stable and led out three horses and two mules. Mrs. Hale came out of the house and confronted the men. She asked if they had left her a horse, and Ferguson said that they did not. Mrs. Hale requested that they leave her a "small, very gentle mule as that was the only animal that I, or any of the women in town, had to go to mill with." Frustrated by the woman, several of the raiders vented that "your men don't care anything about our women and we will not leave you anything." Growing bolder, Mrs. Hale then insisted they either return the animals or pay her what they were worth. Unimpressed, the men warned her not to send men after them, or "they would never come back alive."[12]

It was after dark when the band moved south, out of Albany, and back toward the relative safety of Tennessee. With such a busy day behind them, the men likely relaxed for the night ride back home. However, as they neared the house of Ferguson's mother-in-law just a couple of miles south of town, the men were startled by an armed rider. As it turned out, the horseman was sixteen-year-old Fount Zachary, who was operating as a picket for the Home Guards who were on the lookout for the column. Giving a young, inexperienced boy the responsibility of watching the main road heading back into Tennessee backfired on the unionists. Zachary, apparently thinking the approaching men were Home Guards rather than Confederate guerrillas, rode up to them and announced they would not find the raiders in his sector. Realizing his confusion, the youngster quickly surrendered his weapon. Ferguson, who was mounted nearby when the rider exited the woods, asked his name. He responded, "Fount Zachary." As the Zachary family was one of the county's most prominent unionist clans, Ferguson shot the boy and personalized the act, as he had done several times already that day, by dismounting and stabbing him through the heart.[13] By the end of the day, Ferguson had participated in at least five killings.

When the Zachary family came to claim Fount Zachary's body, they found that it had been taken to the widow Owen's house. Interestingly, Mrs. Owen was Champ Ferguson's mother-in-law. If she supported Champ's activities, she certainly would not have bothered with the corpse. Considering that the divided loyalties of the region even penetrated individual families like Champ Ferguson's, it appears likely that Ferguson's mother-in-law rejected the path chosen by her daughter's husband.[14]

In killing Fount Zachary, Ferguson solidified his place in the history of the region's Civil War. By killing someone so young, even though it was probably dark enough to make discerning Zachary's age doubtful, Ferguson entered a new realm of villainy. He admitted he "shot the lad . . . and stabbed him after he fell to the ground" but dismissed the criminal nature of his actions: "Jim McHenry was in command, and had given us orders to shoot down any person who might be seen with guns." "I shot him on sight in obedience to orders."[15]

Ferguson's newly found habit of stabbing his victims also proved important. Probably done to ensure that none would live to tell the tale (as had Reuben Wood), Ferguson's knifework would become legendary in pro-Union propaganda circles. Mary Catherine Sproul, the young woman whose father and brother had endured the insults of a secessionist mob on election day, recorded in her diary that on the expedition, Ferguson had killed several men and "cut one in twain" and had removed the man's "intrails and throwing them on a log near by."[16] Several days afterward, the news of the raid and the embellishments that followed made it as far as Nashville. The *Daily Nashville Union* reported that Ferguson had taken "a promising little boy, twelve years old, by the name of Zachary" out of his sick bed, and, while held by two guerrillas, "a third cut his abdomen wide open."[17]

J. A. Brents, whose wartime work became drawing Federal attention to Ferguson and the difficulties of unionists living along the border, wrote that Ferguson never took prisoners; instead, "he ordered his satellites to hold them by the arms" and "he deliberately ripped them open with a huge knife, their bowels dropping upon the ground."[18] The day after the column returned to Tennessee, the ladies of Livingston organized a celebration for the raiders. Rumors of Ferguson's treatment of the killed men had traveled with the men back to town and some women were disturbed by the stories. Although one moderate lady criticized Ferguson's actions—"it was enough to kill a man after he had Surrendered without abusing his lifeless body"—another, more patriotic woman offered justification: "Hurra! For Ferguson . . . if we dont kill them, we'll never conquer them."[19] Indeed, the latter sentiment was prevalent in Fentress County, Tennessee. Mary Catherine Sproul wrote, "The rebels in Livingston looked on Ferguson as having few superiors."[20]

Despite the supportive sentiments offered by the ladies of Overton County, the attitude of Amanda McDowell of White County, Tennessee, illustrates the complexity of regional sentiment. A unionist living among secessionists, she felt sick to see her father, also loyal, befriending a man she took to be "one of Ferguson's men." The two, despite their political differences, "had quite a pleasant conversation," but Amanda had "very little faith in the principles of a man that will countenance Ferguson, let alone one who will aid him in his murdering and plundering." Although it is possible that Mr. McDowell and the secessionist had struck up a genuine friendship, it is more likely that Amanda's father saw that developing a relationship with such a man would be possibly beneficial if Ferguson ever threatened to raid his home.[21]

Ferguson's use of a knife is important for another reason: Much mythology grew out of his wartime actions. During the war, numerous, apparently erroneous stories circulated about gifts of knives to Ferguson. Mary Catherine Sproul offered some clarification when she wrote in her diary that Captain James W. McHenry had given Ferguson a knife with the instructions, "here Mr. Furgerson take it and gut the Yankees."[22] Although McHenry's comments on the occasion are questionable, Ferguson admitted that McHenry was the only man who ever gave him a knife, putting to rest rumors of gifts by famous Confederates.[23]

The borderland unrest of late March and early April prodded the Department of the Ohio to react. On April 17, Don Carlos Buell ordered Colonel Edward C. Williams to dispatch four companies of his 9th Pennsylvania Cavalry from Springfield, Tennessee, to Clinton County. Buell wished Williams to assign "the most competent field officer" to lead the men who were "to patrol and protect that section of country from roving bands of marauding troops, horse thieves, and outlaws." He made it clear to Williams that these criminals acted "on both sides," and that "All such parties, whether acting under the name of Union or rebel, will be equally considered enemies to the peace of the country and will be treated accordingly."[24]

For the remainder of April 1862, Ferguson and his men laid low in and around Livingston. Meanwhile, some of the same men of the 1st Kentucky Cavalry (U.S.A.), who had been ordered out of Clinton County only a few weeks before, returned. With the regiment ordered to Nashville, Colonel Frank Wolford received permission to move through Albany en route to his destination. Arriving in Albany only a few days following McHenry's raid, Wolford hoped to return some stability to the embattled region. The column of three to four hundred men crossed the river at Burkesville, Kentucky, and then moved to Albany and camped there for several days. There, they enjoyed the hospitality of the unionist citizens of Clinton County. Apart from feeding the soldiers, the citizens also supplied Wolford and his officers valuable information regarding guerrilla movements. Armed with reliable information, a plan of action was formulated for the company to march on Livingston, Tennessee, which was quickly becoming the center of secessionism in the upcountry region. Near town, Wolford's fast-moving men began arresting pickets who had been placed along the roads to sound the alarm. Feeling confident that the sentries would offer protection against a surprise attack, most of the guerrillas had gone home for the night without concern for their safety. With the pickets swept aside, Wolford's mounted men rode into town and began taking prisoners. By dark, the men of the 1st had captured more than thirty Confederates and established a cordon around town to keep secret the news that the Federals had arrived. After securing Livingston, Wolford called together a small contingent of trusted men to attack Ferguson's camp, estimated to be four miles distant. Traveling through the extraordinarily dark night, the men finally found the camp and surrounded it. Unfortunately for Wolford, the news of his arrival in Livingston had escaped and Ferguson's men had deserted the campfires. Wolford turned his command and spent the night among enemies in Livingston.[25]

While the men slept in private homes and in the Fentress County courthouse, a heavy rain fell. The next morning, the Federals followed the tracks left in the soft roads and began following the Confederate partisans. After a few hours' work, Wolford's men had captured several of Ferguson's followers. The men who recorded the expedition for Wolford's recollections remembered that by noon many men were still out hunting Confederates and small groups were gathering to move back to Livingston, from which they would continue on to Nashville. One of these squads was waiting for more men to come in when two blue-clad soldiers rode up. Milling around for a few moments, the two began to move away when some of the Albany men from company C rode up. "Catch them or shoot them," came the command as the two men reached full gallop; "it is Fergusone." Ferguson made his escape although his companion surrendered to the soldiers. Apparently using captured blue uniforms to learn more about the enemy than was otherwise possible, Ferguson had been recognized by the local men of the company. The chase that followed nearly cost Ferguson his life.

With only a handful of the men mounted on fast horses, Ferguson's pursuers closed ground on him. One of the men came so close that the muzzle of his weapon was within reach of Ferguson, but the jarring of the ride caused his shot to miss. With this, Ferguson jumped off his mount and fled into the thick underbrush, leaving behind his hat, horse, and gun but escaping with his life. His surrendered comrade nearly met a worse fate. Several of Ike Smith's captors were ready to dispense vigilante justice when a small group of soldiers stepped forward to protect him. Although Smith had allegedly killed Federal soldiers who were home on furlough, Wolford refused to allow the mob to kill the prisoner. That night, the company camped several miles west of Livingston and the next morning set out for Nashville, again leaving the region without a significant Union military presence.[26]

In early May, Ferguson embarked on another raid into Kentucky. This time, he rode with his former lawyer, Willis Scott Bledsoe. Born into a prominent Fentress County, Tennessee, family, Bledsoe made his prewar reputation as an attorney based at Jamestown. At the outbreak of hostilities, he organized a Confederate cavalry company and began making raids into unionist regions of Tennessee and Kentucky. Although Ferguson suggested Bledsoe induced him to join his cavalry, no firm evidence exists to corroborate the story. It is certain, however, that Ferguson did join Bledsoe's command sometime shortly after the passage of the Tennessee secession ordinance and that he and Bledsoe participated in a variety of raids together throughout the duration of the war.[27] On this expedition, Ferguson got an opportunity for revenge.

One of the first places the company stopped was at the house of the noted local unionist Alexander Huff. Ferguson had a long and tumultuous history with Huff. The latter was a relative of the Ferguson matriarch, but family ties had not prevented Huff from joining in on the arrest of Ferguson the preceding year. Around Christmastime, Ferguson had partially returned the insult when he took Alexander's son, Preston, prisoner and sent him forward to Zollicoffer's command at Mill Springs. Now, as had been promised to the son in December, Alexander was Ferguson's target. William Williams remembered that he was going to the mill in Fentress County when Confederate pickets placed him under arrest. Depositing him at a nearby farmhouse, they waited for some time before another group rode up with Alexander Huff, their prisoner.[28]

Here, the story becomes confusing. Williams described pickets being deployed after the men arrived with Huff. Shortly, the sound of gunfire was heard coming from the direction of the sentries and a sharp but brief skirmish ensued. Without much elaboration, Williams reported that he and the other prisoners were standing on the porch watching for the return of the pickets when Ferguson reappeared and quickly singled out Huff. Williams, who was standing next to Huff when Ferguson rode up, was ordered to move out of the way. He did not move quickly enough for Ferguson, who had to repeat his order. Realizing the purpose for ordering Williams to step aside, Huff ran into the house. Having dismounted, his pursuer ran around the end of the house hoping to catch his quarry leaving through the back door and yelling "shoot him, shoot him, damn him, shot him."[29]

In the confusion, Williams saw his own opportunity to escape. When Ferguson went around the corner of the house, Williams, who had been left standing on the porch, ran inside and up the stairs. From his perch, he could see very little but heard what happened next. After one shot, probably fired by one of Ferguson's men, Ferguson ran around the end of the house toward Huff. After hearing the man scream, "Oh Lord," Williams heard more gunfire and Huff "continued to hollow, pray, and go on." "The firing of the guns continued a minute or two and the hollowing of Huff continued a minute or two." Having shot Huff numerous times, but without fatal effect, the men stopped firing for several minutes and Williams could still hear the wounded man crying and screaming. He heard one more shot and then silence.[30]

Nancy Brooks filled in the holes of Williams's story. She arrived on the scene in time to see Huff on the ground, "wounded having his arm and ankle broken, in a sitting posture begging for water." She saw Ferguson standing over Huff but noted that he did not fire the fatal bullet. Instead, he ordered one of his men standing nearby to kill Huff. Nancy Brooks's brother tried to pull the triggerman away, but Ferguson warned him "if he didn't get away he would shoot him down." With that, Huff was shot in the back of the head. Marking the time lapse between the first shots and the fatal one as between fifteen and thirty minutes, Brooks's testimony added an air of methodical viciousness to the crime. Apparently, Ferguson and his men intentionally avoided killing Huff right away, preferring instead to watch the man suffer for a while before finally dispatching him. Brooks, who was at her father's house watching the events unfold, clarified that when the pickets came under fire, Huff had made a run for the hills, but had been caught before getting very far. Knowing Ferguson and the threats levied months before, Huff probably expected he would be killed under any circumstance.[31]

After Huff had been shot several times, the Confederates called Williams out of the house. Surely afraid to disobey, he came out and saw the wounded man lying under an apple tree. Several men escorted Williams across the road to another house, where they left him. After a while, a little boy came in and told Williams that Huff was dead. The soldiers had left and Williams walked to Huff's body. "I went back and helped pull his coat off and lay him out. I did not examine the wounds much; he was mighty bloody. His arm was broken. He was shot in a good many places. I noticed his coat, it was a frock coat, there was thirteen or fourteen shots through the skirt of the coat."[32]

Although Ferguson felt strongly that Huff was a dangerous man to his cause, he maintained his innocence regarding the killing. On the eve of his execution, Ferguson alleged that he stayed back with Huff and personally held him as prisoner in order to protect him from Bledsoe's men. This statement may be true as evidenced by Williams's testimony that Ferguson was at the back of the group that left the house to investigate the picket gunfire. However, he followed with the claim that it was not he who shot Huff, but one of the men.[33] His statement can be refuted by the testimony of both Williams and Brooks. More importantly, Ferguson, himself, discredited his own claim by contradicting it in an interview for the *Nashville Union.* As recorded in that piece, when asked whether he killed Alex Huff, Ferguson responded, "He was killed by myself, and some of my men."[34]

As for a reason to kill Alex Huff, the record is vague. Huff did not have a reputation for traveling about armed nor did he keep company with known union partisans. In what was probably a very accurate statement, Nancy Brooks noted that she "don't suppose he [Huff] was friendly [with Ferguson], but I never heard him make any threats against Ferguson."[35] Ferguson's reason for killing Alex Huff was made quite clear in December when he took Preston Huff prisoner. Despite the kinship ties, Ferguson likely killed the man for the single overriding reason that he was "a God-damned old Lincolnite."[36]

Continuing on from the site of Huff's murder, Ferguson and his band ran across Marion Johnson, who was in lower Fentress County collecting debts from men who had avoided payment. Many people saw the Civil War as an opportunity to escape their financial responsibilities. Unionists who borrowed from Confederates, or vice versa, would use the conflict as an excuse to elude repayment, forcing those who extended credit to sometimes send men into enemy territory to recoup the balance of a loan. The perceived arrogance of a Union man traveling inside the Confederacy with the purpose of extracting currency was insulting to southern civil and military officials, so much so that some went to great lengths to curb the practice. In southwestern Virginia, Brigadier General Humphrey Marshall became so disgusted by the practice that he promised to conscript loyal Kentuckians into the Confederate army who traveled into the state for that purpose.[37]

Meeting Johnson at a private home, the column consisting of Ferguson's, Bledsoe's, Hamilton's, and McHenry's men stopped the known unionist and reported member of Eli Hatfield's partisan company and placed him under arrest. Forcing him to accompany them on their journey south, Johnson remembered seeing evidence of the group's activities along the way. Riding at the rear of the column with other prisoners, Johnson arrived at one house as soldiers were leading two horses out of the gate and into the road. He also overheard conversations about the group's activities prior to his arrest. One soldier claimed that they had captured a young man and forced him to tell where he and Hatfield hid their horses. Johnson recognized one of the horses being ridden that day as belonging to Hatfield and saw one man wearing Hatfield's coat. Speaking up, Johnson reminded the men of the Monroe Compromise and asserted that he should not be bothered by the letter of that agreement. The men confirmed that they knew of the compromise and had seen it posted where Alex Huff was killed. Realizing that his captors cared little about such deals and that the actual compromise had been broken long before they arrested him, Johnson dropped his argument. Traveling deeper into Tennessee, the column finally released the prisoners near Sparta.[38]

On April 19, the *Daily Nashville Union* reported Ferguson's recent activities. Although the column contains significant errors, such as reducing Fount Zachary's age to twelve while enhancing the brutality of his death and incorrectly identifying Alex Huff as William Huff, it also added other names of men supposedly killed by Ferguson and his band. Inexplicably, the newspaper report also serves as the end of the historical line for these men. Their deaths were never investigated nor were those counts added to Ferguson's court martial. Also listed as victims were "Henry Johnston, two of the Shellys, John Syms and several others." It is possible that the newspaper mistook the captured, but later released, Marion Johnson for the man it reported as Henry Johnston, but the Shellys, Syms, and others to which it referred are unknown.[39] Since much of Ferguson's wartime activities remains unknown and shrouded in mystery, these men may well be some of his anonymous victims. After all, he did confess to killing many more men than those disclosed on the stand at his postwar trial.

While Ferguson, Scott Bledsoe, and their like were prosecuting their irregular war in the Cumberland region, the broader conflict was escalating around them. The winter and spring of 1862 had not been kind to Confederate operations in the west. In January, Thomas had asserted Union control over the north bank of the Cumberland River in Kentucky, and February saw the fall of Forts Henry and Donelson, paving the way for the Union army to occupy Nashville by the end of the month. To the west, Pea Ridge and New Madrid fell to Union assaults in March. In April, Confederate disappointment reached a nadir with the defeat at Shiloh and the fall of New Orleans. As a result of the numerous military setbacks, north-central Tennessee became an island of secessionist sentiment nearly cordoned by the Federal army. The cause that had shone so brightly less than a year before now languished under the weight of repeated failures.

In the wake of that dismal winter and spring, Confederate raider John Hunt Morgan began planning a raid deep into his home state of Kentucky. The impetuous Morgan, Alabama born but transplanted to Lexington, likely expected that his raid would divert Union attention away from the ongoing campaigns far to the south and toward his attacks deep behind enemy lines. As would become common as the war dragged on, Morgan was wrong. The Federal army did pay attention to his activities but only responded with small mounted forces rather than the grander scale that Morgan expected. Leaving from Corinth, Mississippi, where the southern army had fallen back in the wake of Shiloh, Morgan and more than 300 men moved northward toward the Kentucky-Tennessee border. At Pulaski on May 1, Morgan's men surprised and captured 268 soldiers who were tasked with building a telegraph line to Huntsville. Such an auspicious beginning heartened the commander, but his confidence would be seriously shaken by forthcoming events.[40]

By May 5, Morgan's column had made it as far as Lebanon, Tennessee, twenty-five miles east of Nashville, where they planned to camp overnight before moving on the next morning. Morgan's stay in Lebanon, however, would be affected by what his biographer James Ramage called "headquarterism." Having recently departed from his old habit of living among his men, the commander moved into a hotel while the common soldiers were left to sleep on porches or under the stars. As a result, the effectiveness of communication decreased with each degree of separation. At Lebanon, the problem became acute as Morgan issued orders for the men to be up and in the saddle by 4:00 a.m., but his instructions never made it down as far as the company level. Sleeping well with a steady rain falling around them, the men enjoyed their rest. The pickets stationed along the road left their posts for dry homes and barns as they saw no reason to stand in the rainy night while their commander was apparently warm, dry, and asleep in a comfortable bed.[41]

While Morgan and his men slept, Brigadier General Ebenezer Dumont, an Indiana lawyer, banker, and veteran of the Mexican War, moved on information that Morgan was quartered in Livingston. Colonel Frank Wolford's 1st Kentucky Cavalry was with Dumont that night when the column of about six hundred cavalrymen arrived just outside of town after midnight. The men were exhausted after being in the saddle nearly continuously for twenty hours

and most laid down by the road and slept while waiting for daylight to illuminate the town. The men were awakened before daylight and Wolford's 1st
Kentucky was given the honor of charging through the center of town flanked
by the other attached commands.[42]

Eastham Tarrant remembered the raid as being a complete surprise and
lightning quick, resulting in the "flying pickets" being pushed back so fast that
he and the vedettes "entered town about the same time." The attack, which
would become known as the "Lebanon Races," was underway. "So completely
were they surprised, that he did not meet with serious opposition until he
reached the far side of the public square." By the time the bulk of Dumont's
command arrived, only seconds had passed, but the rout was already on. Behind a "hastily-formed line of dismounted men," Morgan and his staff fled.
Although still shaking out the cobwebs of their rude awakening, Confederates began pouring fire into the advancing Union column from their sleeping
porches and parlors with an intensity sufficient to force back Wolford and his
men. The stand would not last long, however; within a few minutes, the Federals had virtually cleared the town of Confederate soldiers while the outskirts
teemed with scrambling men. By nightfall, Dumont's men had taken an estimated 120 prisoners while scattering the remainder of Morgan's command to
the four winds. Morgan himself was lucky to escape, having been doggedly
pursued thirty miles to the Cumberland River. That night he sat in Carthage,
Tennessee, with only twenty men. For all he knew, they were the only twenty
to survive or escape. Morgan's command and reputation lay in shambles.[43]

Although the arrogant Morgan never openly admitted any responsibility
for the debacle at Lebanon, he did understand the degree of his failure. Within
days, enough of his men straggled in to give him confidence to quickly organize a shorter and safer raid into Kentucky than the one he originally planned.
Knowing that the citizens of Bowling Green were friendly to his cause and being familiar with the area from his earlier scouts, Morgan settled on a plan to
free his captured men. Expecting that the Union army would quickly put the
recently taken prisoners on a train to a northern prison, Morgan targeted the
Louisville and Nashville Railroad that ran through the town. With much of
his command gone and being unfamiliar with the territory through which he
would pass, Morgan enlisted the aid of Confederate guerrillas who operated in
the Cumberland region of Tennessee and Kentucky.[44]

Arriving at Sparta with only about seventy men, Morgan's force more than
doubled with the addition of Bledsoe's and Hamilton's companies. Also along

was Ferguson, who only brought a handful of men with him. Although the extra manpower was important to Morgan, the real reason he embraced the Cumberland partisans was for their geographic knowledge. In order to make his plan work, Morgan had to slip into Kentucky unnoticed. Men like Ferguson and members of his gang had grown up in the region and knew every pass. This was Ferguson's main purpose on the expedition. While John Hunt Morgan's brother-in-law, the martinet Basil Duke, was recovering from a wound received at Shiloh and not on the trip, in his *History of Morgan's Cavalry* he cobbled together accounts of the expedition into Kentucky.[45] Those men whom Morgan had picked up in Sparta were said to be "either new recruits or had never been subjected to any sort of discipline" and the whole mass was poorly equipped. Ferguson and his companions swiftly guided the column through the passes into Kentucky, but not without attracting some attention. In an attempt to warn local unionists of passing Confederates, the Home Guards had begun blowing shells or horns whenever southern soldiers appeared. As the sound moved faster than even Morgan's men, they encountered few people and even fewer enemies along the route.[46]

Once out of the hills and on flatter terrain, Ferguson and the other guides stepped back and allowed Morgan's men, who knew the area around Bowling Green well, to take the lead. At Glasgow, Morgan sent a scout into Bowling Green. Upon his return, he reported that the city held a garrison of five hundred Federals. With that information, Morgan decided not to be part of two debacles in one month and looked for a softer target. His command moved northwest to Cave City. Still on the railroad, but far enough from the soldiers at Bowling Green to render them a nonfactor, Cave City offered Morgan an opportunity to stop a northbound L&N train in relative privacy.

On May 11, less than two weeks after his greatest embarrassment, Morgan got his opportunity for redemption. Arriving at a station near Cave City, Morgan and his men captured an incoming train. Filling the firebox with wood and setting fire to each of the forty-nine cars, they sent it southward hurtling toward Nashville. The explosion was tremendous. Not long after they sent the first train on its way, another pulled in heading to Nashville. Stopping the train and barricading the tracks front and back, Morgan's men entered the passenger cars, which were largely occupied by ladies traveling south to visit Nashville. Morgan, ever the gentleman, treated the women kindly, but he and his men did relieve the express agent of $6,000 and took a few Union officers and enlisted men prisoner.[47] Morgan felt confident when he left Cave City that his reputation had been salvaged. Moving back toward Tennessee along the same route he came, he began thinking about his next move.

For Ferguson, the scout to Bowling Green also proved important. Operating outside of conventional military channels for most of the war, his contact with Morgan brought him close to a man who would allow the partisan to move fluidly between irregular and formal warfare. Ferguson and his men would join Morgan's company several times throughout the rest of the war and, apart from a falling-out with the cavalryman before the Ohio Raid, would blend in well with Morgan's force. In Morgan, Ferguson likely saw an acceptable role model. Just as he took horses and saddles, the cavalryman also tried to leave each raid with more than he had entered with. As an armed representative of the southern cause, Ferguson received affirmation for the way he viewed the world and prosecuted the war.

Upon his return to White County, Tennessee, where he had recently settled, Ferguson spent three weeks quietly. Despite his respite, his comrades in arms continued their activities. In mid-May, the 9th Pennsylvania Cavalry pursued Morgan's retreating column as far as the Cumberland River. After the Confederates crossed into Tennessee, Colonel Edward C. Williams ordered his men back to Tompkinsville. Upon his return to Kentucky, the colonel learned that Confederate guerrilla Captain Oliver Hamilton's men were near Celina, Tennessee. Reversing direction for the second time, Williams's column headed south toward the enemy. Celina, a river town standing on the south bank of the Cumberland, was served by a single ferry, too small to transfer an adequate Federal force across the river. After a brief, cross-river skirmish, a frustrated Williams again reversed direction.[48]

By late May, Ferguson and his men were back on the road toward Kentucky. On Friday, May 29, his men were in Albany, where they again sought out unionists. James Haggard, a former Kentucky state legislator, Cumberland County court clerk, and county judge when the war came, wrote Governor Andrew Johnson of Tennessee in regard to Ferguson's recent activities. Although he wrote from Burkesville, twenty miles from Albany, he relayed that Ferguson had killed a Mr. Story there and a Mr. Long, possibly John Long, a small farmer from Burkesville, had witnessed the murder.[49] Although very little is known about the Story killing, Ferguson was in the area at the time and did murder again during that trip.

The first day of June found the band at the home of one of Ferguson's most vocal enemies. Elijah Kogier captained a Home Guard unit, and although he had known Ferguson since childhood, he was now a sworn enemy. That Sunday morning, Kogier awoke and stepped outside to the spring. While he was a short distance from the house, a small squad, estimated at ten men, rode up to the house and opened fire. Led by Ferguson, the men expected to find Kogier still in bed. Nancy Kogier screamed for her husband to run away, but his pursuers quickly overtook him. She recalled that Elijah had only run about twenty yards when Ferguson shot at him and the entire party gave chase. Running for a fence, Kogier fell short. A neighbor, Jane Walker, was standing at the spring near the action. She recalled seeing Kogier shot twice while running and, after he fell, Ferguson dragging the man's body by the arm before a member of the guerrilla band delivered what likely proved to be the fatal shot. Kogier's terrified wife and children ran to the scene, but the patriarch expired after only a couple of breaths. The family huddled around the dead body near the fence for fifteen minutes while Ferguson and his band lingered around the house.[50]

When Nancy Kogier returned to her house, she found Ferguson sitting and laughing while the others went through her belongings. Calmly, she told him that "it looked like he was going to kill all my friends" to which he frankly responded "there was some more he intended to kill." At that, she returned to her husband's body. Ferguson's men left after remaining there an hour. As they departed, they led away one of the family's horses, and when Nancy reentered the home, she found it ransacked with notes of credit destroyed and a shotgun and pistol stolen.[51]

Preston Huff, the son of Alex Huff whom Ferguson had killed only a month before, corroborated the stories surrounding the death of Elijah Kogier. Having narrowly escaped an intoxicated Ferguson the previous December and understanding that the guerrilla would not waste another opportunity to kill him, Huff and three friends were hiding out near the Kogier farm when Ferguson's band arrived. They heard shots and hurried to a vantage point. Huff recalled that upon hearing the firing he and one other ran toward the sound, arriving within sight of the happenings in time to see Kogier shot down near the fence. As the victim likely ran fewer than fifty yards before he was killed and Huff probably hesitated for a few seconds before deciding to hurry toward the action, he might have embellished his story a bit to help in the prosecution of his father's killer. However questionable Huff's tale of witnessing the actual killings, he did visit the Kogier farm after Ferguson and his men left. There he saw Elijah Kogier's corpse and Kogier's brave but equally bloody eleven-year-old daughter, who had hurried to her father's body and cradled his head while surrounded by his killers. Huff and his friends helped carry Elijah Kogier's body into the house but left quickly, as they were afraid Ferguson's men might return.[52]

Isaac Kogier was apparently at his brother Elijah's house that morning. Obviously he was not a target of that raid, and Jane Walker remembered that Isaac ran away when the raiders rode up. Ferguson's proclamation, "God-damn you, I have [a] load in my gun to kill you," proved enough to halt the fleeing man. Apparently he was considered by Ferguson a nonparticipant in local affairs, and Isaac Kogier only wished to leave the scene. But Ferguson himself wanted to clear out before anyone else so as to beat the spread of news. Ferguson "would not let him go until they got away" and one of the men shot Kogier in the knee to slow him down. It worked; Isaac Kogier did not leave until after Ferguson's band was gone.[53]

Not surprisingly, Ferguson claimed a good reason for killing Elijah Kogier. Proudly pronouncing, "I killed Elijah Kogier and done a good trick when I did it," he added, "He was a treacherous dog, and richly merited his fate." In justification, he argued that Kogier "watched my house day and night, and sometimes until he was nearly frozen, to get to kill me." However compelling Ferguson's allegations, skepticism is warranted, as he had plenty of opportunities to kill Kogier prior to the date of the actual event. If Kogier nearly froze watching the Ferguson house, it had been months before, and Ferguson had visited despite this ubiquitous threat. He closed his statement by adding dryly, "A number of very affecting stories are told in connection with his death."[54]

A couple of hours after killing Elijah Kogier, the band arrived at the home of another old enemy. James Zachary, a Home Guard and participant in that spring's Monroe Compromise, was also the father of Fount Zachary, the young man Ferguson had killed during a raid two months before, to the day. Ferguson had another reason for seeking out Zachary. Just as his killing of Constable Reed had put into motion the machinations that eventually led to his joining the Confederate cause, it also led to Ferguson's visit to the Zachary house that day. Before the war, James Zachary had been a magistrate in Fentress County, Tennessee. As magistrate, he had remanded Ferguson to jail to await trial for the killing of Reed. Perhaps fearing that in the event of a Federal victory, the suit could be resurrected, Ferguson pursued Zachary and threatened to kill him many times before finally accomplishing his goal. Either for revenge or as a preventive measure, Ferguson thought it best to eliminate this man who might be very dangerous to him.[55]

For Zachary, that day was the fulfillment of a bloody prophecy. Shortly before Mill Springs, Ferguson had visited the home, at which time he swore he would kill James Zachary and his son Fount. He had killed Fount; now it was James's turn. Although James had steered clear of the Confederates for the first part of the year, Ferguson's guerrillas finally caught Zachary outside. Busy with something between the house and the stable when the men rode up, he probably did not notice them until one of Ferguson's men fired at him and yelled, "Halt." With Ferguson screaming, "Shoot him! Damn him! Shoot him!" and his band following, Zachary ran into an orchard where he hoped to lose his pursuers. Out of sight of the house, but still within hearing, Zachary's daughter Esther remembered someone saying, "Don't shoot a dead man."[56]

With his work on James Zachary done, Ferguson turned his attention to the house. Walking up to the front door, he almost killed again, but Esther led the family dog out of his path, assuring him that the animal did not bite. Stepping inside, he frankly announced, "we have killed your father," and began his search for Zachary's Colt navy revolver. Esther knew that, unlike Kogier who had been caught outside without arms, her father went nowhere unarmed. She asked Ferguson if her "father did not have his navy with him" and claimed "he had it with him when he left the house." Upon hearing this, Ferguson searched the house and, not finding the pistol, went back outside, retracing Zachary's path through the orchard, where he found the gun. Having witnessed too much killing for one day, Esther attempted to save another life just as she had saved the family pet. When Ferguson arrived at her home, his men were holding a man named Stokely Evans prisoner. While Ferguson loaded her father's gun, she inquired about the band's intentions with Evans. Ferguson claimed that he was going to send him home unharmed.[57]

When Ferguson left the Zachary place, he did so with plunder. From it, he took the revolver, a powder horn, an overcoat, a watch, a bridle, and even a single spur, which Zachary had been wearing when shot.[58] Despite the booty he carried away, Ferguson felt he had a larger and better reason for killing James Zachary. Again, his defense revolved around the issues of mistaken identity and self-defense. Despite his acceptance of responsibility for Zachary's death and that he fired at the fleeing man, he claimed one of his band fired the fatal shot. Ferguson argued that Zachary "was in command of a company of bushwhackers, and was seeking my life," and that he had gone to Zachary's house "for the purpose of killing, in order to save my own life." In final judgment, Ferguson smugly surmised, "He was a clever man before the war, but got over it soon after the war broke out, and arrayed himself in deadly hostility to his old friends and neighbors."[59]

On the morning of June 6, a fight erupted near Tompkinsville, Kentucky. Having camped several miles south of town, Captain Hugh McCullough's Company I, 9th Pennsylvania Cavalry, was surprised as they readied to break camp. The enemy force, estimated between 125 and 200 men, pushed in Mc-Cullough's pickets. The Federals had been traveling light with only sabers and pistols and quickly regrouped and moved forward toward the thick woods where the guerrillas were formed. With only sixty men, McCullough's advance into the brush met the buckshot and rifle fire of a well-hidden and numerically superior force. Despite the disadvantages, the Union troops kept up their charge and scattered the Confederates. McCullough, who had been in front leading his men, was severely wounded. His second-in-command, Lieutenant William H. Longsdorf, continued the pursuit until discovering that his still formidable enemy was reforming a line four miles ahead. Realizing he had only about fifty effectives and that McCullough had died, Longsdorf ordered his men to fall back to Tompkinsville and await support.[60]

Colonel Williams had ordered McCullough to the embattled region to chase the partisans and had sent Major Thomas Jefferson Jordan to Glasgow, Kentucky, to offer logistical support for the operation. Having just arrived with his men in Glasgow as a courier rode into town with the news from Tompkinsville, Jordan ordered his men to ready themselves for more riding. In the saddle all night covering the thirty miles between the two towns, three additional companies of the 9th Pennsylvania arrived at Longsdorf's side early the next morning. With four companies of cavalry, Major Jordan moved out southward to Celina, Tennessee, where Federals had been unable to cross the month before. Upon arriving on the north bank of the Cumberland River, Jordan shouted for the townspeople to send boats over to pick up his men. Confederates hidden among the trees on the south bank responded with gunfire. Unable to cross and realizing the futility of a firefight at that distance, Jordan's men wheeled their horses and headed back to Tompkinsville.[61]

That same evening, Colonel Edward C. Williams arrived in Tompkinsville with the remainder of the 9th Pennsylvania. Williams and his six companies of cavalry had ridden nearly sixty miles from Bowling Green in support of Longsdorf and Jordan. The next day, June 8, the entire regiment rode south and crossed the river at McMillan's Ferry on Turkey Neck Bend. As the ferry could only carry ten men and their horses at a time, all day was spent moving the large force across the river. While their comrades made their way to the opposite shore, one company moved ahead to the town where they "surrounded a Church and kept the inmates prisoners all Day." Knowing that J. M. McMillan was a local Confederate partisan, the men enjoyed dinner at his house that day before releasing their prisoners and moving on.[62]

Arriving at Celina well into the afternoon of June 9, Williams sent three companies to charge the town. Finding little, the 9th took four prisoners, a few horses, and some firearms. On their way out of town, Williams sent a detachment to destroy a local "commissary." There, the men found a large amount of goods that had been taken by guerrillas when they had captured a steamboat shortly before. Jordan reported recouping twenty boxes and ten barrels of army bread, two barrels of sugar, one hundred bags of wheat, and twenty-three hogsheads of tobacco. Although glad to have retaken these stores, the men had no way to carry their treasure. All the goods were dumped into the river.[63] Despite Williams's report specifying that Ferguson was part of the initial attack, it is unknown if the guerrilla personally participated in the fight at Tompkinsville.

As for conditions elsewhere in the hills of north-central Tennessee, Andrew Hall, originally a Vermonter and attorney who had lived in Sparta, Tennessee, in 1860, but wrote from Shelbyville in 1862, penned a letter to Governor Johnson apprising him of the state of things in White, Putnam, and Overton counties. He asked the governor to take an interest in suppressing the southern partisans. He relayed stories that many men from White County had joined guerrilla bands and participated in raids into Kentucky. His letter also alerted Johnson to the activities of Erasmus L. Gardenhire, a member of the Confederate Congress who "is raising a band for some purpose." Whether it was fact or fiction, Hall warned Johnson of a possible attempt on his life. He wrote that two men from White County had recently visited Confederate Colonel George Dibrell's camp, where they told the colonel that Sam Turney, a long-serving state legislator, had approached Ferguson about killing the governor, claiming that he "offered the Notorious Capt Forguson of Overton" $1,000 for the job.[64] At the time, Ferguson likely gave the matter minimal attention; however, a few years later, the memory certainly haunted him.

Away from the travails of politics and intrigue, John Hunt Morgan returned to raiding. Although his attack on the L&N at Cave City had been widely reported as a rousing success, in his heart, the cavalryman knew better. It had initially been planned as his first raid into Kentucky and he had intended to take it as far as his hometown of Lexington, but the "Lebanon Races" had destroyed his vision. Now, just two months after his great embarrassment, Morgan was ready to give his planned raid another try. With nearly nine hundred men, the party left Knoxville, Tennessee, on July 4, 1862, on its way to Sparta where it would turn north into the Cumberland range. After dodging bushwhackers, the column arrived in Ferguson's adopted hometown. There, Morgan and Ferguson reunited for the deep raid into Kentucky.[65]

It was there that Basil Duke got his first look at the guerrilla fighter. Duke, a brother-in-law of Morgan and an interesting character in his own right, recorded that Ferguson's reputation was widely known as early as spring 1862. Duke wrote that Ferguson "Had the reputation of never giving quarter, and no doubt, deserved it." It is likely that Ferguson appalled the rigid Lexingtonian. Writing his recollections shortly after Ferguson's execution, Duke added "(when upon his own private expeditions)" to the previous statement. Describing Ferguson as "a fair specimen of the kind of characters which the wild mountain country produces," Duke added, "He was a man of strong sense, although wholly uneducated, and of . . . intense will and energy."[66]

During Ferguson's postwar court martial, General Joseph Wheeler testified that the Confederacy did not directly grant commissions to cavalry officers but inferred permission once a company was raised and a muster roll submitted. Richard Morgan all but verified the fact that Ferguson was considered part of the Confederate army when he wrote to his brother, "Capt Ferguson has now reported in accordance with your order which I sent him some time since. I do not think he desires much to do so as he prefers roaming where he has been for some time under the pretext of trying to capture Tinker Dave but in reality," he preferred "to steal horses & Negroes & sell them." Unimpressed by the lack of commitment and discipline shown by Ferguson and his men, Richard asked his brother, "If you can do so I would much prefer that you assign [them to] some other Co."[67]

Early in the First Kentucky Raid, Duke, as Morgan's second-in-command and de facto disciplinarian, approached Ferguson wishing to define what would pass as good behavior. With his violent reputation in mind, Duke sought "to impress upon him the necessity of observing—while with us—the rules of civilized warfare, and that he must not attempt to kill prisoners." Nearly offended at the inference, Ferguson responded, "Why Colonel Duke, I've got sense" and added, "I know it ain't looked on as right to treat reg'lar soldiers tuk in battle in that way." With his point made and apparently understood, Duke then wished to satisfy his own curiosity. He asked Ferguson, "Fergusone, how many men have you killed?" The guerrilla responded typically, "I ain't killed nigh as many men as they say I have; folks has lied about me powerful. I ain't killed but thirty-two men since this war commenced."[68] If Ferguson's declaration was true, he had averaged more than two men killed per month of war since Tennessee's secession less than fourteen months before and had killed more than three times the number known up to that point. Rules clarified, curiosity satisfied, and guides secured, Morgan began his move north toward Kentucky.

By the time the column reached Livingston, Tennessee, Morgan was preparing for his first conflict. A small Federal force guarded Tompkinsville, Kentucky, not far across the state line. With only 350 men in the town, Morgan was sure he could brush it aside. With the recent addition of other small forces, such as Oliver Hamilton's partisans, Morgan boasted a nearly three-to-one numerical superiority. On July 9, his men surrounded the Federal position at Tompkinsville and, after a brief battle, took the position and prisoners with it.[69]

For nearly four weeks, Morgan and his men rampaged almost ghostlike from town to town. With the help of his telegrapher, George A. Ellsworth, Morgan's swift movements were combined with a program of misinformation to make the command seem to appear out of thin air miles from its expected location. At Glasgow, Kentucky, he raided a Federal supply depot before moving northeast toward Lebanon. Like Tompkinsville, Lebanon fell quickly under the weight of Morgan's assault. As Ellsworth "milked" information from telegraph lines, Morgan became better informed about potential resistance along his planned path. James Ramage notes that Morgan was misinformed about and surprised by Federal resistance. At Cynthiana, expecting Home Guards, he rode into a small, but well-trained and equipped, garrison of Union troops. Making his turn around the outskirts of Lexington, Morgan headed back toward Tennessee carrying little but destroying what he did not offer up to the citizenry he encountered. By August 1, Morgan's first raid was a rousing success, although it did not bring Kentucky to the Confederate cause, as the grand-thinking cavalryman had hoped.[70] With Morgan, Ferguson finished his first extended tour of regular military duty.

Returning to Tennessee, Ferguson split off from the main party. Back in the familiar territory of Clinton County, Kentucky, he stopped at the farm of Elijah Kogier. Two months after killing Kogier, Ferguson and his men imposed on the dead man's family for a meal. Riding up to the fence, "Ferguson ordered

some victuals sent out to the gate, and I sent them," remembered Nancy Kogier. "He didn't stay long. As soon as he ate he started," but a company of about
two hundred men stayed on the Kogier farm that night and "destroyed nearly
everything I had."[71]

The spring and early summer of 1862 had been a difficult time for the Confederacy. Although he began the season in his traditional role of guerrilla and
partisan, Ferguson also came to realize the urgency of his region's condition.
In addition to his customary independence, he increasingly operated as part
of a larger and, arguably, more legitimate force. He grew closer to John Hughs,
James McHenry, and Scott Bledsoe, riding with them more frequently than
before, and ultimately, he joined in the deepest and most important Confederate cavalry raid of the early war. His work with the heroic Morgan would earn
him a place of legitimacy and honor in the minds of southerners.

STABILITY AND PARTITION

I have killed old Wash Tabor, a damned good Christian, and I don't reckon
he minds dying.
—CHAMP FERGUSON, October 1862

During the first half of 1862, the Civil War had changed for Champ
Ferguson and the other occupants of the Kentucky-Tennessee borderland. Organized warfare had visited them at Mill Springs and
through various cavalry raids into the region. Even Ferguson, the
guerrilla who had recently grown quite comfortable administering extralegal
justice, had ridden in Morgan's First Kentucky Raid as an ordinary horseman.
Although he had neither a commission nor official enlistment, Ferguson's experience with Morgan brought him closer to regular service in the Confederate army. By the close of the year, he would redefine the nature of his service:
regular soldier when convenient, Confederate partisan when otherwise.

As early as the Kentucky raid of July 1862, Colonel Basil Duke took particular notice of Ferguson and his men. Commenting on the complex nature
of Ferguson's style of warfare, he wrote, "Ferguson could hardly be called a
bushwhacker, although in his methods he much resembled them." His men
were "very daring fighters" and "although not enlisted in the Confederate
service, were intensely attached to Ferguson and sworn to aid the Southern
cause." Duke, a disciplinarian who took his job seriously, noted with some
respect that "While Ferguson undertook many expeditions on his own private
account and acknowledged no obedience to Confederate orders generally," the
guerrilla, when riding with regular troops, "strictly obeyed commands and
abstained from evil practices."[1] For the ever informal Ferguson, his time spent
with Morgan constituted regular Confederate service. In fact, he always main-

tained that he belonged to Morgan's Cavalry. While he did accompany Morgan on his raids northward, Ferguson, for the most part, refused to follow the cavalryman farther south than Sparta, Tennessee. When Morgan receded into the Confederacy and returned to organized warfare, Ferguson chose to return to his wife and daughter and his old borderland habits.

After taking a month of ease at home in White County, Ferguson returned to the border. In August, he, along with several others, met Joseph Beck while traveling north of Albany, Kentucky, near the Kogier farm. One morning at nearly 9:00 a.m., Ferguson and his men rode up the road in front of the late Elijah Kogier's house. Jane Walker remembered that Ferguson rode up to the fence and called to the house. Probably terrified at the sight of her husband's killer, Nancy Kogier sent her sister Jane Walker to the door to answer. Ferguson asked Walker if there had been any other armed men passing the house that morning. She responded that she had seen no one. As he turned to leave, Ferguson told the lady, "We have killed a man up there, I don't know him myself, but some of the boys say it is Joe Beck." Giving the woman instructions as to where to find the body, Ferguson's small column rode away. Walker gathered her sister Nancy Kogier and a young man who was at the house and they walked up the road, where they found the body just as Ferguson had described.[2]

The circumstances of Beck's death remain one of the most elusive mysteries of Champ's legend. During Ferguson's postwar trial, Kogier and Walker recounted what they saw when they found Beck's body, but no one outside of the victim, Ferguson, and the seven men riding with him that day witnessed the event. Even after his conviction, in a series of interviews with the condemned man during which he explained the details of all the killings, reporters forgot to question him about Beck's death, leaving only the note, "(Our reporters omitted to make inquiries relative to the murder of Joseph Becks, near Poplar Mountain, Clinton county, Ky., in the Spring of 1862. The Court, however, found him guilty on the charge)."[3]

Ferguson continued his activities into the late summer of 1862 when a brief newspaper article appeared that threw Confederate sympathizers in the region into chaos. The *Louisville Courier Journal* reported that a Captain Morris of the Clinton County Home Guard had "attacked a band of guerrillas a few days since and killed sixteen of them, among whom was the notorious Champ Ferguson." Despite the newspaper's crediting the information to "a source entitled to great credence," Ferguson remained alive and had not "met his deserts in the dominions of his Satanic Majesty." This story was the first during the Civil War that optimistically announced Ferguson's death.[4]

Just as the Confederacy could count on Champ Ferguson to practice his unique brand of warfare in the Cumberland region, the Union could count on men like Colonel William Clift to support its cause in that area. Clift hailed from Hamilton County in southeastern Tennessee and had organized a pro-Union guerrilla band as early as the previous autumn. By November 14, 1861, Clift's activities were known all the way to the state capitol in Nashville, as Governor Isham Harris ordered, "Muster all the armed forces possible without calling on Zollicoffer, and capture Clift and his men, dead or alive."[5] Three days later, Zollicoffer replied, "Three expeditions are moving from different directions upon Clift's men. I fear they will disperse and take to the mountain fastnesses, eluding our forces."[6]

Zollicoffer's fear was well placed; a significant portion of Clift's command had abandoned the fight. Colonel Sterling A. M. Wood of the 7th Regiment, Alabama Volunteers, reported that on November 15, he led a large force to a camp rumored to be used by Colonel Clift and his men. Upon arriving at the campground, Wood found it empty and learned that the enemy force of about two hundred had split up the previous night. Gleaning information from several captured men, Wood learned that on the previous night, Clift's band had met to make a decision about their future actions. He reported that three propositions had been presented to the men. First, only four men had voted to remain in the Hamilton County area and fight (with officers casting half of the votes). Second, almost half of the men voted to march toward the safety of the Kentucky border. Third, the others voted to go home. That night and the next morning, Clift's splintered command filtered out of the camp with a dozen or fewer following the colonel into the mountains, an estimated sixty-five with a captain heading to Kentucky, and the others heading home.[7]

Although Clift's command had abandoned him, he was not through. Seeing a good use for irregular scouts with bushwhacking experience, Brigadier General George Morgan, a native East Tennessean now in command of Federal troops at Cumberland Gap, wrote Secretary of War Edwin Stanton that he had recently "taken steps to organize a partisan regiment, under Colonel Clift . . . in order to annoy the enemy's rear."[8] Having recently heard rumors of a Confederate invasion of Kentucky through Cumberland Gap, Morgan hoped that Clift's guerrillas, along with civilian bushwhackers of East Tennessee, could harass the Confederate supply lines enough to hamper any serious movement toward his position.

By summer of 1862, the paths of Ferguson and Clift would cross. Ordered to Scott County, Tennessee, where he could easily reach into Confederate controlled Tennessee and disrupt lines of supply and communication, Clift constituted a new Union threat moving into a region where Ferguson frequently operated. On August 13, Clift and his band of about 250 men awoke to find themselves staring at a large Confederate force hoping to drive out the enemy and secure a path of retreat after the forthcoming invasion of Kentucky.[9] Losing a significant part of his command, Clift withdrew hoping to fight again. Unbeknown to him, Clift had witnessed the first days of the Kentucky Campaign.

The first half of 1862 had brought little to the Confederacy outside of reversals of previous successes. In late July, Confederate generals Braxton Bragg and Edmund Kirby Smith sought to change that trend by mounting an offensive into Middle Tennessee. Once Bragg secured the heartland, both men would lead their armies into Kentucky. Meeting in Chattanooga, the two men agreed on this plan of action. Bragg would move his army into position for an assault on Middle Tennessee, while Smith would recapture Cumberland Gap. However, instead of retaking the Gap and turning his attention back south and west, Smith, who had an independent command and reveled in his sovereignty, sent part of his command to besiege the Gap while he and a large column of men crossed into Kentucky using lesser-known routes during the middle of August. Smith's premature invasion of Kentucky left Bragg, who had been assured of Kirby Smith's full cooperation, sitting hundreds of miles behind his colleague's swift advance.[10]

Hurriedly, Bragg moved his army north to help Smith's dangerously exposed column. Keeping between Don Carlos Buell's large and well-trained army and Smith's much smaller force, Bragg surmised that Buell, who had been lurking outside of Chattanooga for months until Smith's sudden movement, could not afford to attack within Tennessee with such a pressing threat deep inside of Kentucky. As Bragg moved his army northward in an attempt to catch up with Smith, he effectively used cavalry screens to mask his movements. Only after it was too late did Buell fully realize the size and exact location of his counterpart's force. As expected, the surprised Buell scrambled to constrict his lines in such a way as to protect the commonwealth's seat of government at Frankfort and its most important city at Louisville.[11]

As August turned to September, the tide of the war seemed to be turning. No force, not even Buell's much larger army, had made a serious attempt to check the Confederate invasion of Kentucky. On August 30, 1862, Edmund

Kirby Smith with about 7,000 troops soundly whipped William "Bull" Nelson's Federals in an evenly matched fight at Richmond, Kentucky, resulting in 4,300 Union soldiers being taken prisoner.[12] Having allowed only an estimated 1,200 of the enemy to escape, Kirby Smith's Confederates effectively kicked open the door to Lexington. Two days later, the mayor surrendered his city.[13]

Throughout the month of September, Braxton Bragg led Buell's army around by the nose. Wisely, the Confederate general moved to Bowling Green, squarely between the dual objectives of Nashville and Louisville and astride the railroad. Buell, with his back to Nashville, had a choice to make: Either defend the capitol of Tennessee, now occupied by a governor who hated him and considered the general a traitor, or fight to defend the Kentucky cities of Louisville and Frankfort. Bragg, on the other hand, sought to help Buell make up his mind by backing toward Louisville and settling in at the hamlet of Munfordville, where he could combine with Kirby Smith's force, now only one hundred miles to his east.[14]

Although Bragg felt confident of his chances, circumstances were conspiring against him. First, "Bull" Nelson, who had been wounded in the thigh in the Battle of Richmond, captured by the Confederates, but then had managed to escape, had made his way to Louisville, where he worked feverishly to erect defenses. Second, Smith's army, which Bragg felt would arrive at his side imminently, did not come as he hoped, leaving his own army of 28,000 outnumbered by Buell's 35,000 with another 6,000 men available under George Thomas in Nashville. Overall, Smith's haste had forced an unready Bragg into action, resulting in Bragg moving his army into what, at the outset, had been a strong position on the L&N Railroad. Now, with Smith's army still far off, Nelson working wonders in Louisville, and Buell holding a numerical advantage, Bragg found himself moving away from his supply line while his counterpart moved toward the Union depots in Louisville.[15]

On September 20, Bragg began marching his army east.[16] For the Confederate general, the move was necessary for three reasons. His army, with its supply lines stretched to the breaking point, was in danger of starving if it remained in its former position. Bragg realized that with Nelson in Louisville, his Confederate army might be caught in a vise between the city and Buell's army. And, if he wished to unite with Smith, he should make the move, rather than allow the ever independent-minded Smith the opportunity to again move without Bragg. For the Confederates, an unfortunate result of their move was to allow Buell to reach Louisville, which he did by the end of the month. With a strongly fortified city surrounding Buell, and his army well fed and well equipped, the Union now had a pronounced advantage.

On September 23, Bragg arrived in Bardstown where he expected to meet Smith. However, Smith wrote Bragg that his army must remain in the vicinity of Lexington. Again stuck without Smith's additional 19,000 men, Bragg still had high hopes of meeting and defeating Buell. On October 8, Bragg's Kentucky Campaign culminated in the Battle of Perryville, the largest fight in the state. Buell, now with a massive army of 78,000, sent 20,000 men to Lexington to occupy Smith while the remainder sought out Bragg's 32,000 men. Meeting just west of Perryville, the two forces fought desperately all day, partly due to the legendary acoustic shadow that kept Buell from sending the majority of his forces into the battle. By the end of the day, Bragg had held his own against Buell's comparatively huge army and withdrew to Harrodsburg, where Smith, who began to fear for his safety, finally united with him. Together they retreated through the Cumberland Gap and back into Tennessee, their Kentucky Campaign in shambles behind them.[17]

While the larger war played out on the battlefields of Kentucky, Champ Ferguson's guerrilla war continued in the mountains. During the Kentucky invasion, Confederate partisans operated in the southern part of the state with impunity. From Tompkinsville, Bennett Mearger wrote that two local unionists were killed on the road near his house. He relayed that guerrilla Captain Hamilton's men came to town with two prisoners. Mearger knew both men and recorded how "they shot Austin through the head and his brains was scattered in the road and they shot Heflin in several places."[18] A few days later, several citizens of nearby Burkesville wrote Governor James Robinson telling him of repeated Confederate raids through town within the past few weeks.[19]

Back in Fentress County, life was miserable for unionists, particularly while the Confederate army occupied Kentucky. During the middle of September, a group of Champ Ferguson's men led by Henry Sublett descended on Hale's Mills. With the proprietor and noted unionist J. D. Hale now living in Kentucky and spying for the Union army, the band took out their frustrations on his property. By the end of the day, the more than sixty guerrillas and local citizens had burned the entire community including Hale's house, other homes, all of the outbuildings (with the exception of the corn crib and schoolhouse), and destroyed all of the machinery on the place. The farm was a near total loss estimated at $20,000.[20]

On October 1, Colonel William Clift reacted to the recent violence by sending a scouting party into Ferguson's territory of Scott, Morgan, and Fentress counties, Tennessee. There, they took a few prisoners and some property. Two weeks later, Clift sent out another expedition that spent two weeks passing through the same region, this time meeting Ferguson and his guerrillas. Clift, who was not at the scene of the fight, reported that his men killed four of the Confederates, including one of the more notorious members of Ferguson's band. Heartened by his recent success, Clift ordered a third scout by the end of October, this time originating from Somerset, Kentucky, and moving south along the Tennessee-Kentucky line in an effort to seek out more guerrillas.[21]

One of the men who served with Clift's 7th Tennessee Volunteer Infantry Regiment (U.S.A.) was Lieutenant Preston Huff. Understanding the level of danger he faced as a unionist and identified enemy of Champ Ferguson, Huff had joined Clift's regiment shortly after he had been harassed by a drunk Ferguson the previous December. One biographer suggests that Huff's company probably participated in Clift's first scout into Fentress County, Tennessee, at the beginning of October and within days, he saw an opportunity to visit home in Clinton County, Kentucky, for the first time in months.[22] Having personal experience with Ferguson and knowing that his father had been killed by the guerrilla only months before, Huff certainly understood the risks involved with his return home.

Just as Preston Huff was returning home to Clinton County to visit his mother, Champ Ferguson also had cause to be in the neighborhood. With the Confederate invasion of Kentucky continuing, Ferguson felt comfortable traveling into what was otherwise very dangerous territory. In late September, Ferguson had run into an old friend in Knoxville. Brigadier General Samuel Bell Maxey was a native of Tompkinsville, Kentucky, and a longtime resident of Albany, where he had practiced law in the 1850s. Having graduated from the United States Military Academy at West Point in 1846 with other luminaries such as George McClellan, Dabney Maury, George Pickett, George Stoneman, and the awkward and odd young man who would grow to be "Stonewall" Jackson, Maxey served honorably in the Mexican War. Resigning his commission when the realization of garrison duty set in, he returned to Kentucky and read law under the tutelage of his father. In the late 1850s, both father and son left south-central Kentucky for Texas where they became outspoken advocates for secession during the crisis of 1860–61.[23]

At Knoxville, Maxey ran into Ferguson, who had just reached town from Sparta. Relaying the news to his wife, Maxey told her that Ferguson had seen her father and two of her brothers recently and that all was well at home and that one of her brothers was now riding with Scott Bledsoe's company, but another sibling and he would likely join Ferguson soon. Turning to other business, Ferguson told Maxey, "the Bushwhackers there are still at their murderous work, & probably that if the Govt. will receive his Company he will clear them out." Maxey assured his wife, "I have no doubt he can do it." Upon their parting, Maxey prevailed upon Ferguson to carry a dispatch to "Col. Howard's Regt of Cavalry at Albany," which had been ordered to Clinton County for the dual purposes of offering support to Kirby Smith's command and reporting on the state of affairs there.[24] Ferguson returned to Kentucky carrying Maxey's message.

Before daylight on October 3, Champ Ferguson, having delivered his message and hearing that Preston Huff had returned home, rode up to the Huff farm with about a dozen men in tow. The lieutenant awoke to "Press [Preston Huff], God damn you, come out and surrender yourself up!" Recognizing Ferguson's voice, Huff and one other ran out the back door and into a cornfield where he could hear and observe the goings on at the house. From his position about one hundred yards from the house, Huff heard one man ask "if Press was there," and Ferguson respond, "No he is not here. If he had been, God damn him, we would have had him dead before now."[25]

John Huff, only sixteen years old at the time, had remained inside while his brother Preston ran to the cornfield. He remembered that Ferguson's men surrounded the house before coming inside and ordering someone to get up and build a fire. John responded and made the fire, drawing the question of who else was in the house. Knowing someone had run outside, John could not specifically tell Ferguson who remained inside. One of the raiders then asked specifically for Preston and Andy Huff, promising to kill the two if they were indeed there. Andy Huff had not been there that night, but Union soldiers William Delk, John Crabtree, and John Williams had spent the night and sat in the darkness awaiting their fate. Delk rose and approached the party and asked what they were going to do with him. The Confederates responded that they were going to take him to Albany and try him on an unspecified charge. Without any recourse, Delk, Crabtree, and Williams surrendered.[26]

While the rest of the group ransacked the house, three of the men removed the leather straps from their guns and tied the men's elbows behind their backs. Delk, complaining that the knots were too tight and painful, drew the comment, "damn you, that's what we want to do" from Ferguson. John Huff remembered that the men left his mother's house with "bedclothing and wearing apparel" and Ferguson took a slave girl. Complaining that the girl did not belong to them, Ferguson announced that he knew she was the property of noted unionist Eli Hatfield and he had orders to take her away. Ferguson's men then took axes and chopped up the floor and threatened to burn the house and kill everyone there. Ferguson was more direct. He drew his knife and told Crabtree, "I'm going to cut your throat with this knife." As the men left the house, Crabtree's mother asked Ferguson if he planned to kill the three soldiers. Ferguson assured her that he would.[27]

After a while at the Huff house, Ferguson and his men left taking Delk, Crabtree, and Williams with them, along with the slave girl. It was about daybreak when Preston Huff, hiding in a cornfield, saw the group pass "loaded with clothes and such."[28] The company proceeded to the Alvin Piles farm, which stood from one-quarter to one-half mile from the Huff place. The group had already visited the Piles once that night. Near midnight, they had taken a horse from the family and left. Afraid to lie down and go to sleep, the Piles women were standing in the yard when Ferguson rode up with the soldiers. Passing through the gate and into the Piles's yard, the group went toward the stable. Vina Piles remembered that one of the men came back to where they stood and told them to go inside. Once inside the house, the women heard three shots and saw the crowd leave. At the same time, John Huff, who had stepped outside to make sure Ferguson did not return, saw muzzle flashes and heard gunshots coming from the direction of Piles's farm. After waiting a while, John walked to Piles's corral where he found the three soldiers dead. Williams had been shot squarely in the forehead, Delk shot in the chest with a bayonet wound through the gunshot, and Crabtree, rather than being shot, had been "cut all over the breast and forepart of his shoulder between the neck and collarbone and in the back under the shoulderblade." Apparently, Ferguson's personal threat to kill Crabtree with his knife had been carried out. John Huff remembered that when he found Crabtree's body, it had a cornstalk stuck in the back wound. Vina Piles recalled that Crabtree's mother arrived about an hour after her son had been killed and was left to pull out the cornstalk. Ferguson and his men, one of whom was a cousin to John Crabtree, had apparently turned to senseless mutilation.[29]

Responding to a reporter's questions about his role in the killings of Williams, Delk, and Crabtree, Ferguson contended that he did not torture any of the victims. Illustrating the extent of his activity in the war, Ferguson could not remember if he killed Williams but did recall killing Delk and Crabtree. Not saying much about Williams outside of a denial that he tortured the man, Ferguson matter-of-factly admitted killing Delk, with the caveat that "I killed men to get them out of the way, only; I took no pleasure in torturing them." As had become his patent justification, Ferguson claimed, "Delk had been pursuing me a long time, and I knew the only way to save my life, was to kill him, and I did it." More confounding is Ferguson's excuse for the death of Crabtree. In his own defense, Ferguson "regarded him as a spy . . . He had been piloting Stoke's cavalry[30] through the country, and had acted as informer, when inquiries were made as to the whereabouts of confederate sympathizers." In defense, he claimed to be "justified in killing him, as Federal generals were executing spies." Recycling his claim of self-defense, he added, "He assisted in pursuing me two or three times and I resolved to kill him." Although the guerrilla denied torturing Crabtree, he did offer, "he was a long time in dying." To Ferguson's way of thinking, he simply "put him out of the way."[31]

Interviewed by another reporter within days of his other confession, Ferguson changed his story somewhat. The *Nashville Dispatch* reported that Ferguson had remembered that one of his men, Ben Barton, killed Williams, and that Delk had been "shot by another of our boys," contrary to his recent admission that he had killed Delk. As for Crabtree, a self-righteous Ferguson bluntly confessed "I went to Piles' house in the night and stabbed him, and did another good job when I killed him." He added that Crabtree was "a murderous villain, and had went to men's houses and shot them to get their money."[32] It is worth noting that while Ferguson opposed what he claimed to have been Crabtree's thievery, one witness testified that on the night in question, Ferguson's men stole money and a knife from Delk and Crabtree, not to mention the bedding and clothing from the Huffs.[33]

After leaving the Piles place, Ferguson and his men entered Wayne County, Kentucky, where they met a small group led by Silas Upchurch.[34] The band ordered Upchurch, his wife, son, brother and a few others to stop and pulled out two men, Orphe Williams and a black man called Johnson's Granville, who had fallen in with the family on the road. One of the partisans ordered Williams to hand over his guns and upon doing so, he was immediately shot and killed. The band then tied the black man and took him off of the road about a hundred yards, where they shot him. Upchurch, apparently of no interest to the group, walked closer to the activity and saw the man he would later identify as Ferguson "cutting the negro in the breast and neck after which they wiped the knife on the negros pants." Having made quick work of the two men, Ferguson's men rode to the Upchurch farm where they took ten horses.[35]

Perhaps the most inexplicable of Ferguson's killings, the murders of Williams and Granville are fertile subjects for speculation. Offering little in the way of clarification or reason, Ferguson simply acknowledged that he "killed Offey (Orphe) Williams and a negro man in the mountains. I shot and stabbed them." Wryly adding, "They were scouting for my command, and they found the head of it."[36] When asked about the killing of Granville, a still smug Ferguson stated, "I didn't think the niggers had any business in this war, and I killed him." While the *Nashville Union* stated the black man was a Union soldier, little evidence supports this assertion.[37] The case of Orphe Williams is more interesting in that it is likely that he was John Williams's father; the same man whom Ferguson had killed earlier that morning. One examiner presents these possibilities along with the probability that Williams was an active member of a company of Home Guards.[38]

While in Kentucky, Ferguson reportedly made his way to Burksville, where he kidnapped and held Otho Miller prisoner. Miller recalled that after his capture, he "was ushered into the presence of the rebel thief and catechized and taunted" by Ferguson, who told him "that it was his policy . . . to kill every Union man who fell into his hands." However, before Ferguson could make good on his promise, Confederate officers interceded on his behalf and gained his release. Perhaps the most interesting aspects of Miller's experience as Ferguson's prisoner are his broad statements about the nature of the war in the Cumberland region. Miller relayed that despite the overwhelming support for the Union among the populace, estimated by him at 20:1, small bands like Ferguson's effectively quashed all outward support through the ongoing threat of night visits and the untamed violence that often followed. Echoing longstanding sentiments, he noted that the region of southern Kentucky had sent great numbers of soldiers to the Union army and as a result was relatively unprotected from Confederate depredations because of that fact, "while less loyal districts are protected by Federal troops."[39]

By the end of October, the Confederate threat to Kentucky had lifted. Bragg's defeated army was withdrawing back into Tennessee and an influx of Union soldiers into the countryside signaled a return to relative stability for those who supported the cause. Frank Wolford's 1st Kentucky Cavalry (U.S.A.) returned to the Clinton County area. Seeing an opportunity to visit home while their regiment was stationed nearby, brothers George and William

Thrasher secured permission to go to their father's house for a few days. On the afternoon of October 27, twenty-two men under the command of Champ Ferguson arrested the brothers.[40] Apparently serious about his commitment to the humane treatment of regular soldiers, as he had explained to Basil Duke a few months before, Ferguson held the men nearly one full day before releasing them unharmed. Their ordeal throws light on Ferguson's leadership role and the dynamic within the band.

After spending the night with the group, the Thrasher brothers awoke to breakfast and some unexpected conversation. While waiting to eat, Ferguson walked over and sat down next to William. Either simply curious or wishing to further scare his prisoners, he asked the man what he knew about the murder of James Zachary. Ferguson knew the Thrasher and Zachary boys served together in the Albany company of Wolford's regiment and asked what Zachary's sons were saying about the killing of their father. William told him that the family suspected Fayette Allen, who frequently rode with Ferguson, and alleged that Allen had some prewar reason for wanting Zachary dead. Proud of his role in Zachary's death and disturbed by Thrasher's giving credit to another, Ferguson responded with a snort and claimed responsibility for himself.[41]

After breakfast, the group set off. Early that afternoon, while stopped near Albany, Ferguson spotted evidence that one of his enemies was nearby. Seeing a familiar horse tied several hundred yards off the road, Ferguson said, "Boys, I believe there is somebody there." After moving to a vantage point where he could see a nearby house, he turned to his men and requested, "Boys, I wish five or six of you would ride down there." On Ferguson's orders, six men rode toward the house. George Thrasher recalled that of the six men who went to investigate Ferguson's hunch, an excited five quickly returned, happily claiming, "they had caught one of them." A more sedate Durham Grimes rode up minutes later with the new prisoner on the saddle behind him. Interestingly, neither brother noted any comment coming from Ferguson while the men were gone or upon their return, but when Grimes arrived with old, bald Thomas Washington "Wash" Tabor, the guerrilla quickly dismounted and walked toward the old man.[42]

Ferguson's reasons for killing Wash Tabor are unknown, but several possibilities exist. First, Tabor was an avowed unionist and had spent some time in camp at Albany during the summer of 1861. Tabor's unionism and his remaining at home might have translated into bushwhacking, which Ferguson noted as one of his concerns. More likely however, Ferguson, wishing to instill fanatical obedience in his immature troops and cognizant of his image as a leader, took the matter into his own hands.

The still mounted Grimes realized very quickly that Ferguson meant to kill Tabor immediately and protested "don't kill him behind me." With that, he pushed the old man off the horse and Tabor began begging for his life. Assuring Ferguson, "You know I wouldn't kill you," Tabor received the sarcastic response, "Oh yes, you oughtn't to die, you have done nothing to die for." Pulling his gun, Ferguson shot Tabor twice, once in the chest and once in the stomach. At this point, the seriously wounded Tabor was on the ground with his assailant still standing over him when one of the men screamed to Ferguson, "God damn him, shoot him in the head." Satisfying his men's bloodlust, Ferguson put the gun to Tabor's head and fired. Ferguson's men either understood that their captain reserved for himself the right to kill all the prisoners or they wished to live vicariously through him.[43]

Having watched Ferguson murder an unarmed old man, the Thrasher brothers expected to be next. Apparently, George Thrasher's face told the story, because Ferguson turned to him and assured him, "I am not in favor of killing you Thrasher, you have never been bushwhacking and stealing horses through the country." Turning back to his men, Ferguson declared, "I have killed old Wash Tabor, a damned good Christian, and I don't reckon he minds dying."[44] Ferguson's attempt at comforting Thrasher also served notice of his main reason for killing the old man. Even during his last days, Ferguson maintained that he killed Tabor, whom he called Boswell Tabor, because of his bushwhacking activities. An unrepentant Ferguson alleged that Tabor "had killed three of my men a few days previous" and "He ought to have been killed sooner."[45]

Shortly after the Tabor killing, Ferguson's band was thrown into chaos as a large body of Union guerrillas attacked. Elam Huddleston, originally from Overton and Fentress counties in Tennessee, had endured his own familial trials because of the war. When Huddleston voiced his support for the Union and fled to Kentucky, his cousin, Stokely Huddleston, who held a colonel's commission in the Tennessee State Militia, ordered him arrested if he returned home and locked up all of Elam's belongings. Returning home with James Ferguson and several other unionist friends, he broke open the lock and took his things to Kentucky. Sending his household ahead, Elam and his friends selected a place from which they could fight Colonel Huddleston, who was now pursuing with men. When the colonel drew close, one of Elam's fellows shot him, causing the rest of the militia to turn and flee. Following the close call with his cousin, Elam enlisted at Albany during the summer of 1861. Although he fought bravely at Mill Springs, he left regular service, preferring partisan warfare instead. By stepping away from the U.S. Army, Huddleston could recruit and command men whose primary responsibility was the defense of the borderland.[46] As the war progressed, Huddleston and Tinker Dave Beatty joined forces frequently to seek out Confederate sympathizers.[47] In recalling Huddleston, Basil Duke noted that "Huddlestone and Ferguson sought each other with inveterate animosity, and had several indecisive encounters."[48]

That day, Huddleston's independent company numbered about eighty men to Ferguson's twenty, sans the two prisoners who would be looking for a means of escape. Upon the capture of the Thrashers, Ferguson had ordered his men to immediately shoot the prisoners if attacked. This order, however, was not obeyed. Either the men were too startled to think of anything other than their own skins or some of Ferguson's men, despite their own enjoyment of their captain's exploits, had no urge to draw blood themselves. Huddleston's sizable contingent was augmented by several of the Thrashers' fellow soldiers. Informed of the boys' arrest by their father, Huddleston's posse had ridden the previous night and that morning in search of the men. Finally finding them near the Tabor place, Huddleston's company charged the much smaller band and sent Ferguson's men fleeing. The Thrasher brothers, who were mounted, lived through their captivity.[49]

Following Ferguson's narrow escape from Elam Huddleston's company, the guerrilla band returned to work, this time in Cumberland County, Kentucky. A November 12 dispatch verified Ferguson's presence there and noted that he and another guerrilla leader were in the county with "200 or 300 men, devastating it."[50] While there was no testimony given as to the circumstances of the killing of Dr. William McGlasson, that accusation and Ferguson's confession provide some details. The fifteenth specification against Ferguson noted that at some time in November 1862, Ferguson and his band were near Burkesville when they took three men prisoner, one of whom turned out to be McGlasson. While the fates of the other two men are unknown, McGlasson was reportedly told to run for his life, at which point, Ferguson and his men leveled their guns and shot him down.[51]

In 1864, Thomas Wilson published a collection of fantastic wartime atrocity stories. Several of the stories relate to the Civil War in the Cumberland region with a number of them focusing specifically on Ferguson's deeds. Wilson's tales must be read with considerable skepticism, as his authors were mainly loyal unionists like J. D. Hale and General John B. Rodgers and many of their stories include implausible allegations of torture and barbarism not found in any other source. Rodgers's article on the death of Dr. McGlasson was almost certainly written from hearsay while Ferguson remained at large and was steadily hunted by Union troops.

Rodgers wrote that the trouble started with John Hunt Morgan's invasion of Kentucky in the fall of 1862. In November, a squad of Morgan's men stumbled across a small group of U.S. soldiers near Burksville, Kentucky. After a brief fight, the Confederates took control of three of the men as prisoners of war, including McGlasson, and rode on. After several miles, the Confederates met Champ Ferguson on the road. Ferguson suggested they kill the Federal prisoners and the Confederates agreed. They dismounted and began to mill about the area until one of the men fired his gun and ordered McGlasson to run for his life. At that point, McGlasson ran and the southerners opened fire upon him. As he ran, bullets tore into him, and before long, he found himself at the edge of a deep gully and he fell in. His pursuers ran up to the edge overlooking McGlasson and finished off the doctor.[52]

Surprisingly, during Ferguson's postwar trial, McGlasson's story was lost in the myriad other events of the previous four years; indeed, not a single witness offered testimony on that count. After the proceedings ended and Ferguson prepared to meet his fate, he confessed that he was present when McGlasson was killed. Ferguson confessed to a reporter that he had told McGlasson to run and (although this is highly questionable), "was rather in hopes that he would get away," but some of his men raised their guns and dropped McGlasson quickly. While it is likely that Ferguson did not participate in every killing committed by his men, it is also untrue that he thought McGlasson, on foot, had a reasonable chance of outrunning a bullet or one of the mounted men. In this case, if Ferguson is to be believed, he did not kill McGlasson, he just set him up to be killed by his men.[53]

The *Nashville Dispatch* of October 21, 1865, complicates the issue. In that interview, Ferguson denied knowing anything about the event in question. "I am entirely ignorant of such a man as Dr. McGlosson, [sic] and never heard of him until the charges were read to me." He speculated that McGlasson was in a fight up the Cumberland River in which several men on both sides were killed. Remembering that he had chased a man down a bluff and shot him while the man climbed over a fence, he hypothesized that the man might have been McGlasson, but maintained that he had never captured a man and then sent him running for his life. Casting himself as a victim, he concluded, "I am charged with killing many persons, who fell in battle, and a good many killed by other commands are laid at my door."[54]

Although it is unknown what drew Ferguson back to Kentucky in early November, it is probable that John Hunt Morgan's second raid had some influence. Morgan had spent September in Lexington, Kentucky, with Kirby Smith's army. After a month at home, Morgan retreated back to Tennessee with Smith. Having returned to Confederate territory, Morgan requested and received permission to reenter Kentucky for the purpose of raiding behind Federal lines in the hopes that his disruption would slow the Union's return to Tennessee. On October 18, a little more than a week before Ferguson's men took the Thrasher brothers prisoner and killed Wash Tabor, Morgan entered his home state with 1,800 mounted men. Riding as far as Lexington, he took prisoners, attacked wagon trains, and destroyed railroads and bridges, before making it back to Tennessee on November 1.[55] It is quite possible that Ferguson had advanced with Morgan as far as Clinton County.

In the meantime, Kentucky unionists sought to protect themselves from the Confederate guerrillas. J. A. Morrison, a citizen of Clinton County, but now forced to live in Columbia, Kentucky, had received permission to organize a home guard to protect himself and his neighbors from the depredations of men like "the notorious Ferguson." Unfortunately, the order giving him permission to lead the contingent also restricted its movements to its home county. Angry that the state adjutant general would not allow broader powers, Morrison wrote that his organization was hamstrung by rules while the guerrillas operated freely and with impunity. Noting that he had more than two hundred men scouting after Ferguson, Morrison pled with his superiors to loosen the restrictions.[56]

The late spring, summer, and early fall of 1862 had proven difficult for the people of the border counties. As the region endured the continuing partisan conflict orchestrated by men such as Ferguson, McHenry, and Huddleston, it also quaked under the pressures of the larger war and was visited by large numbers of troops from each army. For Ferguson, that summer had served as a transitional period; he had operated as part of a large-scale regular military force when he guided Morgan through the mountains and likely spent some time with the Kentuckian's command during Morgan's Second Raid. As winter neared, Ferguson would continue to participate in Morgan's adventures, but his own exploits also began to draw more attention from the Union army.

Throughout early 1863, the Federals would send several units into the high-lands to find and capture Ferguson and his band. Just as Governor Andrew Johnson had taken notice of him less than a year before, his reputation would continue to grow in military circles.

A young Martha Ferguson, possibly dressed for her wedding to Champ. In this image she is emblematic of the hard life of an Upper Cumberland farm wife. (Frazier International History Museum, Louisville, Kentucky)

A young, clean-shaven, and fuller-faced Champ Ferguson is shown in this image likely dating to his marriage to Martha in 1848. A portrait of a middling farmer, this ambrotype suggests a man of mountain simplicity but relative success. (Frazier International History Museum, Louisville, Kentucky)

Thomas E. Bramlette was a native of Clinton County, Kentucky. An outspoken unionist, yet still a Democrat, Bramlette resisted the secession impulse and won election as governor of Kentucky in 1863. One of the central concerns of his governorship was minimizing the influence of guerrillas in his state. (Kentucky Historical Society, Frankfort, Kentucky)

George Dibrell, a lifelong resident of White County, Tennessee, served as a unionist delegate to Tennessee's secession convention. Upon the state's departure from the Union, Dibrell enlisted in the Confederate Army as a private. In 1862, he recruited a regiment and began a long and fruitful military relationship with Nathan Bedford Forrest. By the end of the war, he had fought alongside Forrest, Joseph Johnson, and Joe Wheeler and had risen in rank to brigadier general. Champ Ferguson respected Dibrell immensely and cooperated with him numerous times in 1864. (Alabama Department of Archives and History, Montgomery, Alabama)

John A. Brents served for a time as a captain in the 1st Kentucky Cavalry (U.S.A.). In 1863, he resigned his commission and began writing *The Patriots and Guerillas of East Tennessee and Kentucky,* which laid bare Champ Ferguson's activities up to that point in the war. This photograph is of a much older Brents during his service as delegate to the Kentucky Constitutional Convention of 1890–91. (Kentucky Historical Society, Frankfort, Kentucky)

Confederate Colonel John Hunt Morgan in 1862, during the time he frequently used Champ Ferguson as his guide through the Cumberland Mountains. As Morgan's reputation grew, his ambitions expanded, drawing him into conflict with Ferguson. Ironically, Ferguson's break with Morgan most likely saved him from being captured on Morgan's Ohio Raid. (Filson Historical Society, Louisville, Kentucky)

General Joe Wheeler, the famed Confederate cavalryman, provided Champ Ferguson with
an established military organization during the difficult days of late 1864 and early 1865. In
addition to giving Ferguson a military affiliation, Wheeler traveled to Nashville in August
1865, where he testified on Champ's behalf despite receiving a serious beating by a Union
officer on the eve of his taking the stand. (Alabama Department of Archives and History,
Montgomery, Alabama)

Champ Ferguson, a Guerilla
on trial, with guard of 9th Mich. Infy.

Here Champ Ferguson stands with his guard, members of the 9th Michigan Infantry. By all accounts, his relationship with the Union soldiers who guarded him during his confinement was amicable and even friendly at times. (Louis E. Springsteen Collection, Bentley Historical Library, University of Michigan)

In his work on Champ Ferguson, Nicholas Slayton Miles noted that this drawing, while based on the C. C. Hughes photograph, was intentionally altered to portray a more menacing image of Champ Ferguson. Here, a disorderly looking collection of soldiers flank the guerrilla, who has been brought to the fore and given a growth of beard to fit the mountaineer image expected by *Harper's Weekly* readers. (*Harper's Weekly*, September 23, 1865, p. 593)

Champ Ferguson's facial expression suggests a man of seriousness, and his thinness and slouched shoulders belie his fierce nature. (Filson Historical Society, Louisville, Kentucky)

EXECUTION OF CHAMP FERGUSON, THE GUERRILLA, AT NASHVILLE, TENNESSEE, OCTOBER 20, 1865.—[SKETCHED BY J. M. ARNOLD.]

Champ Ferguson's execution was the hottest ticket in Nashville in October 1865. In addition to the military officials and guards, many of the city's citizens came to the yard of the penitentiary to see one of the Civil War's most notorious figures hang. (*Harper's Weekly*, November 11, 1865, p. 716)

This set of iron rings was affixed to the gallows at the Tennessee State Penitentiary during the time that Ferguson and dozens of other inmates were hanged. Thus the rope that hanged Champ Ferguson passed through one of these rings. That the Frazier International History Museum purchased these items and the Tennessee State Museum keeps on display the ball-and-chain worn by Champ while a prisoner speak to the continuing, if not growing, public interest in his memory. (Iron rings: Frazier International History Museum, Louisville, Kentucky; ball-and-chain: Tennessee State Museum)

6

LESSONS OF PERSEVERANCE

Q: Who appeared to have command of the squad?
A: I could not tell you, I believe they all commanded themselves.
   —MOSES HUDDLESTON on Ferguson's company, July 28, 1865

Colonel Wolford has permission to pursue and capture Hamilton and Ferguson, but let him be careful not to get himself caught. By order of Major-General Rosecrans.
   —CHAS. R. THOMPSON, Rosecrans's aide-de-camp, December 15, 1862

As the winter of 1862–1863 approached, Champ Ferguson's infamy continued to grow. In the war's infancy, he was known and feared only locally, but as the conflict matured, his name began to spread throughout the Tennessee-Kentucky theater. Once he operated with Morgan and became the target of pro-union propagandists, his name began to reach the seat of political and military power, driving the Union to redouble its efforts to destroy him, along with other guerrilla operatives, in the Cumberland region.

By the middle of December, Colonel Frank Wolford, frustrated by Ferguson since the beginning of the war, began planning a move against the guerrilla. Having sent scouts to watch the Cumberland River at Hartsville, Tennessee, for signs of Confederate cavalry moving north, he learned little of interest outside of Ferguson and Colonel Oliver Hamilton's partisans crossing the river to the south.[1] Anticipating that the partisans were headed west to Lebanon, Wolford asked permission to set up an ambush for Ferguson. With no Confederate force at Lebanon, Major General William Rosecrans, newly appointed commander of the Army of the Cumberland, authorized Wolford's request to "pursue and capture Hamilton and Ferguson" but cautioned "let him be careful not to get caught himself."[2] Although Wolford did not know it, he was leading his force into the path of John Hunt Morgan's third raid. When Wolford's scouts reported seeing Ferguson's and Hamilton's men moving toward Lebanon, they did not realize that the guerrillas were on their way to join Morgan's invading column.

On December 21, Morgan with more than three thousand men left the staging point of Alexandria, Tennessee, for their third trip into Kentucky in five months. As was the case in all of Morgan's raids, Ferguson and other regional guerrillas rode along. As the brigadier's first two raids opened and closed Bragg's invasion of Kentucky, the Christmas Raid, as it would become popularly known, would also play an important role in that winter's strategic drama. When Abraham Lincoln replaced Don Carlos Buell with William Starke Rosecrans in October 1862, the general took the job with the implicit understanding that Lincoln wished him to be aggressive and press Bragg, now sitting in Murfreesboro, only thirty miles southeast of Rosecrans's Nashville headquarters.[3] Not only did Rosecrans understand the conditions of his appointment, but Bragg also saw the writing on the wall. He knew that a Federal campaign was coming soon and hoped that by acting first, he could neutralize Rosecrans's plan. Sending Morgan into Kentucky to destroy the L&N Railroad, Bragg hoped that the assault on Nashville's communications and supplies would force the Federals out of the city and back toward Louisville.[4]

Despite the fact that Rosecrans had 10,000 troops assigned to the defense of the L&N, Morgan was undeterred. Over the next two weeks, his men and he covered 500 miles, destroying more than 2,200 feet of railroad bridges and thirty-five miles of track and telegraph, along with depots, water towers, and Federal stores. By the time they reentered Tennessee after the new year, Morgan's raiders had taken and paroled nearly 2,000 prisoners and killed and wounded 150, while only losing twenty-six of their own.[5] While Morgan's Christmas Raid was spectacular, it did not accomplish its original objective. With sufficient men and materiel already in Nashville, Rosecrans moved toward Murfreesboro where he and Bragg would close 1862 and open 1863 with the Battle of Stones River, another Union victory.[6]

For Ferguson, Morgan's holiday raid offered another opportunity to return to the Clinton County area. The column entered Kentucky near Tompkinsville and, after more than a week operating within the state, returned to Tennessee via Burkesville, only twenty miles west of Albany. As Morgan's raiders passed through Burkesville, Ferguson and his men used the opportunity to split off from the party and ride for the home of an old enemy in nearby Adair County. John Weatherred, who rode with Ferguson that day, remembered, "At Columbia, old Champ Ferguson asked Morgan for two companies to go with him to capture some bushwhackers." Riding forty miles on a cold and dark night, Ferguson's command arrived at the Huddleston place ready to take their quarry. However dominant Elam Huddleston and his partisans had seemed less than three months before, on New Year's Day, 1863, his luck ran out.[7]

Shortly before midnight, Ferguson's band, accompanied by a major from Morgan's command probably assigned to go with the group to enforce some measure of military discipline, arrived at Huddleston's and quietly encircled the house. Those inside had no idea that something was wrong until Moses Huddleston, brother of Elam and a private in the 1st Kentucky Cavalry (U.S.A.), awoke to see Ferguson looking at him through a window. Yelling through the glass, "Damn you, we've got you now," Ferguson startled the house awake. Moses, Elam, and a cousin ran upstairs with their guns. Weatherred said, "We surrounded the house and demanded his surrender but he answered us by shooting at us with a repeating rifle, so we all fired at him."[8] Within minutes, a full-scale firefight was underway between the guerrillas outside and the Huddleston men on the second floor of the house. All the while, the women and children were huddled on the ground floor hoping to avoid the bullets and putting out the fires Ferguson's men were setting with the goal of smoking the family out.[9]

After an hour, Elam was hit and seriously wounded. Thinking his brother might be saved if the fight ended, Moses Huddleston yelled to the collected Confederates and asked to surrender. Weatherred's captain assured them they would not be harmed and the men came out of the house. Ferguson, however, refused to abide by the captain's promise. Weatherred remembered that Ferguson "broke in the door and rushing upstairs and came dragging Capt. E. Huddleston down the stairs and out in the yard and cut his throat." Weatherred's account, however, is problematic. Although it is unknown precisely when he wrote his recollections, which he called a diary, it was done decades after the war, during his retirement years.[10] His version agrees with testimony during Ferguson's postwar trial until it comes to the method of Huddleston's death. Whereas Weatherred remembered Ferguson slitting Huddleston's throat, others recalled a different end.

Moses Huddleston, Elam's brother who had helped fight the Confederates

that night, told the story differently. Informing Ferguson that Elam was upstairs badly hurt, the guerrilla started for the door followed closely by Moses
and his cousin. Having hauled him down the stairs and out into the yard, the
two were shocked to see Ferguson pull a pistol and shoot Elam just as they laid
him down on the ground. Although severely wounded, Huddleston was alive
when the men brought him outside. Moses testified that when Ferguson shot
his brother, "he moved, sort of drew himself up." While Elam Huddleston lay
dying in the yard, Ferguson and his men turned their attention to the house.[11]
Whatever the course taken by Ferguson that night, it reached its preferred
end. Huddleston was dead.

While some of the band stole Elam Huddleston's boots and took assorted
clothing, some, more sympathetic members helped the women extinguish the
fire set next to the back door. One of Ferguson's men, however, attempted to
overstep himself when he tried to search Huddleston's widow. Not ready to
allow a possible sexual crime to occur, a major from Morgan's command who
had ridden with Ferguson that night put a stop to the attempts on the woman.
Meanwhile, Ferguson ascended the stairs and found another man bedridden
with illness. Pronouncing that he "wouldn't pester him" as "he will die any-
how," Ferguson and his men, loaded with plunder and their two prisoners in
tow, left the Huddleston place, but only after some of the men carried Elam
back into the house out of respect for his widow.[12]

Ferguson then set out toward Creelsboro, Kentucky, but the group stopped
at Cyrus Wheat's store where they stole horses, cloth, shoes, and boots. Calling
for the two prisoners to come to the front of the column, Ferguson asked if
they knew where he could find two other prominent local unionists, Captain
John Morrison and Rufus Dowdy. Apparently scared that the same fate might
befall them as had Elam, the two directed their captors to the nearby Dowdy
house.[13]

Although Rufus Dowdy was not home that night, Ferguson found other
targets. Sarah Dowdy testified that after dark the previous evening, Allen and
Peter Zachary stopped at the house and asked to spend the night. The brothers
were members of Company "C" of Wolford's 1st Kentucky Cavalry who had
probably, like Moses Huddleston, taken a brief "French" leave from their camp
at Bowling Green. Unfortunately, they were also the sons of James Zachary
and brothers to Fount Zachary, both of whom had been killed by Ferguson
six months earlier. Although Ferguson always claimed that his victims were
searching for him and his killing them was done in self defense, in this case,

his fear may have been justified, as the Zachary boys would have certainly killed him if they had gotten the chance.[14]

Leaving the two captives under guard away from the house, Ferguson and his men approached the darkened dwelling. Sarah Dowdy remembered that someone came to the door that night and ordered it opened, but it was stuck. Her mother shouted for them to push it open and when they did, Ferguson and his men poured into the house. Asking the recently awakened men who they were, Ferguson exploded when the question was returned to him. He responded, telling the men, "By God, that is not the question. Get up here." At that, Peter Zachary rose with his pistol and fired at Ferguson. Immediately, gunfire erupted, with Mrs. Dowdy screaming for them not to shoot inside the house. With Peter Zachary's first shot narrowly missing its target, Ferguson grabbed the gun and a scuffle ensued. While his brother was fighting for his life inside the house, Allen Zachary attempted to flee through the front door but was shot down as he crossed the threshold. Peter Zachary, temporarily extricating himself from his fight, also ran for the door as Ferguson held onto his shirttail while "striking at him with something," probably his knife. Once they left the house and porch, Sarah Dowdy saw little else.[15]

Again, Weatherred witnessed the events and offered some conflicting details. At the Dowdy house, Weatherred remembered that "Ferguson and two of his men went into a yard and knocked the door open and cut the throat of two men before they could get up."[16] As often happens with sources written several years after the fact, Weatherred's memory appears to have kept the movements and specific occurrences straight, although the passage of time may have exaggerated Ferguson's actions. Moses Huddleston testified that Ferguson had killed his brother with a gun, rather than Weatherred's recalled knife. During Ferguson's postwar trial in Nashville, Huddleston, an avowed unionist, could have increased the drama of his brother's killing by placing a knife rather than a gun in Ferguson's hand. Alternatively, by the time Weatherred wrote his recollections, the Ferguson legend had grown significantly, changing the guerrilla from mere mortal to a larger than life, nearly invincible figure. It would only be fitting that such a character be intimately attached to the killings by stabbing both men by himself before either could rise from bed.

The element of surprise had worked well that night and after a brief firefight, the prisoners were brought up to the house to identify the bodies. As Moses Huddleston entered the yard, he saw Ferguson bent over wiping a bloody knife across Peter Zachary's chest and heard him say that if it had not been for his knife, "the damned rascal would have killed him." Nearer the porch, Huddleston saw Allen Zachary dead and turned back to see Ferguson drop what he guessed was Peter Zachary's pocketbook onto the dead man's chest.[17]

Upon leaving the Dowdy house, the column headed toward Burkesville where it joined the remainder of Morgan's command. Although Ferguson apparently was torn as to the fates of his prisoners, the major who had ridden along on the mission defended the men and made it clear that he did not think the soldiers should be killed. Once Ferguson's company reached Morgan's camp, the two Federals did not see the guerrilla again. The next day, they were paroled and returned home.[18]

Ferguson was quite proud of his recent expedition. He had killed Elam Huddleston, one of his greatest nemeses, and killed two more members of the Zachary family, both of whom would have relished killing the guerrilla. The day he returned to Morgan's command, Ferguson visited Colonel Basil Duke, who had received a serious head wound during the raid. Sitting down with Duke, he recounted the details of his previous night's work and proudly showed the colonel his knife, covered with dried blood. Duke recalled that the combination of the story and the knife "thoroughly nauseated me."[19]

Unsurprisingly, Ferguson's self-reported role in the New Year's killings changed with each telling. In his interview with the *Nashville Union,* he confessed to killing Huddleston and considered his actions justified "when we take all things into consideration." Similarly, he acknowledged killing the Zachary brothers at Rufus Dowdy's house.[20] However, in the confession he gave to a reporter for the *Nashville Dispatch,* he changed his story considerably. He flatly denied killing Huddleston, placing the weapon in the hands of one of his men rather than his own. Ferguson noted that the victim had shot at him with the ball grazing his coat, but he refused to accept any responsibility for his death. Regarding the killing of Peter Zachary, Ferguson described how he stabbed the soldier "after one of the most desperate struggles that I ever had in my life." During the fight, the two men fell into the floor where Zachary kept trying to shoot him. After a few moments' struggle, Ferguson drew his knife and "stabbed him a few times, killing him."[21]

Whereas Ferguson's appearance in a Confederate camp visiting with officers may have stood out as odd early in the war, since Morgan's first raid in July 1862, he had grown increasingly comfortable with the regular military ideal. By no means does this suggest Ferguson began to behave as a commissioned officer bound by larger strategy and the rules of war, but his personal attachment to Morgan and Duke influenced his behavior and methodology. To Ferguson, they were three Kentucky expatriates attempting not only to save the state for the Confederacy, but also to defend their homes and families from what they considered foreign aggressors. On a more pragmatic level, the pursuit of wealth and power also drove Ferguson and Morgan. The fact that both men were considered martyrs for the southern cause during the postwar years helped elevate the level of respect given them and quieted dissenting voices. With the passage of time, however, historians have been more willing to promote evidence over emotion. Ferguson's habit of stealing money, guns, horses, and clothes is well documented in this study. As for Morgan, the passage of time has allowed scholars to critique his often questionable behavior. For example, Morgan biographer James A. Ramage quite accurately describes the inherent lack of discipline within the cavalryman's command and notes several instances, particularly during Morgan's Last Kentucky Raid, when military exigency gave way to bank robbery and armed theft from private citizens.[22] Even devoted Confederate ideologues like young Edward O. Guerrant, who began his career wanting to ride with the Lexingtonian, came to become "perfectly disgusted with Morganism."[23]

After Ferguson's New Year's killings, evidence becomes sparse regarding his independent operations. Surely he retained his autonomy and continued raiding borderland communities, but his broader military experience likely impacted him by forcing him to reckon with the Civil War as a national conflict in addition to the localized, community and kinship oriented fight he had been participating in up to that point. While Ferguson began to broaden his interpretation of the war, the Federal army in the borderland region began to narrow its focus. As the guerrilla transitioned to sometime soldier, his enemy began to increase its use of irregular tactics to flush him out.

During the first four months of 1863, following the Confederate defeat at Stones River and Ferguson's killings of Huddleston and the Zachary brothers, the notorious guerrilla nearly disappears from the record, either the result of his slowing his activities or temporarily relocating due to the pressing war. However, in April, Ferguson reappeared, through a letter written by "J. O." of Lebanon, Kentucky, to the *Louisville Daily Journal*. J. O. reported a dire situation in southern Kentucky with 1,500 Confederate cavalrymen in Wayne County and part of Pulaski County, with "six hundred in Whitley, and enough in Clinton to hold the county all the time." He estimated that since December 1861, both the Union and Confederate armies had decimated Clinton County, with the Union taking five hundred men into the army while the Confederate guerrillas preyed on the remaining sixty men, "about half of whom are too old to get out of Champ Ferguson's way, and the balance kept out of his reach." He attributed fifty citizens' deaths to "Champ Ferguson & Co."[24]

By early May, Ferguson made another personal appearance in southern Kentucky. News of his presence near Monticello, Kentucky, spurred Colonel Richard T. Jacob, commander of the 9th Kentucky Cavalry (U.S.A.), to order Captain Wendell D. Wiltsie to organize a force of one hundred men from his own 20th Michigan Infantry, 9th Kentucky Cavalry, and 12th Kentucky Cavalry to go into the mountains south of the Cumberland River and search out Ferguson and his men.[25]

With his small force zigzagging southeast deeper into the mountains, Wiltsie's men failed to locate Ferguson, although they took twelve prisoners whom they found scattered along their route and destroyed a still which Wiltsie suspected served as a gathering place for the guerrillas. Having received a report that a company of enemy cavalry had been seen on the road behind him, Wiltsie sent a picket back toward Monticello to watch the crossroads. Within minutes of arriving at their station overlooking the road, the picket force was attacked by a large cavalry contingent. Instead of finding a small band of Ferguson's guerrillas, Wiltsie's men had stumbled upon three hundred men under John Hunt Morgan. Having made the mistake of sending out small squads to investigate the isolated hollows and farms, the captain found himself with only about forty men. Realizing his perilous position, Wiltsie's small force positioned itself well and proceeded to attack the thinly spread and generally disorganized Confederates until he found an opportunity to fall back nearer Union lines.[26]

Although Wiltsie did not know it that day, he had located part of Morgan's command, which was encamped in Wayne County, Kentucky, near the town of Williamsburg, readying itself for its greatest raid. With characteristic audacity, Morgan fancied taking his unique, and now, frequently illegal, brand of warfare north of the Ohio River. Beginning on July 2, 1863, Morgan and 2,500 men embarked on the most audacious invasion of his career. Two days later, the general took heavy casualties in a fight with Federal cavalry at a ford on the Green River. Having to withdraw and find another crossing, Morgan and his men fought the next day at Lebanon, Kentucky, where again he lost a substantial number of men, including his younger brother. At Brandenburg on July 8, Morgan and his men ferried across the Ohio River into Indiana. For the next ten days, the Confederates raced from town to town through southern Indiana and Ohio with Federal cavalry in constant pursuit. Bypassing a terrified Cincinnati, Morgan's men rode east, hoping to recross the Ohio at Buffington but found the fords well protected. Now desperate, he turned northward and rode hard. Finally, on July 26, Morgan surrendered his command outside of the small village of West Point, Ohio, only five miles from the Pennsylvania border. Only 400 of the 2,500 he had left Tennessee with avoided capture and made it back home.[27] Morgan's luster had clearly worn off. Fortunately for Champ Ferguson, he had chosen to remain behind rather than participate in Morgan's wild scheme.

Ferguson's absence, however, is fertile ground for speculation. He had accompanied Morgan on all of his raids up to the ill-fated Ohio foray but did not move northward with the cavalryman that July. During his postwar trial, Ferguson mentioned his relationship with Morgan only once. In an interview during the height of the proceedings, he stated, "I always acted under orders from John Morgan up to the time he made the raid into Ohio." Perhaps importantly, he added that when Morgan left for Ohio, "he took forty of my men and I was left with only a small force."[28] With no military training and probably a limited understanding of protocol, he may have objected to Morgan leaving him with so few men with which to operate while he was gone. It is also possible that jealousy played a role in the sudden split between the men. Having accompanied Morgan on his previous raids, Ferguson knew very well how Morgan's men behaved when they rode into Kentucky towns. When Morgan began pulling men from Ferguson to take them on what became looting expeditions, Ferguson may have felt threatened by this suave and debonair new southern hero. Though they both at times fought for their own pockets, in the eyes of many southerners, Ferguson was the rough and vulgar version of the handsome and cultured Morgan. Tellingly, Basil Duke wrote with some subtle aversion to Ferguson's decision not to accompany Morgan on his raid that "at the time, no Confederate troops in that country [north central Tennessee], and Champ Ferguson was resting in inglorious ease at Sparta."[29] Duke was right on both counts; Morgan had left the region unprotected by his impetuous decision to enhance his own reputation and Ferguson was living the comparative high life well away from the dangers that would befall Morgan's column.

Having failed to find Ferguson with Wiltsie's scout, Federal commanders in the area redoubled their efforts. Brigadier General Samuel Powhatan Carter, the East Tennessean who temporarily traded in his naval commission for an army post, cautioned Brigadier General Orlando Willcox about the dangers of meeting the guerrillas on familiar ground. Carter pointed out the geographic complexity when he wrote,

> An examination of a map of Wayne and Clinton Counties will show you how exceedingly difficult it will be to meet the rebels now there on any-thing like equal terms, if acted against only from this direction. From Monticello there is the right-hand road, leading to Albany, another run-ning east, called the "Jacksborough road," from which a road branches leading to Jamestown, Tenn. Going south from Monticello is the main Jamestown road. One mile out there is another, branching from this to the left, leading to the same place. Five miles out on main Jamestown road there is a fork, the right hand going to Albany, and coming into the Albany road first mentioned about 7 miles to south and west of Monticello. If the enemy is unwilling to fight, he can take one of all the above-mentioned ways, and concentrate at Jamestown or Livingston, or he can fall back to some of the almost impregnable positions on the main Jamestown and Albany roads, and there make a stand.[30]

Given Carter's description of transportation routes in and around Albany, it is little wonder that guerrillas on both sides operated so freely in the region.

Realizing that the extensive network of escape routes was second nature to Ferguson and his men, Carter all but confessed that a frontal assault would never bring complete victory. He suggested instead that a force be sent across the river to the west and move back east finding itself on the southern edge of Ferguson's usual area of operation. At that point, the Federals would move northward, cutting off escape routes to Livingston and Jamestown along the way, and drive the guerrillas toward Federal lines. Despite the depth of Cart-er's planning and the level of his conviction, he admitted that the task would not be easy. He expected that "our communication over so long a line will be constantly interrupted," and that "The marauding gangs of Champ. Ferguson, numbering about 150, are from Wayne and Clinton Counties, and will in all probability give us much trouble."[31]

For much of the summer of 1863, Ferguson rested in Sparta while the war escalated around him. By August, the conflict moved into his backyard when Brigadier General Nathan Bedford Forrest ordered Colonel George G. Dibrell out of Chattanooga to Sparta with orders to scout enemy positions and harass their foragers and pickets. The move was fortuitous for Dibrell, whose farm was located only two miles north of town and provided a perfect setting for his encampment. It also gave him an opportunity to become acquainted with Ferguson, although the two men might have met prior to August 1863.[32]

George Dibrell, a native of White County, Tennessee, had no military training prior to the Civil War. He had spent his adulthood as a farmer and merchant, and when Tennessee called its secession convention in 1861, he took a seat as a unionist. When Tennessee left the Union, Dibrell went with it and joined the fledgling Confederate army as a private. Soon elevated to lieutenant colonel, and then colonel of partisan rangers, Dibrell fought alongside of Forrest throughout Tennessee and northern Alabama through 1863.[33]

Settling in on their commander's farm, the men of Dibrell's 8th Tennessee Cavalry (C.S.A.) were startled when distant pickets retreated into camp closely pursued by a Union cavalry force at daylight on August 9. The force Dibrell's men found that morning was that of Colonel Robert H. G. Minty's 4th Michigan Cavalry. Originally from Ireland, Minty joined the British army when he was only eighteen years old. Over the course of his career, he served in British Honduras, the West Indies, and along the coast of West Africa. His career came to a premature end with chronic liver trouble, which improved after he immigrated to the United States in 1853. Upon the outbreak of war in 1861, he joined a Michigan regiment and quickly rose through the ranks, finally settling at lieutenant colonel commanding a cavalry regiment in Tennessee.[34] With nearly eight hundred men traveling light, Minty moved toward Sparta in the hopes that he could take Dibrell's camp by surprise. When the Federal presence was discovered, Dibrell's men quickly retreated across a creek and took a position on a hill overlooking a small bridge, the only convenient route across the stream, and thus commenced the Battle of Wild Cat Creek.[35] Over the next few hours, Minty's men tried several times to cross the creek in Dibrell's front, but they repeatedly failed in the face of steady Confederate resistance. Accepting that his men would not take Dibrell's position from the front, Minty sent a detachment downstream to find a ford and attack the enemy's flank, but the Confederate commander chose to withdraw his estimated three hundred men rather than continue the fight against a force twice his size.[36] Although Dibrell pulled his men back and abandoned his position overlooking the creek, he had made his point: despite Minty's superior numbers, his lightly armed and equipped force could not compete directly with Dibrell's firepower. As quickly as Minty's Federals had appeared, they withdrew to find less defensible prey.

In his report on the fight, Dibrell noted that at some time during the battle, the strength of his force was increased when Champ Ferguson arrived with several of his men and a number of Sparta men. Celebrating their victory with a breakfast cooked by the women of town, Dibrell reveled in his small success.[37] Ferguson also likely felt significant pride. It had been eight months since he had operated with a formal Confederate force. His recent falling out with John Hunt Morgan, combined with the fact that Morgan was now sitting in an Ohio prison, hinted that his movement toward legitimacy had stalled. With his participation in the engagement near the Dibrell farm, he solidified a relationship with the colonel that he would cultivate and maintain throughout the war, and that would help bring Ferguson face to face with his destiny.

Ferguson's new relationship with Dibrell should not be surprising. He clearly enjoyed working with Morgan up the point of the Ohio Raid and certainly understood the benefit he might gain from receiving a regular commission as a Confederate officer. With Morgan now in prison, he saw an opportunity to align himself with another who might help him gain legitimacy. Although he certainly craved the legal recognition a commission would bestow on him, it is unknown how actively he pursued it. Despite the fact he was not comfortable with losing his autonomy, as evidenced by his displeasure with Morgan over the raider's taking some of Ferguson's men, he sought official standing, which he apparently achieved when he chose to fill out his company's first muster roll.

Ferguson also remained close with his old Cumberland raiding friends. One of the more notorious was Colonel John Hughs of Overton County, Tennessee. Only twenty-nine years old at the outbreak of the war, Hughs humbly joined Company D of the 25th Tennessee Infantry (C.S.A.). Due to a combination of fortune and effort, he rose quickly from private to first lieutenant to captain and then to colonel. He participated in Bragg's Kentucky invasion of September 1862, during which his men came into contact with and destroyed a unionist guerrilla company. Having killed most of the men in the fight and captured the remainder, Hughs ordered those still alive to be killed, except for one boy whom Hughs considered too young to be held to the standards of warfare. Wounded at Stones River in January 1863, he recovered sufficiently to be operating near Sparta during the spring, rounding up mountaineers who were avoiding Confederate service.[38] Although no evidence points to Ferguson's men helping Hughs in this endeavor, it is possible that Ferguson participated to some degree.

In the wake of the fight at Sparta, Ferguson and the other guerrilla leaders of north central Tennessee became mobilized. On August 13, Union Brigadier General and future President of the United States James A. Garfield was notified that Federal cavalry had been sent into the Cumberland region as "Small parties are reported to be prowling about the country north of us."[39] While much of this information was gained from sympathetic travelers or paroled Confederates, some Federal scouts did yeoman's work gathering intelligence.

One of the more productive Union operatives was Ferguson's old nemesis, Dr. Jonathan Hale. Hale, the man who had written several anti-Ferguson pamphlets in 1862 in an attempt to draw Federal attention to the Cumberland guerrilla, spent much of the war in the employ of the Union army. Throughout the war, he provided invaluable information to commanders like James Garfield, George Thomas, and William Rosecrans. While it is certain that the bulk of information Hale provided to Union sources became part of the Federal effort in Kentucky and Tennessee, the level of his participation and his importance can only be estimated. Frequently, Hale would collect information from men traveling through the region and he also made good use of his political common ground with Tinker Dave Beatty. He also periodically asked local residents to write reports of the wartime goings on in their neighborhoods, including requesting specific information about Champ Ferguson and the men who rode with him.[40] So valuable was Hale's work, George Thomas referred to him as his "chief of scouts."[41] During the coming months, Thomas would need more good scouts.

On the home front, however, Ferguson maintained sovereignty, even over the Hale household. Although the family had gone away from Tennessee months before, they had left their possessions under the protection of friends and neighbors. At some time "a good while after the battle of Mill Spring" and further estimated as September 1863, Ferguson found and loaded Pheroba Hale's piano on a wagon and took it to Julia Ann Williams in Yankeetown, White County, Tennessee. Williams operated a shop there and Ferguson asked her to sell the instrument for him. Although she had no idea of its worth, especially in the region's turbulent wartime economic climate, she guessed it would bring $300 to $500. Williams testified that she knew the instrument belonged to the Hales, but Ferguson assured her that "Dr. Hale was in the Yankee army holding some position and we needn't apprehend any danger about his coming back or claiming his piano."[42]

After a while, a likely frustrated Ferguson sent word that he had sold the instrument for $200 and a local woman arrived at the Williams store, paid, and took the piano. Interestingly, Ferguson's wife, who remains an anonymous figure standing next to her infamous husband, may have known more about Champ's activities than has previously been revealed. Williams could not remember if she paid the money to either Ferguson or his wife. By Williams's placing Martha Ferguson as the recipient of the cash, it is likely that Mrs. Ferguson assisted her husband with the financial part of his activities or that she had collected payment previously for other, ill-gotten, items sold in the Williams shop.[43]

A letter dated October 24, 1863, places Ferguson in Greensburg and Munfordville, Kentucky, in the company of Colonel Oliver Hamilton and a collection of other partisans. The writer, "M. D. C.," wrote that the southern guerrillas arrived after dark and "commenced immediately to rob and pillage." Breaking into a Union man's store and house, the men stole furniture, cash, and even private papers before moving on to other quarry. By the time the bandits rode out of town, they had relieved other stores and homes of goods and cash, stealing approximately $14,000 from Confederate sympathizers. The writer noted that on their way to Munfordville, the group stopped and robbed private citizens along the way, including one man from whom they took eleven cents, "being too chivalric to insult him by giving it back."[44]

On their retreat back to Tennessee after the Munfordville Raid, the motley collection of raiders visited Adair County. A correspondent reported that a group of more than fifty bandits entered town under the command of a locally famous partisan named Dillsbury and after they had been gone a few days, he returned with the Munfordville party in tow. Oliver Hamilton and Champ Ferguson supposedly led more than 250 men between them and sacked the town. The Confederates robbed all the people they found in the streets without concern for their status. The writer noted that slaves were harassed as freely as was the son-in-law and secretary of state of former Governor Beriah Magoffin, a man with well-known Confederate sympathies. The gangs broke into safes, set offices ablaze, and even burned the Clinton county court, which had been moved to Adair County for safekeeping. As the mayhem began to subside, it was noted that the men had strewn Governor Thomas Bramlette's personal library along the road for two miles out of town. Surprisingly, and for one of the few times during the war, witnesses claimed that "Champ Ferguson, a murder spotted fiend, was the best-behaved of the group."[45]

By November, several Confederate missions had been made into the region, but with mixed results. One byproduct of Colonel John M. Hughs's brief expeditions into Kentucky was the general instability he left behind in Tennessee. Unionists had rejoiced when the Federal Army began to take an active interest in their condition, but the recent increase in partisan activity hinted that Union success might not be as quick in coming as some expected. On November 7, Colonel Henry Gilbert of the 19th Michigan Infantry wrote Tennessee Governor Andrew Johnson from McMinnville with an update on the condition of the area. He informed the governor, "the Counties of Van Buren White & DeKalb is dominated over by Champ Ferguson, Muncy,[46] Carter & other outlaws." Applying pressure to Johnson, he continued, "It is a disgrace to our Government that Union men cant live at home when their homes are 50 or 60 miles inside the lines of the Union army." Volunteering the services of his regiment to go to Sparta, where the pro-Confederate guerrillas had established their de facto headquarters, and "clean them all out," Gilbert estimated he could do the job with "300 good cavalry."[47]

Emboldened by his recent work, Hughs wasted little time getting back in the saddle and returning to Kentucky. Within two weeks, he attacked Monticello, Scottsville, and Columbia, Kentucky, frustrating Union Brigadier General Edward H. Hobson, who had doggedly pursued Morgan through Kentucky, Indiana, and Ohio only a few months before.[48] Dispatching companies to find and stop Hughs, Hobson's work proved futile as the Confederates stole back across the river and into the safety of Tennessee without incident.

By late November, Hughs was at it again. On November 27, he attacked a garrison at Monticello, Kentucky, with 149 men and claimed to have taken 153 prisoners. This engagement proved disappointing, as he left with little in the way of stores. Importantly, Major W. Scott Bledsoe, Ferguson's old attorney and commander, "was severely wounded by accident." The details are unknown.[49] While at Monticello, Ferguson and Hughs took the opportunity to refresh their horses. H. W. Tuttle wrote later that the two entered town with about 100 men and proceeded to steal his "horse, saddle and bridle and left a worn out horse" in exchange. Later, Tuttle found it branded "U.S." indicating that it had been stolen from the Federals in the first place.[50]

Although no direct mention is made of Ferguson's participation in Hughs's raid on Monticello, two days prior, Lieutenant Colonel James Brownlow of the

1st Tennessee Cavalry (U.S.A.), son of the locally famous "Parson," reported a victory in a skirmish near Sparta, placing Ferguson in the vicinity.[51] He tellingly noted that his adversary "has sent for forces under Hughs, Hamilton, Daugherty, Ferguson, and others," suggesting that the grouping of guerrillas were all operating together in Kentucky.[52] Responding to the situation near Sparta, Hughs returned to Tennessee quickly and on November 30 fought Brownlow's Tennesseans in what he described as a "very severe" engagement.[53]

After the Sparta fight, Hughs apparently turned around and headed back into Kentucky, probably thinking that his raids would relieve Federal pressure in Tennessee. On December 8, he attacked a Federal position at Scottsville, Kentucky, capturing eighty-six men along with "a considerable quantity of quartermaster and commissary stores" and hundreds of weapons and cavalry accoutrements. One week later found him back in Tennessee at Livingston, where he attacked a detachment of the 13th Kentucky Mounted Infantry (U.S.A.).[54] If he had lacked excitement in the months preceding his meeting Dibrell and riding with Hughs, Champ Ferguson had surely found it in the late summer and fall of 1863.

By Christmas, Hobson's frustration with Hughs boiled over. On December 22, the Federal general reported, "I have at last succeeded in alarming the rebels, south of the Cumberland River. My orders to scouting parties sent over the river to take no prisoners has had a good effect." Having given his men authority to operate under the black flag had surprised Hughs, who "complains of my order." Hobson wrote that Hughs "says that I should not hold him responsible for the conduct of Ferguson, Richardson, and Hamilton, and the cause of his now being in Tennessee is that he cannot get out." Hobson, feeling smug, added, "I think I will demand his surrender."[55]

Despite Hobson's apparently strong position, Hughs was not ready to give up. Over the course of the next several months, the Confederate retained his band and continued to be a thorn in the side of Union forces in his part of Tennessee. Likely with the help of Ferguson and other Cumberland partisans, Hughs remained effective. In turn, Champ Ferguson, who had turned his back to Morgan during the summer, had found a new military home. For the remainder of the war, he would remain active, often fighting beside Hughs and Dibrell, two men with whom he spent much of the last half of 1863.

7

THE BORDERLAND
GUERRILLA LIFESTYLE

I have to fight rebel soldiers and citizens, the former carrying the arms and doing the open fighting; the latter carrying news and ambushing.
—COL. WILLIAM B. STOKES, U.S.A., February 24, 1864

I was badly wounded in one of these fights . . . once thought I should die, but the Lord appeared to be on my side; how long he will stay of that way of thinking, I cant tell.
—CHAMP FERGUSON, shortly before his execution

The new year of 1864 opened with the same guerrilla warfare that had plagued the Cumberland region for the preceding three years. For Champ Ferguson, however, the nature of the war had changed significantly. Having made a quick transition from the lone man seeking retribution to the leader of a small pro-Confederate band, he saw the benefit of attaching himself to a charismatic and popular officer with whom he could operate semiautonomously. While his first such relationship with John Hunt Morgan had ended fortuitously on the eve of the raider's disastrous ride into Kentucky, Indiana, and Ohio, Ferguson then found George Dibrell to be a man with whom he could work. During the last months of 1863 and most of 1864, Ferguson and Dibrell would maintain a mutually beneficial association: Dibrell could avail himself of Ferguson's help whenever needed and Ferguson could continue to operate independently while enjoying periodic recognition from the Confederacy.

With the Union noose now tightening, Federal commanders focused their attention on the guerrilla warfare now commonplace in the Cumberland region. Andrew Cropsey of the 129th Illinois Infantry wrote Military Governor Andrew Johnson, reporting little guerrilla activity up the Cumberland River to Jackson County, but once there, a high level of partisanship could be found. On the south side of the river were "Hamilton Hughes,[1] Ferguson and other guerilla leaders, who by their robberies and murders . . . keep that region in perfect terror." Cropsey added that the bands "occasionaly make robbing raids into distant parts of the Country especialy up into Kentucky" and commonly mustered "some two hundred and fifty *fighting* men, and twice that number for robbing excursions."[2] As early as January 10, Major General George H. Thomas reported to Johnson that he intended to send Colonel William Stokes to White County in an effort to break up the guerrilla bands nested there. Specifying Ferguson as a main target, Thomas, who had spent the preceding two years sharing much of the same ground with the southern partisans, had grown to respect the effectiveness of these irregular soldiers.[3] Even Ulysses Grant, only weeks before his promotion to lieutenant general and elevation to Chief of the Armies of the United States, voiced concern to Johnson regarding Ferguson, Hughs, and Hamilton's operations in White County. Urging Stokes to be sent in to scatter them, he added, "The work is Important," and all other cavalry regiments were occupied outside of the target area.[4]

In many ways, William B. Stokes was the anti–Champ Ferguson. While Ferguson claimed to have supported the Union cause initially before becoming a Confederate, Stokes had supported secession, at first, but decided to remain loyal to the United States by the time of Tennessee's convention. In late 1861 or early 1862, he organized the 5th Tennessee Cavalry (U.S.A.) which gained a reputation for brutality similar to Ferguson's band of renegades. A brief biography noted that the 5th was made up of "bad men . . . a considerable number" and that "The conduct of a number of Stokes's men toward their former neighbors cannot be condoned."[5] As 1864 opened, Stokes's 5th Tennessee began its campaign to root out Confederate guerrillas, particularly Champ Ferguson.

On January 4, Colonel Thomas J. Harrison, commander of the 8th Indiana Cavalry, led a small contingent across the Cumberland Mountains toward Sparta, a growing enclave for Confederate expatriates from southern Kentucky and northern Tennessee counties. Dividing his force of only two hundred men in four parts, he sent each company to a designated point with orders to converge on Sparta beginning at dawn on January 5. On their way toward the seat of White County, Harrison's men were under orders to arrest all the men they came across. Specifically, Harrison was looking for four guerrilla leaders and local men loyal to them: George Carter, Scott Bledsoe, John P. Murray,[6] and Champ Ferguson. Harrison reported, "Our move resulted in considerable skirmishing," but they had some significant success during their five-day stay in the area. His men killed four bushwhackers, wounded another five or six, and captured more than a dozen, including two officers. Additionally, the Federals raided guerrilla households, making off with thirty horses and twenty stands of arms. The troopers even visited Champ Ferguson's house twice and confiscated some goods that Ferguson had taken from James P. Brownlow's company sutler. Ferguson also lost five horses and what Harrison cryptically described as "many valuable articles."[7]

To be sure, Harrison had enjoyed overwhelming success during his Calfkiller expedition, not losing a single man from his entire force. He did admit that two stragglers were captured by the enemy but released unharmed after having everything of value taken from them. Despite his boast that "Before we left the valley these bandits would fly to the mountains on the approach of even a squad of my men," his victory surely seemed hollow.[8] He did not meet any of the region's guerrilla leaders, any of whom would have likely been able to field enough men to give each one of his four detachments a stiff fight. Although Harrison probably envisioned Ferguson, Bledsoe, Murray, and Carter hiding in the bushes waiting for his departure, the more likely scenario is that the four were not in the vicinity of Sparta during the week of his visit.

Emboldened by their recent success but still unsatisfied, the Union army ordered a grand invasion of the Cumberland region of Tennessee in an attempt to root out the guerrillas. Dispatching three forces into different regions, the union hoped to drive the bandits out of their hiding places and into the teeth of the other Union forces. Colonel William B. Stokes entered the White, Putnam, and Overton county region, Brigadier General Eleazer A. Paine scoured the Tennessee-Kentucky border counties, and Colonel Henry McConnell moved into Jackson County.

"Wild Bill of the Hills," Colonel William B. Stokes of the 5th Tennessee Cavalry, arrived in Sparta on February 2 with two hundred men. As they entered town, the colonel estimated about thirty Confederates fled in all directions. Stokes followed Harrison's earlier tactic by following the road along the Calfkiller River hoping to catch Ferguson. He moved up the river to Putnam County, then returned by the same route, even stopping and camping near Ferguson's house. Returning to Yankeetown, north of Sparta, Stokes boasted of his success. His men killed "17 of the worst men in the country" and "took 12 prisoners, and captured about 20 horses and mules." In closing, Stokes assured his headquarters, "It will take some time and continued scouting to break up these bands, but . . . no time will be lost and no effort spared to rid the country of them."[9]

Brigadier General Eleazer A. Paine left Gallatin, Tennessee, en route to the state border with Kentucky. Through the first week of February, Paine's men spread throughout the hills and watched the roads for suspicious activity. By the end of the expedition in the middle of the month, Paine could boast of thirty-three guerrillas killed and sixty-three captured, one of whom was Colonel Thomas B. Murray, "a politician of some note, who was on the Breckinridge electoral ticket."[10]

In an attempt to close the trap on local guerrillas, General Paine ordered Colonel Henry McConnell's 71st Ohio Infantry on a similar scout to that of Paine and Stokes. Moving toward Flynn's Lick in Jackson County, Tennessee, McConnell realized he was getting close to his target as Captain Oliver Hamilton's skirmishers repeatedly attacked the Union pickets. After killing and capturing an estimated twenty of Hamilton's men, McConnell arrived at Flynn's Lick on January 31. There, he found Hamilton with forty of his men. Past experience had taught the Federal commanders that guerrilla bands would not fight unless they felt sure of their advantage over the enemy. Knowing this, McConnell selected thirty men to advance on Hamilton, hoping the partisan would feel comfortable enough with his numerical advantage to do battle. Holding considerable numbers in reserve two miles back, McConnell advanced on the Confederate position. Just as McConnell feared, the enemy withdrew rather than taking a chance in open combat.[11]

For the next two days McConnell awaited orders, and on the morning of February 2, they finally came. He was given permission to move toward Livingston where he expected to find both Oliver Hamilton and John Hughs. Three days later, he arrived at Livingston and commenced his scouting operations. Separating his force into squads, he sent his men out "to sweep the country between the road on which we had come and the Cumberland River back to Flynn's Lick." His expedition had resulted in thirty-three of the enemy killed, eight wounded, and 102 prisoners taken. McConnell had "no means of knowing the number of mules and horses taken," only that "It was considerable, but the quality and condition of the stock was so inferior that its only importance to us was to get them out of the hands of the enemy." In one community, McConnell brought "hard war" to a house he described as "the veriest den of thieves and murderers" when he "removed the women and children and burned it."[12]

Apart from McConnell's report on his activities while in the counties of Jackson and Overton, he also offered one of the few wartime descriptions of the state of life in the region. He informed his commander, General Paine, "the country between Carthage and the Cumberland Mountains . . . is bordering on famine. Families without regard to politics are eaten out and plundered by those common enemies of mankind (rangers) until even those formerly wealthy are utterly reduced, and many of the poorer are now actually starving." McConnell also reported that Confederate guerrillas from Jackson, Overton, and Fentress counties frequently traveled into Kentucky where they bought everything they needed without any restriction, but added that his expedition probably crippled such efforts in the immediate future.[13]

As Paine, Harrison, Stokes, and McConnell learned on their expeditions into partisan country, the curse of the guerrilla fighter is to be captured or killed. To prevent that end, irregulars typically refused to fight unless either the circumstances were ideal or the action unavoidable. On February 13, the prerequisites were met. That morning, Ferguson and an old nemesis, Rufus Dowdy, became involved in a partisan fight in Fentress County. The skirmish involved men who rode with Hughs, Carter, Bledsoe, and Ferguson, who fought a unionist force of Rufus Dowdy's and some of Tinker Dave Beatty's men. Although fierce, the engagement was brief and little detail has survived. Daniel Garrett was not in the fight but remembered seeing the graves afterward. With the same imprecision with which the guerrilla war was fought and remembered, Garrett placed their number at "three, four, or five."[14]

One mile away, Daniel Garrett was getting ready to start work at the Isham Richards farm, when three men appeared. Jackson Garner, Dallas Beatty, and James Templeton had seemingly come out of nowhere. While both Daniel Garrett and Isham Richards knew the men who showed up at the place around midmorning, neither man could speak confidently about their purpose. Although no evidence was presented linking any of the three men to the fight that had taken place nearby, Garrett confirmed that Garner and Templeton were probably armed, as was their habit, and all three men were solid unionists. His level of knowledge is suspect, however, as he claimed not to know that Dallas Beatty was the son of locally famous union partisan, Tinker Dave Beatty.[15]

Not long after the three men came to the Richards farm, Ferguson and several others rode up. The unionists took cover when they heard the horsemen approach, but Ferguson had an idea they were at the farm and began searching for them. He found Dallas Beatty near the woodpile, and although Garrett, who was inside the house at the time, could not see or hear the goings on, he heard two shots coming from that part of the yard. Ferguson then approached the house and from the porch ordered Jackson Garner outside. As Garner hesitated, a member of the household requested that if Ferguson planned to kill Garner, he not do it inside of the house. An enraged Ferguson responded with the warning that if ever questioned again, Ferguson would kill him "if he was the best friend he ever had." With that, Ferguson shot Garner twice, killing him on the porch. As for James Templeton, guerrilla captain George Carter took him away and returned shortly without him. No testimony was offered regarding ever finding his body or hearing other shots fired, making it likely that Templeton was either released by Carter or delivered to another nearby group.[16] While in jail at Jamestown, Tennessee, in early July 1866, Columbus German acknowledged that he had witnessed Ferguson's killing of Dallas Beatty. German recalled that Ferguson, chillingly, made Beatty look down the barrel of his gun and asked him if he would like to eat the powder just before he pulled the trigger.[17]

Within days, Ferguson and the other partisan bands were back in the vicinity of Sparta, followed closely by Colonel Stokes. Now commanding six companies of the 5th Tennessee Cavalry, Stokes moved into town and quartered his men in Sparta's deserted houses. Having "barricaded the streets strongly, and fortified around my artillery," the colonel was prepared to comb the guerrillas out of White County. This task would not be easy, however, as Stokes reported, "the country is infested with a great number [of] rebel soldiers under Colonels Hughs, Hamilton, Ferguson, Carter, and Bledsoe, the whole force being under Colonel Hughs, a brave, vigilant, and energetic officer." Additionally, Stokes noted that the guerrillas had virtually stopped their plundering, instead turning their attention and efforts against Federal soldiers venturing into the countryside in search of food and forage.[18]

At this time, Hughs commanded around six hundred men equipped with excellent arms taken during one of their raids into Kentucky. On February 22, some of his troopers got an opportunity to meet their enemy. Stokes had sent two companies up the Calfkiller River through the Dug Hill community on a scout. W. B. Hyder, a pilot for Stokes, recalled that Ferguson and Hughs divided their force and sent the men into the bushes where they lay in wait for the approaching Federals. When the young captain who led the expedition guided the men into "this Narrow Place between the River and the hill," the Confederates blocked the road in front and behind. Trapped by a much larger force with only sixty men of his own, Hyder suggested that the captain entertain the idea of surrendering but deferred when he saw "their would be no quarters showed." Completely trapped, he ordered his men to "Bust through the Rebel Ranks as it was nothing but Death anyway."[19]

The Battle of Dug Hill,[20] as it would become known, was a slaughter for the Federals. With their quarry trapped in the gorge, the Confederates began cutting them to pieces from their superior positions at the top of a long, steep hill, at one point even rolling large rocks and throwing smaller ones down on the men of the 5th Tennessee.[21] At the end of the day, Hughs counted forty-seven of the enemy killed, thirteen wounded, and four taken prisoner, while he lost only two men to wounds.[22] Hyder remembered, "the Rebels then Cut the throats of the Boys from Ear to Ear. It was every Man for him selfe." By the next day, Stokes clearly saw the completeness of his defeat. He reported that although all six of his officers escaped, only forty-five other men had made it through the hills back to town.[23] Hyder offered more detail: "they took to the Woods and Brush . . . Scattered all over the Neighborhood and worked they [their] way Back to Sparta sum of them changing their Clothes for Citizens Clothes in order to git on to Sparta."[24] The Battle of Dug Hill illustrated to the Federal army that the guerrilla menace would not cease to exist in the Cumberland region despite the overall Union success throughout Tennessee.

Although not identified in any official account, it appears that Ferguson's nemesis Tinker Dave Beatty was on the field that day fighting alongside Stokes.[25] Indeed, much of Beatty's wartime service remains unknown or historically obscured, although fragments of his service suggest an active and effective partisan leader. In verifying Martin Eldridge's military service, W. W. Windle recalled, "Tinker Beatty's men killed his brother in law George Franklin in cold blood in the fall of 1864."[26] In the months that followed the Federal victory on the Calfkiller, John Farris joined a Confederate company out to "keep Tinker Dan Beaty in check."[27] L. S. Poston was wounded in an undated skirmish with "Tinker Dave Beatty's crowd."[28] And John Newton Vance took the oath of allegiance to the United States in early 1865 after learning that his friends "Tom Bohanon, Buck Holford, and others were killed by Tinker Dave Beatty's band."[29] As the most prominent Union guerrilla fighter in the region,

Beatty avoided some of the same ridicule that would later be laid at Ferguson's feet because of the U.S. victory. Whereas the Confederate defeat shined a bright, critical light on Confederate guerrilla activities, the Union victory sanitized and sometimes obscured the actions of men like Beatty.

The embarrassment from the rout at Dug Hill resonated throughout Middle Tennessee and its occupying army. Two weeks later, Brigadier General Alvan C. Gillem wrote unionist governor Andrew Johnson about the fight and claimed, "The disaster is charged to the ignorance & cowardice of the officers." Suggesting the escape of all six officers was more than coincidence, he clearly did not understand that between one-half and one-third of their men had been killed on the field that day.[30]

Rather than claim unprofessional behavior on the part of Stokes's officers, Champ Ferguson's testimony, along with W. B. Hyder's statement, suggests that the Confederate attackers may have killed several enemy soldiers who had given themselves up.[31] In an interview with a newspaper reporter, Ferguson addressed the fourth charge of his indictment, which accused him of hanging nineteen members of Stokes's 5th Cavalry after the Battle of Dug Hill. Ferguson denied responsibility but acknowledged, "I was told they were hanged, but I never saw them." During those terrible months of the war, a self-justifying Ferguson said, "Both sides hung their prisoners." He alleged, "if they had found me, I know they would have killed me . . . Stoke's men all swore I should hang, if they caught me, and I retaliated."[32] Although Ferguson initially denied taking part in the hangings, his later statements suggest he played some role in either executing the prisoners or ordering the act.

Although the Confederates had already done their real damage in the ravine at Dug Hill, the next day, Stokes reported that the enemy was continuing to press for whatever advantage they could muster. In an attempt at deception, six Confederate raiders, dressed in Union uniforms, ran toward a picket post screaming for them not to shoot, "that the rebels were after them." Within seconds, gray-clad men rushed up as if in pursuit; however, their goal was not what it seemed. The southerners in blue immediately attacked the reserve pickets, while those following behind wearing gray hit the forward post. Together, they attacked both sets of videttes with very little forewarning. In his report, Stokes complained that the enemy, whom he thought was Colonel George Carter's company, killed several of the men after they had been captured. He noted, "Hughs himself does not allow this barbarity, but his subordinate officers practice it."[33]

Echoing past sentiments, Stokes reported the terrible condition of White County and the pro-Confederate sentiment that prevailed despite the local hardships. As in past months, he had "to fight for every ear of corn and blade of fodder I get." He also saw considerable strengthening of Hughs's force, reporting that "Deserters from the rebel army are constantly joining" him. As for the citizenry, they were "thoroughly and decidedly disloyal," although "a great many are taking the oath." Indeed, the nature of the local war had forced many White Countians to be Janus-faced. When Stokes's men searched the bodies of the enemy troops they killed, they frequently found a signed oath of allegiance to the United States government. Complaining about the terrain, Union commanders in the region expressed their frustration with the duplicity of the largely Confederate population. "I have to fight rebel soldiers and citizens, the former carrying the arms and doing the open fighting; the latter carrying news and ambushing."[34]

Not allowing the Federals to rest, Ferguson immediately resumed his operations. The afternoon of February 25 found nearly one hundred men under Ferguson and Carter thirty miles southeast of Sparta, in Pikeville, Tennessee. The *Chattanooga Gazette* reported that three of the men "went to Judge Frazier's robbed him, presented a pistol at his breast and said they had come to kill him." The judge survived, however, due to "the tears and entreaties of his wife and children." Another group robbed "Mr. Lee and Col. Bridgeman, trying the strength of their pistols over the aforesaid gentlemen's heads." After spending several hours in town stealing what they could carry and destroying the rest, the bandits returned to their commands.[35]

After camping north of town, Carter and Ferguson separated. Columbus German recalled that the split was not a friendly one. In the wake of the Battle of Dug Hill, most of Ferguson's men had remained behind to round up and sell the dead Federals' horses. German wrote, "After we got on the mountain Col. Hughs and Champ had some difficulty because Champ could not rob." As a result, "Hughs ordered him back." With only about a dozen men with him, Ferguson returned to White County, but not without incident.[36] Stopping to plunder along the way, the band "killed a Mr. Hall, he being the only man they found that was not of their own way of thinking."[37] Carter, however, would lead a much more exciting expedition.

George W. Carter's wartime exploits were daring. Only thirty years old when the war began, the former blacksmith carried his heart on his sleeve. He was arrested several times in 1862 for fighting and by August 1862, he was listed as a captain in the 4th Tennessee Cavalry (C.S.A.). By the end of the year, he was listed as a prisoner of war and reportedly exchanged. However, in August 1863, it was reported that "Capt. George Carter had been captured and put in Fort Delaware Prison, but escaped, swam the bay and came to us while at Chattanooga."[38]

On the night of February 26, 1864, the returned Carter, with 150 men, raided the courier line connecting Union forces at Washington and Sulphur Springs, Tennessee. Killing the provost marshal, wounding two others, and taking several prisoners, Carter's company made off with nearly a dozen repeating rifles and an equal number of horses. At Sulphur Springs, they killed two more men before crossing over the mountain into the Sequatchie Valley and overwhelmed a company of Home Guards.[39] The Union army was growing tired of these small groups of partisans.

On March 11, Stokes's past disappointments were forgotten when he parleyed intelligence about enemy movements into an important victory. That morning, he learned that a small enemy contingent was ten miles up the Calfkiller River, near where his men had been slaughtered at Dug Hill only two weeks before. Sending a contingent of eighty men toward the position, they found about a hundred Confederate partisans. After a crisp, one-hour fight, the two sides lost one man each killed and several others wounded. Hughs, who was preparing many of his men to move south within a few days, was not on the field and his absence likely increased the Federal advantage. By the end of the fight, the Confederate defenders had borne the brunt of the affair.[40]

The *Louisville Daily Journal* reported that Stokes's command had won retribution along with its victory. With the questionable Confederate victory fresh in his mind, Stokes apparently vowed to repay his enemy if the opportunity presented itself. In the aftermath of the short fight, seventeen prisoners were taken and "were immediately taken out and shot, in retaliation for their recent murders." The newsman justified these actions by writing, "This act of severity was demanded by the dreadful circumstance; it is the only manner in which the lives of loyal men can be protected. If men will become murderers, let them meet a homicide's doom, and that without ceremony."[41]

More good news for the Union arrived when an ecstatic *Nashville Daily Union* reported on March 29, 1864, that Ferguson had been "shot through the abdomen and mortally wounded and at first secreted in a cave." The information originated from a local physician who dressed the wounds and was later found and questioned by Colonel Stokes. W. B. Hyder, who was probably on the scene during the battle, wrote, "Old Champ charged up and on their Horses fired out all of their shots from their pistals But the boys in the Blue held to their trees and stumps and Champ fell Back out of Gun Shot and reloaded and here they came again hard as their horses could run yelling like wildmen came up in a few steps & Old Champ spoke in a loud coarse voice to Blackman and said Surrender or I will Kill you and Blackman hollered out to him Go to Hell God Dam you." At that point, some of the Federal soldiers fired at the guerrilla and he "sunk down on his Saddle and turned his horse and ran off." Unaware of the extent of Ferguson's wound, Colonel Stokes called for Hyder two days later and informed him that if Ferguson was seriously wounded, he would not go far and the local doctor would have probably been called to treat him. Stokes sent Hyder "their to Night With 50 Men and take the old Doctor out and Maik him tell where Champ is and if he Refuses to tell Maik him think that you are a going to hang him." Cautioning Hyder not to "hang him till he is ded," Stokes instructed the scout that he did not want the man killed, just scared into giving the required information.[42] After the doctor informed Hyder and the others of Ferguson's whereabouts, the men went to a cave where they only found an empty bed.[43]

By March 27, the news became more dramatic as the *Nashville Daily Union* reported that Ferguson had been killed in the fracas. The story recounted how Ferguson's men had scattered but were hunted down by the Federals and "Whenever one was taken, he was shot without ceremony." Although the newspaper claimed Stokes did not know the wounded Ferguson's whereabouts, it reported that one of his own men betrayed the guerrilla chieftain. Fabricating a story about a captured soldier who begged for his life and managed to broker a deal with Stokes in exchange for Ferguson, the paper reported that the cowardly partisan informed on his captain and the colonel quickly dispatched a scout to the appointed house. The Federals "entered and found Ferguson lying on a bed in one of the rooms, suffering from the wound received the day before." Upon orders from Stokes, "They immediately surrounded the bed and riddled his body with pistol balls."[44] Although premature and patently false, the newspaper published other reports confirming his death. Their "authentic source" validated the physician's claim of the severity of the wound and the newspaper cheerily announced, "Union men will no more be persecuted by him."[45]

Although the Nashville newspaper could not have been more wrong about Ferguson's demise, his injury was indeed life threatening. For more than three months following the fight, Ferguson seemingly disappeared into thin air. The next year, he remembered, "I was badly wounded in one of these fights" and "once thought I should die, but the Lord appeared to be on my side; how long he will stay of that way of thinking, I cant tell."[46]

The day following Ferguson's wounding, Stokes sent out another detachment hoping to locate those who had scattered from the previous day's fight. Writing to the *Confederate Veteran* more than thirty years later, L. W. Chapin of Livingston, Tennessee, remembered his part in the raid. A Lieutenant Gulue who headed a small band who frequently rode with Hughs left Hughs's command and took six of his men to William Officer's house in Overton County where he planned to stay the night. The next morning, the Federals found Gulue and his men in the house and placed them under arrest. Taking them a little way from the house, they drew their guns and killed the Confederates. Chapin wrote his letter "in order that his friends or relatives may know what became of him."[47] After a brief return to camp, Stokes sent the men back out, this time in pursuit of Hughs, who was moving out of the mountains toward a vantage point from which he could harass the Nashville and Chattanooga Railroad.[48]

Early on March 18, Stokes's detachment surprised Hughs's sleepy camp. Catching the men just out of bed, the Federals completely routed the Confederates, causing the fleeing troops to throw away "saddles, blankets, clothing, and arms." Stokes reported, "The entire force would have been captured or killed if they had not run up in the mountains, where it was almost impossible for men to travel." The end result of the brief fight was seven dead Confederates, while the attackers lost only two men. They also recouped a sizable amount of stolen Federal property and made off with "Colonel Hughs' portfolio and papers," surely a special prize for someone who had been pursuing Hughs as long as Stokes had and possibly a useful tool in formulating future Union strategy. The only missing piece, however was the colonel himself, who had been out the previous night on a scout to the railroad and completely missed the excitement.[49]

Two days later, Stokes sent out a force of his reserves "for the purpose of picking up stragglers and preventing them from again concentrating." Fanning out through Putnam, Overton, and Jackson counties, they spent five days either raiding farms or capturing the dispersed Confederates. During the expedition, Stokes's men killed several local guerrilla leaders and verified that the Confederate resistance in the region had been at least temporarily broken.

Summing up the effectiveness of his mission, Stokes wrote, "Hughs' command is scattered over the entire country, no 10 of his men being together. They are merely trying to keep out of my way."[50]

Within days of Hughs's defeat at the hands of Stokes's cavalry, the colonel, who had been cut off from the Confederate army for months but had thrived in his circumstance, began making serious preparations to return south after his demoralizing loss. With Confederate forces pushed into north Georgia by now, Hughs was forced to undertake desperate measures. He ordered his men to divide into small groups of twenty to thirty and filter through the Union lines to Dalton, Georgia. By the end of April, Hughs and the majority of his men had made it back to the southern army.[51]

Just as Hughs had to escape the mountains, so did Stokes. For months, his men and he had faced nearly daily dangers. The pressure on them had built constantly in the face of frequent fights and the near absence of food and forage. By the time he left the area in early April, half of his men were without mounts, "having worn out their horses by constant duty." Moving his command to Chestnut Mound, halfway between Sparta and Nashville, he found supplies easier to get and sustenance more available. Although Stokes had done more for the Union army to eliminate the guerrilla presence in the Cumberland region than any of his contemporaries, his efforts were quickly forgotten as the war moved south out of Tennessee and much larger trophies became available. Stokes and his small contingent spent much of the remainder of the war watching it from a distance.[52]

While Ferguson was laid up with his serious wound, his old Fentress County nemesis David Beatty was courting Military Governor Andrew Johnson. Knowing the governor was sensitive to the plight of the embattled unionists Beatty claimed to protect, Tinker Dave wrote him in Nashville with several important requests. Recalling his unpaid duty since the advent of hostilities, Beatty asked for help from Johnson providing subsistence to the people of the region. He explained, "This county, as you are awear, has been hemed in without any outlet to supply herself with the necessaries of life." Recalling that "The citizens have done all they can do" to feed Beatty and his men, he informed the governor, "now I think it is my turn to do all I can for them." Beatty asked Johnson to send supplies upriver to Mill Springs where he and his men would carry the food overland into his section of Tennessee. In addition to asking for "corn, flour, *crackers,* or anything that will sustain life," he also requested the government begin paying him for his service. Although it is possible he was asking on behalf of himself and his men, Beatty only specifically noted his own need and want of funding.[53]

On May 2, Captain Christopher M. Degenfeld of the 12th Ohio Cavalry was dispatched with a company of cavalrymen to the Cumberland region to locate Ferguson. Not knowing about Ferguson's wound, Frank Mason, in his regimental history, recalled, "For four days the captain (Degenfeld) harassed and chased him; but Ferguson eluded him, and, finally, made good his escape from Kentucky."[54] Whether Mason or Degenfeld created the roaring good story, it was all untrue. Ferguson was still laid up.

By early July, Champ Ferguson had healed enough to resume his activities. On July 9, Major Thomas H. Reeves of the 4th Tennessee Infantry (U.S.A.) reported that two days earlier he had been notified that a band of guerrillas was stealing horses in the vicinity of Post Oak, Tennessee, five miles north of Cookeville. Upon receiving the news of Ferguson's sighting, Reeves personally led a small scout to the area. There, he found the guerrilla still in the area with twenty mounted men. With a force only half the size of Ferguson's, Reeves returned to the safety of his camp and gathered a larger company. By the time he returned to Post Oak, he had fifty additional mounted men but had lost the advantage of time. He estimated that Ferguson was hours ahead of him with "113 U.S. horses, which were in pasture there," and returning to the mountains.[55]

Halting that night, Reeves learned of four hundred more army mounts at a mountain farm nearby. Hoping to reach the animals before Ferguson, the major was disappointed. Now leading more than five hundred U.S. army horses and mules, Ferguson stayed ahead of the rapidly tiring Federals. Slipping into the mountains with the stolen stock, Ferguson left Reeves behind with his exhausted mounts and men. Although Reeves sought to paint as bright a picture as possible, he undoubtedly understood the level of his failure. While he could claim that his men "captured 1 prisoner, retook two, and several horses, 1 gun &c," and lost none of his men in the process, he had watched the reinvigorated Ferguson make off with a large collection of one of the most valuable commodities in the mountains.[56]

Reeves's report to General Jacob Ammen refocused Federal attention onto a problem the region's commanders probably had thought solved. Ammen responded aggressively by ordering Reeves to rest his command but return to the mountains and retake the stock before Ferguson had a chance to sell it.

Two days later, Reeves sent another contingent into White County where he had heard the horses were being held. Once in the valley near Ferguson's home and the infamous Dug Hill, Reeves's men found themselves periodically attacked by bushwhackers who quickly fled into the mountains. Failing to find the horses, Reeves guessed that they had been divided among the raiders and sent into the hills where it would be impossible to retake them.[57]

While their inability to recapture the horses and mules frustrated the Federals, the opposition of the citizenry angered the soldiers. Reeves reported, "The citizens would not give any information about the stock nor against the guerrillas, and denied of knowing that any had been brought into that valley." The commander on the ground in White County "found that the citizens were all aiders and abettors to the thieving band." The unnamed officer, angered by the local apathy toward his cause, "commenced to show them the rewards given to such people, and had their stock (private) and everything that his command could consume seized, and plundered every house from there to Sparta." Proud of the "hard war" that his subordinate had brought to the disloyal people along the Calfkiller, Reeves enumerated the guns, ammunition, and other articles of war uncovered by his command, and bragged, "For a distance of fifteen miles down the valley every house where good stock, arms, or goods of a contraband nature could be found, the most unparalleled plunder was committed."[58]

The track of their plunder likely took them to Ferguson's house and led straight to Sparta, the epicenter of pro-southern sentiment in the region. Reeves reported that his men rode into town on the evening of July 15 and declared martial law but failed to find any of the enemy. The news of the Federal raids upstream frightened the townspeople terribly. "For two hours the cries of women and children were intense, for they all expected the town to be burnt up and all the citizens killed." The next day, the Federals left Sparta with fewer than a dozen prisoners and equal parts of twenty-five head of recaptured army mounts and confiscated private stock.[59]

On August 1, Governor Johnson issued an order that made many loyal Tennesseans happy. That day, he placed Brigadier General Alvan Gillem in command of the "Governor's Guard." Since Gillem now answered only to the governor, Johnson ordered him to lead the 9th and 13th Tennessee Cavalry regiments and two batteries of light artillery into the hills of eastern Tennessee to "kill or drive out all bands of lawless persons, or bands which now infest that portion of the State." Mustering all his power as Tennessee's executive,

Johnson commanded that all organized Tennessee troops obey Gillem's orders, gave the general authority to impress any Tennessee regiments or companies as he saw fit, and authorized Gillem a blank check with commissaries and quartermasters. Johnson wanted the guerrillas and he would get them.[60]

Updating Governor Johnson, Alvan Gillem described the state of affairs in the White County region when he visited in early August: "Sparta is most emphatically a 'deserted village.' One half of it was burned by Stokes & the other half is abandoned, there is I believe but four families in this once flourishing village. So much for the practical working of Secession." While Gillem gave Stokes's men credit where Reeves's were due, there remained no question as to the condition of the town.[61] The Union army had made the subjugation of White County a priority, and over the preceding seven months, had waged a fierce fight to do so. By late July 1864, Sparta and White County, while remaining a strong Confederate enclave and popular guerrilla hideout, had been virtually destroyed by the war.

Although Gillem had complete autonomy on his expedition against the partisans, he understood the political nature of his task and practiced unusual discretion while on the march. Having moved east from Sparta through White County, he informed the governor that the previously lax discipline of his men was improving and the column was making a "very favorable impression . . . on the loyal men of the county." Though many White County residents were beginning to accept the inevitability of their situation, some retained their southern patriotism. With the aplomb of an expectant conqueror, Gillem reported, "Three Bushwhackers have died suddenly near our line of march since leaving Sparta."[62]

Where conventional warfare had met serious difficulty in fighting guerrillas, irregular bands enjoyed more success. Men like Tinker Dave Beatty of Fentress County had been fighting as a partisan since early in the war and Gillem proudly reported other practitioners in White County. Abraham E. Garrett was in White, Macon, and DeKalb counties recruiting men for what would become the 1st Tennessee Mounted Infantry (U.S.A.) when he and his local recruits began prosecuting partisan warfare. Garrett's men were no more than a powerful, but localized unit in August 1864. Gillem, who had "not heard of a single instance of depredation by them" complimented them and noted, "they are killing many of the worst men in this part of the State, & will soon drive all the Guerrillas out." Fighting like their counterparts, Garrett's partisans moved throughout the region in small groups, "killing (they take none [prisoners]) all the robbers & Coundrels."[63]

The increased Federal attention to Sparta and White County did not faze Ferguson. Within days, he and Captain George Carter resumed their work. Joseph Blackburn, a captain in the 5th Tennessee Cavalry (U.S.A.) who was in the Cumberland region trying to raise a regiment, reported to Governor Andrew Johnson that on August 3, he had learned that Ferguson and Carter were moving toward Tracy City, Tennessee, south of Sparta, with the intention of attacking it. Riding fast in pursuit with only fifteen men, Blackburn arrested a man near Spencer, Tennessee, "who Seemed to know where Carter was." The prisoner informed his captor, who, by then, had ridden hours ahead of the rest of his men and told him that Carter and his band, Ferguson probably included, had already raided Tracy City and were now at Hemlock Hollow, twelve miles away. Pressing on in disguise hoping to sneak up on the partisans, Blackburn and another man made four miles before they stopped at a house where they found southern partisans. Claiming to be "a Southern Soldier" who "wanted to find Captain Carter," Blackburn was told by the residents to "go to the Stable and feed our horses and have dinner." While eating and wait- ing for the chance to meet Captain Carter, Blackburn's lagging men rode into view, effectively blowing their captain's hastily planned ruse. A wild skirmish ensued with Blackburn's men quickly driving away Carter's group. Although the officer failed to take his prisoner, he did leave with "all their horses and equipments also a large mount of goods that he had captured at Tracy City." Searching the house and grounds after Carter's men left, Blackburn reported finding "about five wagon loads of arms and ammunition which I had piled and burnd for the want of transportation."[64]

The Federal presence was so strong that even Ferguson's home became a target. In late August, Rufus Dowdy visited the Ferguson place in the company of other unionist guerrillas, where they "found some bolts of flannels outside the farm in the woods, together with some casimeres, silks, coffee, shoes, and other articles." Their being stowed "under logs, in hollow trees, and under rocks, where they could be kept dry, exacerbated the suspicious nature of the items being found in the woods."[65] Although Dowdy could not directly place Ferguson with the goods, little imagination is needed to see these items as sto- len and hidden by the guerrilla until he got an opportunity to either sell or use them. It is also quite possible that the booty found in the woods was placed there in an attempt to conceal it from men like Dowdy, who, like Ferguson, had his own partisan intentions. While no conclusive date exists more precise than the summer of 1864, this raid likely resulted in the burning of Fergu- son's house.

By August 1864, the larger war had moved into northern Georgia, leaving pro-Confederate pockets like White County, Tennessee, far behind. In an effort to disrupt the Union war effort and slow the enemy's advance, the newly appointed commander of the Army of Tennessee, General John Bell Hood, sent Major General Joseph Wheeler with 4,500 cavalrymen into Tennessee to cut Federal Major General William Tecumseh Sherman's lines of supply and hopefully force him out of his earthworks and back into Tennessee. For Hood, the decision to give the command to Wheeler was logical. "Fighting" Joe had conducted a similar incursion the previous year when he spent nearly two weeks raiding Federal supply trains in the vicinities of Stevenson, Alabama, and Chattanooga and McMinnville, Tennessee. The success of his early October 1863 raid made him a wise choice for the summer 1864 expedition.[66]

Leaving Covington, Georgia, on August 10, 1864, Wheeler and his command, which included Champ Ferguson and his squad of men, successively struck the rails at Marietta, Cassville, Calhoun, and Resaca destroying track, taking Union prisoners, and confiscating livestock. By August 14, he stood outside Dalton, Georgia, where he hoped to take the Federal garrison, but moved on two days later when enemy reinforcements arrived. Entering Tennessee east of Chattanooga, he rode northward in the direction of Knoxville before circling west toward the tracks of the Nashville and Chattanooga Railroad where he destroyed several sections. Then, he moved to Franklin and tore up parts of the Nashville and Decatur Railroad before bearing south and crossing into Alabama near Tuscumbia on September 10.[67]

However impressive Wheeler's Raid appears, it was a decided failure. By the time he returned to Georgia, Wheeler found that his expedition had only weakened Hood's cavalry and that Sherman had taken Atlanta in his absence. Furthermore, the extensive damage done to the rails in Tennessee did not include bridges or tunnels and was quickly and easily repaired. Additionally, he returned to the manpower-strapped Confederate lines without three brigades he left behind in eastern Tennessee.[68]

Despite the strategic disappointment of Wheeler's Raid, Champ Ferguson could consider it successful. During Wheeler's movements, Ferguson and his men had joined the cavalryman. For Ferguson, his recent attachment to Wheeler was predictable. He had entered the war following Scott Bledsoe, prosecuted much of it with John Hunt Morgan until the raider overstepped his bounds in regard to Ferguson's men, and then began working closely with John Hughs. When Hughs returned to Confederate lines, Ferguson was left without the legitimacy a military mentor provided. He attached himself to Wheeler's column and went to Georgia likely expecting to reunite with Hughs or remain in the service of Wheeler if the situation proved pleasant.

Late the next year, Joseph Wheeler testified as to his knowledge of Ferguson. He recalled that at some time in August 1864, he accepted part of Ferguson's company into his cavalry command. In the closing days of the raid into Tennessee, Ferguson and his men marched with Wheeler back into Georgia and subsequently into South Carolina during the Confederate retreat. Ferguson did not stay with Wheeler long. After getting "into some trouble with some of the guard" and being arrested, Ferguson was attached to the command of Colonel George Dibrell.[69]

Wheeler remembered that after being released from confinement, Ferguson "conducted himself with the greatest propriety," but that level-headedness would not last. In late September, Dibrell's command was ordered into eastern Tennessee but was soon rerouted into Virginia to face a large raiding force led by Union Brigadier General Stephen G. Burbridge.[70]

A TERRIBLE CAREER'S
GRAND CLIMAX

All our troops behaved well.

    —CONFEDERATE SECRETARY OF WAR JAMES A. SEDDON on the
    Battle of Saltville

He is much pained to hear of the treatment the negro prisoners are reported to have received, and agrees with you in entirely condemning it.

    —LIEUTENANT COLONEL CHARLES MARSHALL, writing on General
    Robert E. Lee's reaction to the events at Saltville

f Champ Ferguson spent much time in contemplation during the late
summer and early fall 1864, the recent course of the war would have
surprised him. Tennessee was, by then, mostly Union territory. The
Confederate army could freely roam only Georgia, the Carolinas, and
Virginia. And Ferguson, a localized guerrilla from the Tennessee-Kentucky
borderland, stood in Georgia as part of Joe Wheeler's command. However
radical the recent changes, Ferguson felt compelled to return home to Tennessee. By late September, he would again be on familiar soil and well on the
unfortunate path toward his final destiny.

In August, Joe Wheeler raided deep into Tennessee from Georgia. His
cavalry corps swung east, then north, around Knoxville, before turning west-
ward toward Middle Tennessee. On his trip around the city, he allowed Brigadier General John S. Williams, a Kentucky attorney to whom military command came quite naturally, to take two brigades and half of the artillery to
Strawberry Plains. There, Williams planned to assault the Federal garrison
and bridge over the Holston River. Finding the position too strong for the

proposed strike, he could not move his column fast enough to catch up with Wheeler and thus the commander lost a full one-third of his force. As for Williams, he would be left in East Tennessee for more than a month. An apparent loss for the Confederates in north Georgia turned to good fortune as the Union army planned a raid on the prized salt works at Saltville, Virginia.[1]

Whereas Williams spent the month of September 1864 virtually trapped behind enemy lines in eastern Tennessee, Union Major General Stephen Gano Burbridge sat comfortably deep within his home state of Kentucky planning a raid into Virginia. Like Williams, a civilian whose military star had risen quickly, Burbridge earned a gallant reputation at Shiloh and in the fight for control of the Mississippi River. After the fall of Vicksburg in July 1863, he remained with the Department of the Gulf until named commander of the District of Kentucky in the Department of the Ohio in April 1864. Within weeks of his arrival home, John Hunt Morgan's final raid brought Burbridge in pursuit. His autocratic nature aided him while pursuing and ultimately splintering Morgan's command, but it hindered him as an administrator. His heavy-handedness when dealing with civilians quickly made him a scourge to his fellow citizens.[2]

After his promotion to major general in August 1864, the zealous Burbridge began to hatch a plan for the invasion of the Confederacy. Specifically, he sought permission from his superiors, XXIII Corps, Department of Ohio, Commander John M. Schofield and Army Chief of Staff Henry Halleck, to invade mountainous southwestern Virginia and attack the Confederacy's most valuable salt works. Though Schofield doubted the merit of the plan and the quality of its advocate, he acquiesced to Burbridge's wishes after Halleck's support was secured. Burbridge received authorization from the Federal high command on September 19 and began moving toward his goal.[3]

Not wanting to waste any time, Burbridge immediately ordered Brigadier General Nathaniel C. McLean to move his 1st Division out of Mount Sterling into the eastern Kentucky mountains toward the Virginia border. At Prestonsburg, Kentucky, two other Kentucky regiments and, significantly, an estimated six hundred still-green troopers of the cobbled-together 5th U.S. Colored Cavalry joined Burbridge.[4]

With an invading force of 5,200 men united near the Kentucky-Virginia border, other, smaller forces under Brigadier Generals Jacob Ammen and Alvan C. Gillem moved out of Knoxville, Tennessee, in the direction of Saltville to offer both diversion and support. After a spirited march across the rugged mountain terrain, Burbridge's column drove off a small group of Kentucky Confederates guarding Laurel Gap on October 1 and camped within easy reach of the salt works. Burbridge preferred to wait until morning for the full assault.[5]

In the meantime, Confederate Brigadier General John Echols, who had been commander of the Department of Southwestern Virginia for less than a month, worked feverishly to consolidate the men scattered throughout his area. Though he spent the day requesting various forces to be reassigned to his command for the defense of the salt works, the overwhelming majority of those men had yet to make it to Saltville. Brigadier General John S. Williams had 1,700 men, including Champ Ferguson and his band, marching toward the works and another 300 reserves were en route by train, but if Burbridge struck quickly, the battle would be finished before Williams and the reinforcements arrived.[6]

On the field, the 54th Virginia Infantry's Colonel Robert Trigg initially took command and began setting up defenses. After a few hours, Brigadier General Alfred E. Jackson arrived and assumed command. Jackson, who had picked up the not-so-flattering nickname "Mudwall," proved himself worthy of his command that day. He calmly ordered fortifications built, trenches dug, and artillery placed. During the night, Colonel Robert T. Preston arrived with three hundred Tennesseans, whom he ominously described as "in a state of perfect insubordination," and the Confederates remained outnumbered by ten to one.[7] With the Confederate emplacements prepared for the coming fight, "Mudwall" prepared to get some sleep before morning. Before turning in, however, he stopped to ask Preston and Lieutenant John S. Wise a question. "Kernel, my men tell me the Yanks have got a lot of nigger soldiers along. Do you think your reserves will fight niggers?" Confidently, Preston responded, "Fight em? . . . they'll eat 'em up! No! not eat 'em up! That's too much! . . . we'll cut 'em up."[8] Though Preston's men spent the following day far away from the heated action that the men of the 5th U.S. Colored Cavalry experienced and probably did not see a black soldier until after the incidents in question had already taken place, the sentiments and overtones are unmistakable.

Early the next morning, the battle began in earnest about three miles in front of the Confederate preparations. The Union forces advanced but were slowed by enemy skirmishers. This delay gave 250 men, who had left Williams's force the day before, time to arrive on the field and take a position near the right side of the Confederate line. Commanding this assemblage was Brigadier General Felix H. Robertson, a Texan who at twenty-five had become one of the youngest general officers in the Confederacy.[9] Robertson's small column was mainly made up of parts of the 8th and 11th Texas Cavalry, but Champ Ferguson and a group of his men arrived on the field with Robertson's command. A couple of hours after Robertson's arrival, General Williams showed up with his van of 1,700.[10] What most would have thought to be a dire situation for the Confederates the night before began to look much better by 10:00 a.m.

As senior officer on the field, John S. Williams began placing his troops. Following the blueprint established the evening before by Jackson, he strengthened the line by deploying Robertson's men to the right of the main road guarding the ford on the Holston River. Arraying his forces across the high ground overlooking the ford, Williams placed Brigadier General George Dibrell's Tennesseans on the extreme right flank. There, it can be expected, Ferguson reunited with Dibrell. For Ferguson, the placement of Dibrell's command proved fateful. Ferguson and the other Tennesseans found themselves directly facing the men of the 5th U.S. Colored Cavalry.[11] There, the war, which was rooted in the dual issues of race and labor, would be fought in a very personal way for these soldiers.

The makeup of Dibrell's command that day was a recipe for disaster. Apart from Confederate guerrillas, the bulk of his force was made up of about three hundred relatively untrained recruits. Not used to military discipline, these green troops had initially refused to follow the orders of officers on the field until either Dibrell or Williams arrived.[12] The inherent lack of order in the guerrillas and new recruits would prove fateful the following morning.

John Williams had only had his full force on the field for an hour and a half when the battle moved toward the Confederate positions outside of Saltville and intensified. Robertson and Dibrell's men had been ordered to the east side of Cedar Creek, but that position proved untenable as soon as the Federal column began moving. Retreating hastily across the creek, the Confederates recrossed Cedar Creek but were quickly caught by members of the 4th Brigade (11th Michigan, 12th Ohio, and 5th U.S. Colored Cavalry). The bottomland to the Confederate right of the ford erupted in hand-to-hand combat. In that creek bottom, the black soldiers who had never before seen action distinguished themselves and drove Robertson and Dibrell's men into the log and stone fortifications halfway up the hill behind them.[13]

Although the 5th U.S. Colored Cavalry had begun the battle to the right of Dibrell's Tennesseans, by the time they reached Cedar Creek, the black soldiers had moved to the center of the line and were facing both Dibrell and Robertson. Here, color became all-important. William C. Davis described Dibrell's 8th Tennessee as becoming "exasperated" at the sight of black soldiers climbing the hill toward them and several let their irrational anger get the best of them and left the security of the works to fight a black man personally. The men of the 8th Tennessee paid a heavy price for their intense hatred as the regiment had four of its officers killed and another captured during the first half-hour of the fighting. For three hours, the fighting raged, with both Robertson and Dibrell paying particular attention to the hated black soldiers in their front.[14]

By early afternoon, Felix Robertson created a crisis for the Confederate effort by apparently panicking during the attack and withdrawing further up the hill without informing Dibrell, who remained engaged on his right. A gap developed between the brigades, forcing Dibrell to withdraw hurriedly to save his command. The Federals, along with the 5th U.S. Colored Cavalry, moved up the hill closer to the enemy. Colonel Robert Ratliff commanded the 4th Brigade that day and seized the momentum offered by Robertson's mistake. Within a few minutes, the Confederates were forced out of their trenches and had taken a tenuous position at the top of the hill. The 4th Brigade pushed the Confederates back toward town before a severe shortage of ammunition ended the Union threat. In his haste to move on Saltville, Burbridge had neglected to accumulate enough ammunition for a long assault. By 5:00 p.m., the battle was over.[15]

As the evening drew to a close, both armies began to assess their damage. Burbridge, who had arrived on the field with 5,200 men and had a full two-thirds of his force engaged with the enemy, lost an estimated 350 men during the fight. The Confederates, owing to their more defensible fortifications, lost fewer than 100 of their 2,800 active participants. Although Burbridge's men had finally come to control the Confederate right by the end of the day, the shortage of ammunition closed the fight for them. With a superior force looking down on the town of Saltville and the works just beyond it, Ratliff's 4th Brigade was powerless to press on and moved back across the Holston River. During the night, a frustrated and embarrassed Burbridge planned to extract himself from what might become a rout if fresh Confederate reinforcements arrived as expected. Filling the bottomland across the river from the Confederate positions with campfires, Union soldiers began a midnight retreat.[16] In the overwhelming majority of military battles, when the actual fighting draws to a close, the battle is considered over. At Saltville, the real crisis occurred the following morning when Confederates roaming the battlefield reportedly began executing wounded enemy soldiers, most of whom were black troops.

As no information exists regarding Ferguson's role in the actual combat that took place that day, it can be assumed that he performed as did any other soldier. Early the next morning, however, the sounds of battle were gone and so was the remainder of Burbridge's command. George Dallas Mosgrove would witness the beginning of a new fight. Upon waking, he "heard a shot, then another and another until the firing swelled to the volume of . . . a skirmish line." Asking if the enemy had returned and being told that it had not, Mosgrove made his way toward the sound of the firing. Finding himself in front of Robertson's and Dibrell's positions, he realized that "the Tennesseans were killing negroes . . . they were shooting every wounded Negro they could find."[17] Writing about the killings that followed the battle, Mosgrove believed his fellow Kentuckians behaved well after the battle because they had not met the black soldiers in battle, and therefore, "had not the same provocation as the Tennesseans."[18] Edward O. Guerrant echoed and expanded elements of Mosgrove's story. "Scouts were sent, & went all over the field, and the continued ring of the rifle, sung the death knell of many a poor Negro who was unfortunate enough not be killed yesterday." He added, "Our men took no Negro prisoners. Great numbers of them were killed yesterday & today."[19]

Although no individual soldier was named in the aforementioned accounts, at Champ Ferguson's trial in the summer of 1865, Henry Shocker of the 12th Ohio Cavalry placed the defendant on the field as an active participant in the slaughter. Shocker recalled, "I saw the prisoner [Ferguson] in the morning pointing his revolver down at the prisoners laying on the field." Understanding what was taking place, Shocker, who had been wounded the previous evening, crawled out of the path of the slowly approaching Ferguson. Keeping quiet and probably feigning death, he heard Ferguson ask his friend, Crawford Henselwood, "what he was doing there. And why he came down there to fight with the damned niggers." With that, Ferguson pulled out his pistol and asked Henselwood, "where will you have it, in the back or in the face?" Henselwood, now begging for his life, could not sway Ferguson. Having heard such pleas many times before, Ferguson shot the wounded trooper in mid-plea.[20]

Still playing dead, Shocker felt Ferguson walk past him and watched him go to a small log building nearby that was serving as a hospital. For several minutes, Shocker lost sight of Ferguson, and when two harmless-looking Confed-

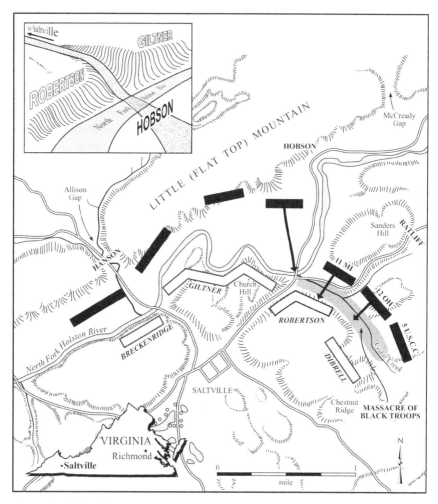

The Battle of Saltville, October 1864 (Map by Mary Lee Eggart)

erates came near, the wounded Union soldier asked them if they would take
him into the hospital. As the two soldiers neared the building with Shocker,
Ferguson came out with two black soldiers. "Wait and see what he does with
them," commented one of the men. Shocker testified that Ferguson took the
men several yards away and killed them with a revolver. He then returned to
the hospital and took two more, whom he killed in a similar way.[21]

More insightful was Lieutenant George Cutler's account. Cutler's 11th
Michigan Cavalry was separated from the 5th U.S. Colored Cavalry on the

battlefield by the 12th Ohio, but on the morning following the fight, the lieutenant "saw some colored soldiers killed, eight or nine of them." Recalling that all of the Federals on the field were now prisoners and no longer armed, Cutler claimed he then saw several of the prisoners killed. Confused by the unprofessional nature of the southern soldiers, Cutler recalled, "I couldn't tell whether or not citizens or soldiers did the killing of the prisoners, as all seemed to be dressed alike." Unsurprisingly, the profound breakdown of discipline and command within Confederate ranks that morning was also noted. Cutler did not "know that anybody had command" and recalled, "They all appeared to be commanding themselves."[22]

That morning, some Confederate soldiers doubtlessly allowed their anger to boil over and killed some of the white and black soldiers who had opposed them the day before. Ferguson, as claimed by Shocker and as had been his habit since the earliest days of the war, certainly participated in the killings. While some historians have sought to vindicate Ferguson, they have frequently done so based largely on speculation. William Marvel's work on Saltville attempted to do so by attacking Shocker's credibility. His most pressing complaint about Shocker was the fact that the young man turned to falsehoods rather than the truth at several points in his life. Although Marvel did not directly condemn him for lying about his age in order to enlist and later reenlist in the Union army, he did use Shocker's actions, whether they grew out of a patriotic urge or a desire to escape a difficult home life, to build the foundation that the young man became a persistent liar. Despite Marvel's allegations, many of the points at which he finds ethical problems in Shocker's life are circumstantial and without firm evidence. Marvel's central issue with Shocker appears to be the young man's willingness to testify at Ferguson's postwar trial. It is true that Ferguson probably had no real hope of escaping conviction and severe punishment, but that estimation is the logical conclusion based on the myriad of crimes he committed throughout the war and confessed to afterward, rather than the grand conspiracy foisted upon an innocent man, which Marvel's argument infers.

Marvel's criticisms of Shocker are weak considering the corroboration of his story by another Union soldier who was also an eyewitness to the events and offered eerily similar testimony. William H. Gardner came to Virginia with Burbridge as a surgeon in the 30th Kentucky Infantry (U.S.A.). Either captured by the enemy or left behind by his unit to treat wounded Federals, Gardner was inside the hospital doing his job when "Ferguson came there with several armed men." The guerrilla then "took 5 men, privates, wounded (Negroes), and shot them."[23] Interestingly, Marvel did not take issue with Gardner's statement even though it nearly mirrored Shocker's, and he failed to reconsider Shocker's allegations despite Gardner's corroboration of events.[24]

Ferguson, however, was not finished with the Saltville fight. Long after dark on the night of October 7, four days after the battlefield killings, Ferguson and several others ascended the stairs of nearby Wiley Hall on the campus of Emory and Henry College. The building had been converted to a hospital and was now serving those wounded prisoners who had been carried off the field. Orange Sells, a member of the 12th Ohio Cavalry, recalled three men burst into his room. With one holding a candle and the others carrying revolvers, they were clearly looking for someone specific. After looking at each prisoner's face, one of the men said, "There are none of them here," and left the room. Within seconds, Sells heard gunfire in the room next door and a black soldier wrapped in a sheet ran frantically into his room.[25] Apparently still angered by his experience fighting black troops, Ferguson had found two wounded black soldiers on the second floor and shot them in their beds.[26]

If a single person could be credited with sending Ferguson to the gallows, it would be Elza Smith. A lieutenant in the 13th Kentucky Cavalry (U.S.A.), Smith, a relative of Ferguson's first wife, hailed from Clinton County, Kentucky. About 4:00 p.m., the day after Ferguson came to the hospital and killed the two black soldiers, he returned with some of his men. Ordinarily, guards would be stationed in each stairwell to prevent escape attempts, but after the previous night's excitement, they were also on the lookout for incoming vigilantes. Attempting to climb one of the stairs, Ferguson was stopped by a Confederate guard. Dr. James B. Murfree, a Tennessean who was assigned to the hospital at Emory and Henry College, remembered that when the guard told Ferguson and the others they could not go upstairs, the guerrilla replied, "they would go up the steps in spite of him." Undeterred, the guard leveled his gun on the small group and warned them not to advance. Without knowing it, the guard, whom Murfree colorfully described as "an Irishman . . . as brave as Julius Caesar," had accomplished a rare feat by forcing Champ Ferguson to back down. Ferguson, still wanting to go upstairs but unwilling to fight for the chance, changed his tack. Leaving the Irish guard who was watching the stairwell at one end of the building, he and his men walked to the other end where they ascended a second stairwell over the protestations of a less committed guard.[27]

On the third floor, Ferguson found the man for whom he was apparently

looking. The "badly wounded and perfectly helpless" Lieutenant Smith was lying in a bed in a room with two other ailing prisoners. Orange Sells, a soldier
in the 12th Ohio Cavalry, was in the room when Ferguson entered. Though
seriously wounded, Smith recognized Ferguson and asked, "Champ, is that
you?" Without a word, Ferguson approached the bed while pulling up a gun
with one hand and hitting the breech with the other. Ferguson asked, "Smith,
do you see this?" while leveling the weapon on the soldier. Smith begged,
"Champ! For God's sake, don't shoot me here." Pushing the muzzle of the gun
to within a foot of Smith's head, Ferguson pulled the trigger three times before it finally fired. Sells watched as Ferguson and another man inspected the
wound to make sure it was mortal before they left.[28]

However, Frank Mason's history of the 12th Ohio Cavalry both verifies Ferguson's relationship with Smith and suggests a different reason for the guerrilla's presence at the hospital. Mason wrote that Ferguson, "the prince of guerrillas, entered and murdered in his bed, a wounded Lieutenant of the Thirteenth
Kentucky Regiment whom he had known previous to the war." He also noted
that the intended victim was Captain Christopher Degenfeld, who had spent
part of that spring chasing Ferguson and his men out of southern Kentucky.
Ferguson reportedly "demanded Captain Degenfeld and Colonel Hanson of
the hospital authorities but not knowing the former by sight, passed him without recognition, and before the opportunity returned again the two intended
victims had been slipped away into another building by the hospital authorities. Mason went further to note that a Major Springfield, of the 18th Virginia,
organized men and "were able to defend their wards against the marauder."
Degenfeld and Hansen were soon transferred to Richmond's Libby Prison.[29]

More than a year after that turbulent week in southwestern Virginia,
Champ Ferguson, already convicted of fifty-three counts of murder and only
days away from hanging, addressed the individual charges with a reporter. Responding to the charge of killing twelve black soldiers on the morning of October 3, Ferguson matter-of-factly stated, "I only killed one of them," placing
the blame for the others on some of his men. While this statement appears in-
nocuous at first glance, Ferguson's patent acceptance of twelve men killed suggests that he was aware of a level of violence that might produce such a result.[30]

After Ferguson had offered one story of the events of October 3, as was
his habit, he followed with a conflicting interpretation. In an interview with
the *Nashville Dispatch*, he denied any culpability in what happened following the Battle at Saltville. He claimed, "I was not in the fight, and did not kill

any Negroes as charged."[31] Despite Ferguson's protestations, his presence on the battlefield as early as the day prior has been verified by several different sources who fought on both sides that day, and his activities after the battle are well documented.

The *Nashville Union* interviewer then asked about the killing of the two black soldiers in the hospital at Emory and Henry College. Ferguson again sought to separate himself from the incident by passing the blame to his unidentified men, replying, "They were killed by my men, as I afterward heard, but without my order, or my knowledge." Challenging the prisoner, the newspaperman asked, "Did you punish your men for the act, when you heard of it?" Seeking to further shift the responsibility, the strong-armed and strong-willed guerrilla responded, "No. I never either approved or disapproved the act. It was their work, and they are responsible."[32]

The specification related to the killing of Lieutenant Elza C. Smith was the most important yet least understood and Ferguson made no real attempt to clarify his thoughts on the matter. He ambiguously confessed, "Yes, I killed him, but it was to save my own life; Smith had sworn to kill me, if he found me. He was wounded, and in the hospital. I knew he would get well, and my life wouldn't be safe, so I killed him."[33]

In one of his late-hour interviews, Ferguson assigned revenge as his motive. "He captured a number of my men at different times, and always killed the last one of them." While Ferguson's inconsistencies preclude any possibility of patent acceptance of any of his statements, the guerrilla war as it was fought in the Cumberland region is filled with such stories of no quarter. However, he returned again to his habit of separating himself, if only by degree, from the crime by claiming, "I was instigated to kill him, but I will not say by whom as I do not wish to criminate my friends."[34]

Another possibility lies in a brief note in the Southern Historical Collection's Leroy Moncure Nutt Papers. The passage refers to the killing of Lieutenant Colonel Oliver P. Hamilton, a Confederate guerrilla with whom Ferguson operated extensively throughout the first two years of the war. Hamilton, who had been captured in September, was being transported between Lexington and Lebanon, Kentucky, when a Federal soldier shot and killed him. The account in the Nutt Papers places Lieutenant Smith in command of the guard and alleges that Smith shot Hamilton himself after the prisoner attempted an escape.[35]

Whatever Ferguson's motivations, the aftermath of the Saltville fight resonated throughout the Confederacy's military machine. The ultimate and official blame for the battlefield killings came to rest on the shoulders of Felix Robertson, who, if he did not participate himself, apparently did little to calm the frenzied situation.[36] Major General John C. Breckinridge, who had investigated the source of the gunfire on the foggy morning following the fight, had been appalled by the behavior and ordered it to be halted.[37] Apparently hoping the news of the post-fight killings would not travel far, he initially reported the results of the battle to Robert E. Lee in glowing terms. On the morning of October 4, Lee, led to believe all was well, relayed news of the "bloody repulse" to Confederate Secretary of War James A. Seddon, adding, "All our troops behaved well." The secrecy did not last, however.[38] Within days, newspapers from Lynchburg and Richmond were reporting astronomical numbers of black soldiers killed during the battle and afterward. With the news out, Breckinridge had to reveal the indiscretions to Lee and denounce the behavior.[39]

Although Lee's own words have not survived, Lieutenant Colonel Charles Marshall wrote to Breckinridge on October 21 that Lee was "much pained to hear of the treatment the negro prisoners are reported to have received, and agrees with you in entirely condemning it." On Lee's behalf, Marshall added, "That a general officer should have been guilty of the crime you mention meets with his unqualified reprobation." Lee took the matter further. He dictated that Breckinridge should bring the officer up on charges if he was still under Breckinridge's jurisdiction, and if not, he should forward the charges to the responsible department.[40] Although neither Lee nor Breckinridge named the guilty party, William C. Davis, in his 1971 article, offered strong evidence that Felix Robertson was responsible.[41]

Despite his apparent guilt and Lee's order for his arrest, Robertson escaped to Georgia. After joining John Bell Hood's command, a severe wound at Buckhead Creek saved Robertson from trial.[42] Ferguson, however, was not so lucky. As an unofficial participant in the battle and killer of a wounded Federal officer, he did not warrant the protection of the Confederacy. Leaving Virginia with Robertson, Ferguson rejoined Wheeler's command in Georgia, but the march from Saltville was not without controversy. En route to Georgia, a scuffle broke out between men of Dibrell's 8th Tennessee (C.S.A.) and a member of Ferguson's company. The argument escalated to gunplay, leaving at least one soldier wounded.[43] Such turmoil is not uncommon when mixing trained soldiers with guerrilla fighters.

His stay in Georgia would not last long. Shortly, Ferguson was ordered to return to Virginia, where Confederate authorities arrested him. Although Confederate authorities wished to prosecute Ferguson for the hospital killings, his unofficial status also presented formidable problems. Milton P. Jarrigan, judge advocate in Abingdon, Virginia, wrote a month later naming Ferguson and William Hildreth as the two central figures in the murders but judged that "a military court has no jurisdiction over Ferguson and Hildreth." Unimpressed, Brigadier General John C. Vaughn replied, "The outrage committed at Emory Hospital . . . demands the punishment of the offenders." Upon his own investigation, Vaughn informed Jarrigan, "those charged by name left this Dept with Williams' command which returned to Genl Hood's army shortly after this act was perpetrated." In closing, Vaughn wrote, "I respectfully urge that the men Ferguson and Hildreth be arrested and sent to Abingdon for trial."[44]

Angry and embarrassed by the killing of an unarmed and wounded enemy officer, Breckinridge ordered the arrest of Ferguson and Hildreth, demanding they return to his department to face justice. On February 8, 1865, they reported to jail at Wytheville, Virginia, where they would remain, awaiting trial, until the waning days of the Confederacy. During the two-month imprisonment, Breckinridge wrestled with his duty as an army officer and as protector of the southern cause. He devoted all the time he could to the investigation of the happenings at Emory and Henry but was also wrapped up in the unfolding drama of the war's final weeks. Seeking answers from Wheeler, Breckinridge asked the cavalry commander the question that would ultimately decide Ferguson's fate: Under whose authority had Ferguson raised his company?

The answer to this plaguing question would not be simple. Responding to both Breckinridge and the court that tried Ferguson later that year, Wheeler claimed he understood Edmund Kirby Smith had initially allowed the guerrilla to form his band and operate along the Tennessee-Kentucky border. It appears that Ferguson's legitimacy within Confederate circles was assumed, and only under close scrutiny, such as that of Judge Advocate Jarrigan in Abingdon, did Ferguson's unofficial status become apparent.

On April 5, as Robert E. Lee's tattered army was retreating across southside Virginia hoping to reach the railroad at Danville, Brigadier General John Echols ordered Ferguson's release from his confinement.[45] With the Confederacy certainly fading, Echols likely considered dealing with such mundane business counterproductive in light of the state of the nation. Joseph Wheeler, who had been apprised of Ferguson's release, credited the difficulty of securing witnesses against the guerrilla as being another factor motivating Echols.[46]

From the time of his release from jail in early April through much of the month, Ferguson's whereabouts are unknown. Although Echols had turned him loose with orders to return to Wheeler, the guerrilla would not have had enough time to travel from Wytheville, Virginia, to Georgia or South Carolina, rejoin the fading fight, and make it back to Middle Tennessee by late April. It is more likely that Ferguson either heard of the Army of Northern Virginia's demise and returned home, or, having become jaded with regular service by his arrest and imprisonment, had no intention of returning to the field of formal battle. Whatever his reason, by late April, Ferguson returned to the Cumberland region and resumed his personal style of warfare.

REVELATION OF A CLEAR CONSCIENCE

I sleep but very little at night, and never through the day. I am wakeful and have dreams but they are not unpleasant. My mind is cheerful and I do not grieve or fret as you suppose.
    —Champ Ferguson on his state of mind during the trial

It is said that Champ Ferguson is dying. Well, let him, if he will, die of his own accord.
    —*Louisville Daily Journal,* September 1, 1865

In the two months following General Robert E. Lee's surrender of his Army of Northern Virginia at Appomattox, Virginia, myriad other Confederate commands accepted Union terms and laid down their arms. On April 18, outside of Durham, North Carolina, Generals Joseph Johnston and William Tecumseh Sherman agreed to surrender terms. Three days later, John Singleton Mosby disbanded his partisans in Virginia. On April 26, Johnston officially surrendered his command to Sherman outside of Durham. As April stretched into May, other southern forces gave up the ghost. Richard Taylor surrendered his Department of Alabama, Mississippi, and East Louisiana on May 4. Finally, on May 26, Simon Bolivar Buckner and the Trans-Mississippi Department capitulated, the last major Confederate command remaining. That same day, nearly six hundred miles north of Buckner's camp in New Orleans, Champ Ferguson was arrested at home in White County.[1]

During the unraveling of the Confederacy, Ferguson was released from his confinement in Wytheville, Virginia. He and one of his longtime lieutenants,

William Hildreth, who entered the room with Ferguson when the guerrilla shot Lieutenant Smith, had spent the final two months of the war jailed for the crime. Four days before Robert E. Lee gave up his command at a small Virginia hamlet, Ferguson and Hildreth were released and ordered to report to Wheeler. By either their own determination or the evident fading of the southern war effort, they instead returned to Middle Tennessee.

Despite the apparent winding down of hostilities, Ferguson and his band continued prosecuting their unique brand of warfare in Tennessee's Cumberland Highlands and even increased their numbers. After the battle at Waynesboro, Georgia, a protracted fight stretching from late November into early December 1864 in which Joseph Wheeler, with Dibrell's regiment in tow, met Judson Kilpatrick's cavalry and slowed its advance on Augusta, several Tennesseans left their regiments and returned home. Thomas Farris had been separated from his unit at Waynesboro and joined a small independent command until news of Lee's surrender made it into the ranks. Farris then joined Champ Ferguson's band "until the end of hostilities."[2] William Sliger behaved similarly when he returned to Tennessee in April "and got with Champ Ferguson's company."[3]

"About three weeks after the surrender at Richmond," Champ Ferguson spotted Tinker Dave Beatty in Fentress County. Beatty was stopping for a meal at a friend's house near Jamestown, Tennessee, when Ferguson and five others rode up, drew their weapons, and ordered him to give up his arms. The Confederates then ordered Beatty to mount his horse and lead them to a nearby farm. Ferguson, who had survived many scrapes with Beatty during the war years, resolved to exercise extreme caution in dealing with his nemesis. Beatty, aware Ferguson "knew where the Taylor place was as well as I did," held no confidence that he might escape alive. Riding away, the men flanked Beatty, with Ferguson riding on his left. Particularly concerned about Ferguson's position in the column (evidence suggests that Ferguson was left-handed), and not wishing to either take the group to the Taylor place where they might harm others or be conveniently led to a private spot for his own execution, Beatty realized he had to act fast.[4]

Suddenly, Beatty spun his horse to the rear and spurred it back in the direction from which he had just come. With men on both sides, he used the split second that fire would be held for fear the bandits would hit each other to its fullest advantage. One man did fire at him but only the cap went off, probably sparing Beatty's life. Ferguson and his cohorts had reacted quickly and by the time they got their horses turned, their quarry was still only a few steps ahead. Beatty recalled that he rode for his life as the men fired about twenty shots at him with three finding their mark. Although he escaped that day, he was seriously wounded in the action. He had been hit in his upper right back with the bullet lodging and later cut out "just at the left of the right nipple." The second wound was in his left shoulder and exited above the left collarbone and the last in his right hip and left through the groin.[5]

Not long after Ferguson lost Tinker Dave on the road outside of Jamestown, he was involved in another scrape with old enemies. Like many others during the war, Van Duvall had left Clinton County in an attempt to save his family from the partisan warfare that permeated that section. After moving his wife and children to Taylor County, Kentucky, Van joined the 12th Kentucky Infantry (U.S.A.) with his brother Bug. In the weeks following Lee's surrender, the brothers had returned to Clinton County to care for their elderly and ill father.[6]

On the morning of either April 30 or May 1, 1865, Ferguson and an estimated twelve or fifteen men arrived at the Duvall farm. Standing together at the spring, the two Duvall brothers and John Hurt saw two men ride down the road and onto the farm, stopping near where the family kept their horses. Awakened by the sound of horsemen, Martin Hurt, John's brother, hid underneath the floor of the house and witnessed the raid. From there, he saw two men at the horse lot dismount and go into the stable, while others swarmed the farm with some examining the house. Behind this small advance group, a larger column left the road and galloped toward the Duvalls and Hurt. Riding up to the men, Ferguson ordered them to surrender. Van Duvall responded by asking the company's identity. Two of the farm men were armed and did not give up after being ordered to do so three times. Frustrated, Ferguson, with his pistol already leveled on the men, shot once. Unhurt, the men drew their guns and returned fire. Ferguson quickly rode away, yelling back down the road, "Hurry up here with the command." Taking advantage of the raiders' lack of attention, Bug Duvall ran down the creek while his brother and Hurt fled up a small hill. It did not take long, however, for the partisans to catch Bug, but to his surprise, he heard Ferguson instruct the men, "Don't hurt that man, that's Bug Duvall."[7]

Leaving a lone guard to watch Duvall, the small command continued in the direction of the others. While waiting, the guard asked which command the two men belonged to. Noting, quite rightly since the war had apparently closed in Tennessee, that they were part of no unit, Duvall was shocked when the man responded angrily, "Don't commence telling your God-damned lies, I'll blow your brains out in a minute." Fortunately, as the guard drew his pistol and appeared ready to shoot Duvall, another man rode up and volunteered to watch the prisoner. Ferguson returned to Bug Duvall and ordered the men standing around to go to the house. Exchanging pleasantries with the man, Ferguson asked the names of the men he was chasing and told Duvall that "they are killed up yonder." Despite Ferguson's attempt at friendliness with Bug, one of his sisters refused to allow the killing of her brother to pass as if unnoticed. Apparently, she began berating the guerrilla to which he, in a feeble attempt at defense, claimed, "They started it with me." With that, Ferguson and his men rode off with a few animals from the stable, leaving the family to find and bury the bodies.[8]

Interestingly, Ferguson's claim that Van Duvall and John Hurt initiated the conflict does possess some suggestion of legitimacy. It was the Duvall brothers and Hurt who were in the group that took Ferguson prisoner early in the conflict and attempted to turn him over to Federal authorities before he escaped their clutches. The incident at the Duvall place as reported, however, does have some inconsistencies. While Bug was with the group in 1861, Ferguson apparently harbored no ill will toward him or he would have treated him as he did his brother and Hurt. It is also possible that since Bug carried no weapons that day, Ferguson saw him as either no threat or a noncombatant. Despite rumors that Ferguson had sworn revenge on those who had taken him in 1861, his lack of interest in Bug Duvall while killing Van and Hurt indicates that revenge might have been only a partial motive.

On May 1, the same day Ferguson killed his last man, Major General George Thomas, who had spent most of the war in Tennessee and Kentucky and had heard Ferguson's name throughout it all, authorized his subordinate commanders to publish surrender terms for independent bands in the newspapers. In Nashville, Major General Lovell Rousseau obeyed his commander's order and offered Tennessee partisans similar terms that Grant had given to Lee. By accepting the terms, these men would be allowed to return home peacefully; however, if they continued their activities, they would "be regarded as outlaws and be proceeded against, pursued, and when captured, be treated as outlaws."[9]

While Thomas and Rousseau were offering liberal terms to the mass of Upper Cumberland partisans, Ferguson was an exception to their policy. At the point Thomas ordered the publication of the terms of surrender, Ferguson had already fought his last fight. Therefore, those terms would embrace all participants who agreed to avoid partisan activities from that time forward, which Ferguson evidently did. However, when news of Ferguson's post-Appomattox, but pre-surrender, attacks reached Thomas, the general made the guerrilla an exception to the rule and ordered Rousseau to refuse his surrender under the terms offered to the others. On May 16, Rousseau made the decision a matter of public record when he declared, "Champ Ferguson and his gang of cutthroats having refused to surrender are denounced as outlaws, and the military forces of this district will deal with and treat them accordingly."[10]

In the weeks following the surrender at Appomattox, southern partisans had quietly explored their options. On May 13, one newspaper reported Ferguson in Sparta, Tennessee, "with a troop of less than one hundred men" committing depredations, while a week later, a second report credited him "with about twenty five men," while it noted the partisan Captain John P. Gatewood "has not got over thirty men with him."[11] While neither of these stories originates from confirmable sources, they do suggest that many of the wartime partisans were leaving their units and returning home.

During the first part of May, Captain Henry Shook at McMinnville, Tennessee, had been in near-constant contact with various guerrilla bands wishing to capitulate. Rousseau appreciated Shook's work, but he reminded the captain that Ferguson and his men were outlaws and were not to be accepted. Additionally, Shook was instructed to make a roll of all the men surrendered to him with their name, regiment or company, length of service, age, rank, and place of surrender.[12]

Knowing that many guerrilla activities during the conflict fell outside the bounds of proper warfare, in some cases men were sent to ask Federal officers about their fate if they agreed to give up. Colonel Joseph H. Blackburn of the 4th Tennessee Mounted Infantry was a popular correspondent in the Upper Cumberland. Having operated in the region, he knew many of the enemy, if only by name and reputation, but apparently his prosecution of the war made the Confederate guerrillas feel confident that they would receive fair treatment from him. With General Thomas's permission, Blackburn began extending terms of surrender to the southern raiders from his headquarters in Alexandria, Tennessee.[13]

During the second week of May, Captain James Walker, a Confederate guerrilla, wrote Blackburn requesting permission to surrender at Sparta. On

May 15, Blackburn wrote the captain promising to meet him and his men on May 24, at which time his men would have to give up their weapons and mounts but would otherwise be paroled and allowed to return to their homes and farms. Having met with both Thomas and Rousseau to inform them of the impending surrender, Blackburn received a telegram from Rousseau when he returned to camp specifying that all of the other men could surrender, but not Ferguson. On the appointed day, Blackburn and his detail met Walker and his men along the Calfkiller River, outside of Sparta, where Blackburn informed them that Ferguson would not be allowed to capitulate.[14]

Meeting the Federals with Walker that day was Scott Bledsoe, Ferguson's old attorney and Confederate patron, who also wished to end his role in the war. Having heard about the terms offered to Walker by Blackburn, Ferguson, who had no idea of his status as the exception to the rule, had also brought his men to the meeting, although they kept out of sight until assured all was well. Being told that Ferguson was also ready to give up his command, Blackburn requested that Ferguson come to the gathering and discuss it. Ferguson, however, did not trust Blackburn and his Union soldiers and insisted that Walker bring Blackburn to meet him. After riding about a mile through the woods, Blackburn and Walker found Ferguson with nearly thirty men along a road in a small grove of trees.[15]

Having grown moderately comfortable with his former enemy, Walker challenged Blackburn to identify Ferguson while approaching the group. Probably having received a description of the guerrilla, Colonel Blackburn immediately pointed out his subject. Upon explaining his order against accepting Ferguson's arms, Blackburn asked that he and Ferguson step aside and speak privately. Reiterating Thomas's and Rousseau's order, the colonel urged Ferguson to come in anyway. Ferguson refused to give up without assurances that he would be treated well and paroled like the others. Ferguson asked Blackburn for protection if he went out among the men, the colonel agreed, and the guerrilla gathered with Walker, Bledsoe, and the others. There, all those in attendance, both military and civilian, begged him to give himself up rather than bring an armed Union force back into their community to search of him.[16]

Ferguson, the guerrilla whose wartime experience had been filled with narrow escapes, was stuck. He appealed to his old enemy Rufus Dowdy, who had ridden to Sparta with Blackburn. Stepping away from the others, the two men discussed their "old scrapes." After their small talk, Ferguson confided in Dowdy that he wished to surrender and be paroled, but it would not be accepted. He then asked Dowdy for advice as to his course. Dowdy responded that he "would leave the country." With that, Ferguson told Dowdy that he was going to return home, but if his surrender was not to be accepted, he would "leave the country and do no more fighting."[17]

After several minutes, Blackburn walked over to the two men. Hoping for an answer in the affirmative, he asked what Ferguson had decided. In response, the guerrilla asked that both Dowdy and Blackburn personally request General Thomas to reconsider his order of exclusion and to allow Ferguson to surrender like everyone else. Promising that he would go home until a reply came, he was reportedly warned by Blackburn that "it was not best to trust us too far." Promising to fight no more "unless some of them Home Guards came there after him," Ferguson's men tossed their weapons into a pile and marched off to receive their paroles.[18] Two days later, Blackburn, upon arriving at his headquarters, sent five men back to the Calfkiller to bring Ferguson in.[19]

Having sent the detachment on its way to White County in late evening, Blackburn expected them to cover the forty miles to Ferguson's house in darkness and arrive in time to arrest him at first light. However, the Federals became lost in the night and finally arrived at the Ferguson place around midday. Surprisingly, Ferguson had apparently taken his promise seriously, for the men found him in his stable and, maybe for the first time in several years, without arms. It is unlikely that the Federals told Ferguson the true nature of their visit, preferring instead to allow the guerrilla to believe that his parole was forthcoming. Before leaving, they permitted him to return to his house and retrieve his pistols, which were inside and unloaded, and carry them with him on his way to meet Blackburn. However, the ruse did not last long. Probably nervous that this man, about whom they had heard so much, was again carrying weapons, the five Federals took time early in their journey to disarm him and tie him to his horse. The next morning, the small group arrived at Blackburn's headquarters in Alexandria, where the commander forwarded his charge to the prison in Nashville.[20]

Writing from Nashville, Robert Johnson informed his father in the White House that "Yesterday, Col. Blackburn brought to the city, as a prisoner, the notorious *Champ Ferguson*." The elder Johnson, having first heard Ferguson's name in the spring of 1862, was surely interested in the guerrilla's fate, since many of his depredations had been perpetrated on Johnson's watch in Nashville. Robert added that the president's nephew, Andrew Johnson, Jr., had been recently elected "*Keeper* of the *Penitentiary*" by the state legislature, a position he would maintain throughout Ferguson's trial.[21]

As Ferguson settled into life as a prisoner, Federal officers rejoiced in his capture. On May 30, after notifying General Thomas that the guerrilla was now in jail, Brigadier General William Whipple wrote Thomas updating previously issued plans for the Cumberland region. Since Thomas had declared Ferguson an outlaw nearly two weeks before, plans had been laid to move into White County and take him. Now, Whipple could cancel Rousseau's expedition. He bragged, somewhat prematurely since Ferguson had only been under arrest for four days, that "The capture of Champ Ferguson and surrender of his guerrillas has restored complete quiet to Overton and Fentress Counties."[22]

Even though Ferguson arrived in Nashville secretly, the public clamored for information about him. To meet this demand, the city's daily newspapers vowed to cover the trial in great detail. In one of the first reports of the trial, a correspondent offered a detailed physical description of the guerrilla:

a tall, well built man, of about forty-five years of age. His hair is black and tolerably short, and seems from long habit to have grown in one direction, at an angle of 45 degrees backward from the surface of his head. This gives him a somewhat fierce appearance. His forehead is large, white and well proportioned. Beneath it are two dark penetrating eyes which look as though they were little accustomed to tears. His cheek bones are rather prominent, suggesting to one's mind a well formed half-bred Indian. Adding to those features, is a well formed nose, prominent, and slightly acquiline. Beneath this is a large bulging lip covered with black bristles of about two week's growth. The lower lip is small, and when the mouth is shut give the latter a compressed and somewhat puckered appearance. The small chin aside from its knottiness does not indicate great firmness, but the whole face betokens an immense amount of it. His beard is short and seems to be about a fortnight old. Its blackness renders the small space of clear skin upon the upper portion of the cheeks doubly transparent. If we mistake not there are signs of pretty free drinking in little blood-shot net-work resembling the hectic flush of a consumptive. A coarse, heavy rusty sack coat covers his broad shoulders while a checked flannel shirt and dark blue pants with his half heavy boots all pretty well worn, make up the balance of his wardrobe.[23]

The detailed description of Ferguson's condition betrays the toll that illness and confinement had taken on him. During the first month of his incarceration, Ferguson's health had been poor; however, he slowly regained his strength over the course of the summer.

As if the facts of Ferguson's wartime deeds were not enough, contemporary events conspired against his acquittal. The weeks preceding his arrest had riveted attention on the search for John Wilkes Booth and the growing knowledge of the conspiracy behind Lincoln's assassination. The murder of the president demanded punishment. Additionally, on May 7, the U.S. Army arrested Major Henry Wirz, commandant of the Confederate prison at Andersonville, Georgia, on charges of murder and conspiracy to kill the prisoners in his charge.[24] Wirz's arrest was clearly a question of war crimes, similar in principle to those upon which Ferguson would stand trial. However, the frenzied state of affairs following Lincoln's assassination surely fanned the flames of retribution for both Wirz and Ferguson, particularly since George Atzerodt, David Herold, Lewis Powell, and Mary Surratt were hanged on July 7, only four days before the Ferguson tribunal met.[25]

As preparations for the trial progressed, former Confederates mobilized for Ferguson's defense. Angered by the duplicitous nature of Ferguson's capture and the fact that he had been singled out to be punished while others, both Union and Confederate, who bore similar guilt were allowed to go free, volunteers began preparing to defend the mountaineer. Foremost among those willing to take up the cause célèbre was Judge Josephus Conn Guild. One of Nashville's most respected legal minds before the war, Guild had practiced law there for years, where he had come into contact with some of the state's most famous men. An ardent secessionist, Guild spent much of Tennessee's secession crisis speaking on behalf of the Confederacy. When the Union army took Nashville and offered the loyalty oath to residents, Guild stubbornly refused it, earning for himself arrest and confinement at Fort Mackinac, Michigan. One of only three prisoners on the island, Guild held out for six months before signing the Oath of Allegiance to the United States and was released and allowed to return to Nashville. Assisting Guild in his defense was recently paroled Confederate officer, Captain R. M. Goodwin. Although young and without significant experience, Goodwin acquitted himself well enough to be allowed to make the defense's final statements.[26]

In postwar Nashville, finding Federal officers to serve on the commission was no difficult task. Rousseau judiciously put together a panel of sober and responsible officers and ordered them to meet on July 3. In referring to Ferguson's trial, one chronicler derisively described it as "a kangaroo court."[27] Indeed, Ferguson's chances for acquittal were slim, but that probably had more to do with his admittedly extralegal wartime activities than a prejudiced and conspiratorial judicial body. Another historian put it more directly: "If Rousseau and Thomas had intended to hold a kangaroo court to try and hang Ferguson, they picked the wrong men for the commission." Although the Federal government had a vested interest in Ferguson's conviction, they could have chosen partisan unionists like David Beatty to administer justice. The aforementioned chronicler succinctly wrote that if local unionists had sat on the commission, "the hearing would have probably lasted just long enough for them to find a rope, a tree, and a horse."[28]

The commission detailed to hear Ferguson's case was made up of five Union officers. On July 11, Captain H. C. Blackman of the 42nd U.S. Colored Infantry was chosen judge advocate, who, in military cases, acted as prosecutor. He then swore in the commission, which was presided over by Major Collin Ford and consisted of Captain E. C. Hatton, Captain Thomas H. Osborn, Second Lieutenant William O. Bateman, and Second Lieutenant E. P. Leiter. Within days, however, the makeup of the body changed as Osborn and Bateman left the service and Captain O. B. Simmons and Captain Martin B. Thompson took their places.[29] Overall, Ferguson's jury was an eclectic and qualified group.

Major Ford, a native of Lebanon, Ohio, had been an attorney and educator before the war called him away. Joining the 79th Ohio Infantry in August 1862, the lieutenant slowly advanced until he earned a promotion to major in 1864 and transferred to the 100th Ohio U.S. Colored Infantry Captain Hatton, a prominent prewar Democrat, spent much of the early war with the 22nd Michigan Infantry. Appointed by Major General William Rosecrans to handle civilian claims against the Federal army, Hatton, at the time of the trial, had very recently been appointed as Assistant Adjutant General of Volunteers by President Andrew Johnson. Simmons came to the commission after initially enlisting in the 46th Pennsylvania Infantry. Attaining the rank of first lieutenant during an early stint with McClellan's Army of the Potomac, he resigned after being wounded at Chancellorsville. He returned to service in 1864 with the 15th U.S. Colored Infantry and later served with the Department of the Gulf. Thompson, originally an Illinois lawyer, began the war with the 25th Illinois Infantry but later transferred to the 154th Illinois Infantry. Lieutenant Leiter had been an Ohio carpenter before the war and joined the 15th Ohio Infantry as a private. During the final year of the war, he was promoted to lieutenant while serving in the Atlanta Campaign at Pickett's Mill, where a severe wounding cost him his right hand and part of his arm.[30]

Upon the opening of court at 8:00 a.m., on July 11, the full indictment was read. The United States was trying Ferguson on the general charge of being a guerrilla and on twenty-three specifications of murder totaling fifty-three men, to which Ferguson would plead "not guilty." After a short morning session, court was adjourned until 2:00 p.m., when the defense promised to submit an affidavit for continuance. When they returned, Goodwin submitted his request based on the grounds that Ferguson had not been given enough time to secure defense witnesses to clear him of the various murder charges. Second, Goodwin initiated the claim that Ferguson had not operated as a guerrilla but had been regularly commissioned as a captain in the Confederate army. The latter point would be more difficult to prove since his defense argued that Union raiders had taken the documented proof of his commission from his home in 1862. With that, the two sides established their central arguments; the prosecution contended that because of Ferguson's irregular service and absence of a formal commission, his killings were unsanctioned murder, while the defense argued that he had indeed been a Confederate officer and should be treated as all others had been treated under Grant's terms at Appomattox.[31]

Although the defense had provided the affidavit requesting a continuance to procure witnesses, the court refused to consider it as no timetable was supplied for the gathering of witnesses and the return to court. Despite this omission, Guild and Goodwin had given specifics regarding the location of each prospective witness and exactly what the proceedings would likely hear from each. In accordance with military law, the judge advocate corrected the document to say that the court considered the listed individuals within reasonable reach of the court and gave them until September 1 to appear in Nashville. The next morning, the court reconvened and Blackman formally rejected the defense's plea for a continuance. While military legal precedent supported his decision, the wishes of Generals Thomas and Rousseau that Ferguson meet a tribunal quickly probably served as Blackman's primary motivation.[32]

With the continuance initially rejected, Guild turned to delaying tactics to secure a sort of continuation. Citing problems with Ferguson's capture and the various promises allegedly offered him in return for his surrender, the defense repeatedly requested various forms of the same continuance they had first drawn up. Finally, Guild and Blackman negotiated a settlement that allowed the trial to continue. Accepting General Thomas's order authorizing the surrender of "every band of armed men in your vicinity," the court also considered the nature of the declaration.[33] Thomas only extended this offer to those men who immediately ceased their guerrilla activities, but in Ferguson's defense, his attack at the Duvall place, if, in fact, it had been his last fight, may have preceded the order. If so, Ferguson should have been offered immunity like the rest of his upcountry comrades.

Failing to delay the proceedings, on July 17, Ferguson's defense reversed course and submitted a plea that argued that the military tribunal had no authority to try a private citizen. Having spent the previous weeks trying to convince the court that Ferguson was a commissioned officer, and therefore, an official participant in the war, their change in tack further frustrated the court. An irritated Blackman agreed to let Guild speak his piece, hoping that whatever the old judge had to say would satisfy him and allow the proceedings to continue. For more than two hours, the man delivered an eloquent oratory revolving around the three central points of the case. First, the military commission had no jurisdiction to try Ferguson. Second, as a captain in the Confederacy, Ferguson had surrendered properly to Blackburn at Alexandria and was entitled to protection by the United States. Third, General Thomas's order of May 1 was a blanket promise that Ferguson had abided by in good faith.[34]

By July 20, the defense had exhausted all of its delaying tactics. That day, the court received its first witness: Tinker Dave Beatty. For the next seven weeks, a parade of men and women visited the courtroom with sometimes dramatic results. Additionally, Ferguson's trial garnered an incredible amount of newspaper coverage. Various Nashville dailies recounted for their audiences the witness testimony and legal maneuverings. Even representatives of the nationally circulating *Frank Leslie's Illustrated Weekly* attended court early in the proceedings for the purpose of seeing "the Mosby of the West," and published an article and picture of the defendant for the entire nation to see in mid-September.[35] *Harper's Weekly* also covered the trial.[36] Local photographers even got in on the action by selling what they called "Splendid photographs of Champ Ferguson" to his growing band of admirers.[37]

Curiously, Ferguson appeared quite comfortable, almost peaceful and content, during the trial that would ultimately decide his fate. On one occasion, an interested man approached an uncuffed Ferguson and his guard and asked them to point out the infamous guerrilla. Seeing an opportunity to amuse themselves with little real harm to be done, they identified Judge Blackman as the bloodthirsty Confederate. After the visitor took a long look at Blackman, he agreed, "Well, he does look ferocious, and I expect that he is a very bad man." Having seen the notorious figure, the man was satisfied and went home.[38]

Further evidence of Ferguson's unique perspective can be gleaned from an interview he gave to a reporter from the *Nashville Dispatch*. The story, which ran on August 19, introduced the public to a vastly different figure than it had been prepared to meet. The reporter noted how when he entered the cell, "Ferguson rose to his feet and advanced at the same time extending his hand to us in a cordial manner" and "asked for our name," commenting that he had heard it in the courtroom some time before. As the interview commenced, Ferguson the lion appeared more like a lamb. He complained that he had only had one visit from his wife and daughter since his arrest "and that was shortly after I got in this scrape." Lamenting their inability to visit, he felt "very lonesome in not seeing them oftener."[39]

While Ferguson's emaciated appearance surprised the reporters to the point that they asked for an explanation, his answer was even more shocking. Painting a vivid portrait of a man possessing a crystal clear conscience, the prisoner explained that mental anguish had nothing to do with his failing health, that the spartan fare at the prison had brought about diarrhea, which had weakened him to the point that he had caught a serious cold. For more than two months, he had fought these physical maladies, but his state of mind had apparently not suffered. He noted that while sleeping, "I am wakeful, and have dreams, but they are not unpleasant." He went on, "My mind is cheerful and I do not grieve or fret as you suppose."[40]

The reason for Ferguson's easy state of mind might have to do with his religious beliefs. After initially thinking the reporter was not serious about his inquiry as to the confined man's religion, Ferguson finally agreed to answer. Speaking like a man ignorant of theology but still confident in his faith, he smiled gently as he explained, "I believe that there is a God, who governs and rules the universe, and that we are all held responsible for our acts in this world." He continued, "I think, in fact, that the 'Old Man' has been on my side this far in life, and I believe he will stay with me, and bring me out of this trouble all right." Subtly suggesting a belief in predestination, he noted, "I have been mighty lucky through life, and I always thought that God favored me. I place all my hope in Him, and I don't believe 'the Old Man' will throw me now." To complete his answer, he informed the reporters that he "always thought that the Campbellites (Disciples of Christ) were just as good as any of them, and a little better."[41]

Ferguson's state of mind, as evidenced by his playful nature inside the courtroom and his calmness and confidence while being interviewed, suggests a man completely comfortable with his precarious situation. In contrast to his wartime character, which was filled with anxiety and anger, he never became desperate in prison. To the contrary, he apparently grew close to his Federal guards throughout his nearly four months of incarceration. To his rigidly Manichean mind, the war was over, he had no existing trouble with them personally, and therefore, they were no longer enemies. The confidence and comfort offered by spiritual thought also may have played a major role in his approach to the final months of his life.

During the course of the trial, the prosecution seated forty-three witnesses, including old enemies like David Beatty against whom Ferguson had fought during the war and Nancy Kogier, whose father Ferguson had killed. He also faced many old friends who now chose to work with the Federal government, possibly out of fear that they might become subject to prosecution. The Capps brothers had ridden with McHenry's band during the war and had operated with Ferguson on occasion, but they eagerly testified against him. Even Wilburn Goodpasture, who had spent the entire war espousing the southern cause, told how Ferguson played a role in breaking the compromise, which further destabilized the upcountry region.[42]

Whereas the prosecution had no trouble finding men and women to speak out against Ferguson's wartime activities, the defense had a more difficult job. Guild and Goodwin subpoenaed eighty-four witnesses on their client's behalf, among those, Dibrell, Bledsoe, McHenry, and Hughs. In the end, however, only four would appear in his defense. Certainly, men like Dibrell and Hughs feared the hostility that they might face in a Federal courtroom, but others, those who had spent the conflict as civilians, "had nothing to fear from the authorities." In the words of one historian, "Their silence spoke volumes."[43]

Despite the handful of defense witnesses, one luminary appeared in Nashville to speak on the guerrilla's behalf. Joseph Wheeler, the great Confederate cavalry commander, arrived in Nashville on August 20 and checked into the City Hotel. Having spent time in prison after his capture in early May, the diminutive Wheeler, probably still weak from his postwar experiences, used that night and much of the following day to rest. At nearly 4:00 p.m. on August 21, Wheeler was awakened from a nap by a knock on the door. Rising, he stepped to the door and opened it to find two U.S. Army officers standing before him. One thanked the cavalryman for his gentle treatment while a prisoner and the other claimed to have met Wheeler previously. After a few minutes of conversation, the men made their exit, noting to their host that they had heard he was unwell. With this peculiar meeting behind him, Wheeler prepared to relax again when another knock came. Opening the door, he found two more Federal officers. One immediately stepped forward into his room and as if an old acquaintance, grabbed the general's hand, shook it and asked, "Is this General Wheeler?" When Wheeler verified his identity, the first man announced himself as Colonel Joseph Blackburn as the other grabbed him by the arms and held him. Blackburn then began hitting Wheeler in the head with a cane and the injured man broke away from his assailants. The other officer drew a pistol while Blackburn beat Wheeler out of his own room and into the one across the hall. The physician who attended to Wheeler's injuries verified that the beating had been severe. When he arrived at the general's room, he found Wheeler "lying on a bed, bleeding profusely." Apparently, the root of the conflict lay in a directive reportedly issued by Wheeler a year before. Blackburn, who commanded a unit in the Cumberland region during the last year of the war, was still angered by rumors that he and his men were subject to hanging if caught by Wheeler's men.[44] Although it is unknown if Wheeler's order was ever carried out, it surely affected Blackburn enough to continue to anger him a year later.

The injured Wheeler appeared before the court on August 24, one day after Henry Wirz's trial began in Washington, D.C. Despite the sympathy Wheeler's beaten appearance likely elicited, there was little he could do for Ferguson. Having no experience with the guerrilla or his band prior to August 1864, the general could only testify that he had considered Ferguson an officer in the Confederate army during the final phase of the war, whether or not official documentation existed.[45]

The last week of August was spent listening to testimony offered by additional witnesses for the defense. By September 1, Ferguson's attorneys requested another continuance in order to give subpoenaed witnesses an opportunity to travel to Nashville and testify. Asking for ten days, Guild and Goodwin could not have been surprised when the court refused their request: After all, the witnesses had been summoned several weeks before and clearly were not willing to testify. For good measure, however, the prosecution recalled Rufus Dowdy, one of their star witnesses, whose testimony reiterated the strong case the Federal government had against Ferguson.[46]

While Ferguson stood trial for his life in Nashville, his wife and daughter were barely surviving. Used to being left alone for long periods of time while her husband was off raiding, Martha Ferguson was readjusting to life as the now impoverished wife of a national enemy. Hoping to ease her financial burden, she sold Champ's part of a tract of land that he and his brother Jim had bought together before the war. With Champ's fierce reputation having become a burden for his mother and siblings back in Kentucky, there was no real possibility of his or his family's use of the land, particularly since Jim's widow and son lived upon it. The $49.63 that Martha collected in the deal likely eased immediate difficulties but did not provide a long-term solution to her tenuous financial condition.[47]

The trial began to draw to an end on September 11, when the young attorney Goodwin offered the closing arguments for the defense. Attempting to focus the court on Ferguson's status within the Confederate army as a proper reason to acquit him, Goodwin contended that Ferguson had served as a commissioned officer and that he had killed only in self-defense. Although the self-defense argument was without merit, Goodwin offered the tenuous and fluid nature of the borderland as Ferguson's foundation. With no civil law or military control in the Upper Cumberland, Ferguson had to kill others in order to survive himself. Goodwin also pointed out an issue that has troubled many Ferguson defenders. While Ferguson's crimes were publicized and their perpetrator punished, unionists like David Beatty, who had committed similar crimes, were allowed to go free. Finally, Goodwin introduced a legal tactic that would gain infamy after World War II as the "Nuremberg Defense." Arguing that Ferguson was only following the orders of his superiors, Goodwin suggested the court try his commanders rather than the man himself. Although this was a useless ploy since it was abundantly clear that Ferguson had never worked closely with any regimental level officers for any considerable length of time, it did illustrate the commitment of the defense to Ferguson's sinking cause.[48]

Five days later, the prosecution closed its case. Reminding all in attendance of the individual charges, the witnesses, and their testimony, Blackman noted that the defense had done little to refute any of the evidence offered in the trial. Second, Blackman addressed the defense's notion that Ferguson should have been given the opportunity to surrender and be paroled under the same terms as Lee. Astutely, he reminded the court that Ferguson could have surrendered with John S. Williams's command (with whom he had fought at Saltville) but refused, preferring instead to return to the Cumberland region and continue his raids.[49]

On September 18, Ferguson stood to make his own statement. Although he had paid close attention to the proceedings since his first day in court, the rustic mountaineer was no match for the arcanum of law. With neither of his attorneys in the room, Ferguson stood and began recounting his wartime activities. It did not take long for Ferguson to venture into dangerous territory and begin to inflict damage on his case. Fortunately, he had only a few minutes before the court when Goodwin entered the courtroom and insisted the statement be halted. Fearing the damage Ferguson, a novice in such circumstances, could do to himself, the young lawyer pled his case with the court and then advised his client of the dangers of frank talk inside a court of law. Although Guild and Goodwin wanted him to stay quiet on this, the final day of the trial, Ferguson apparently wanted to tell his story in open court. A newspaper reported that when the court ordered the room cleared for deliberation, "Champ Ferguson cast a long wishful look at his counsel and at the President of the Commission, as he rose to leave."[50]

Within hours, the commission had made its decision and forwarded it to the headquarters of the Department of Tennessee in Knoxville for approval. Although the defense did not yet know the verdict, such a quick decision did not bode well for them. Indeed, the commission had found Ferguson guilty on the first charge of being a guerrilla and twenty-one of the twenty-three specifications of murder. On the second specification of killing twelve soldiers at the field hospital at Saltville, Virginia, they only found him responsible for the death of Crawford Henselwood. On the fourth specification of killing nineteen of Stokes's men after they had surrendered, he was found not guilty. Finally, in regard to the killing of Dr. McGlasson, he was also not guilty. On September 30, the headquarters approved the work of the commission in Nashville and returned the verdict to be read in court.[51]

On October 10, the court reconvened for the decision. During the three weeks that had passed since the case had closed, Ferguson prepared himself for the worst. Standing in the courtroom that day, he listened as the convictions were pronounced. Finally, the sentence was read. He would "be hanged by the neck until he is dead, at such time and place as the General commanding may order."[52] Throughout it all, Ferguson maintained a steely façade in the face of the decision of his impending execution. For the next ten days, he would divide his time between pleading for mercy and preparing for death.

On the same day the court presented its findings and condemned Champ Ferguson to death, his attorneys and he crafted a request for clemency to be sent to a man who, if sympathetic, would become an unlikely ally. Since President Abraham Lincoln's assassination within days of Lee's surrender at Appomattox, Andrew Johnson had occupied the White House as the chief executive. Now Ferguson, the same man whom rumor had credited with planning to assassinate Governor Johnson in June 1862, asked President Johnson for compassion and forgiveness. Not bringing up details such as his rumored acceptance of a bounty on Johnson's head while the latter served as governor of Tennessee during the war, Ferguson presented his most compelling argument that, upon being notified of General Thomas's intention to offer pardons to all Confederate partisans, Ferguson attempted to surrender.[53]

In the ten days between the announcement of Ferguson's sentence and the execution date, President Johnson received several letters imploring him to exercise forgiveness and commute the sentence to imprisonment rather than death. John McClelland, a resident of Nashville, wrote Johnson with a mysterious story that had compelled him to write on Ferguson's behalf. On the night of October 14, a stranger had come to his door and asked one of the children for something to eat. McClelland invited the man inside, but "he stepped back & stood away from the door as if to avoid the light." Given food, the stranger vanished into the night. When one of the children suggested that the man might have been Champ Ferguson escaping from prison, McClelland, feeling sympathy for the condemned man, took up his pen and wrote Johnson urging the pardon of Ferguson as an act of reconciliation. He suggested, "Would it not be better to commute his sentence to 20 years imprisonment, and then in a year, or 2 or 3 let him out." Acknowledging, "I have no doubt of his guilt," he implored the president to "look at the surroundings—The feuds in his section— the entire want of all law—the raids by irresponsible bodies of men, of both sides through that portion of country, and we can more properly estimate the temptation of crime."[54]

Others wrote with simpler requests. "M. Winbourne, Lyle Preston, and others," informed the president of the court's decision and the proposed speedy execution, and asked Johnson "to suspend his execution for 30 days giving him time to lay his case before you, hoping that you may commute his sentence."[55] R. M. Goodwin, Ferguson's junior counsel, even sought to offer every ounce of aid to his former client. Without revealing his role in the trial, he wrote Johnson asking for a two-week extension.[56] Sympathetic letters also arrived at the White House from farther afield than Nashville. Maclain L. J. DeVillia, a Louisianan writing from Lexington, Kentucky, requested that the sentence of "Gen. Champion Ferguson of the Confederate Army" be commuted to imprisonment.[57] Urbana, Ohioan, John W. James, Jr., also wrote the president with a similar request.[58]

The warden of the prison, James Johnson, Jr., even spoke on Ferguson's behalf. While Ferguson prepared for his impending death, Johnson took the train to Washington, D.C., where he asked his uncle, President Andrew Johnson, to grant the guerrilla clemency. Many years later, a clearly sympathetic and possibly confused James Johnson remembered that the president patently refused to hear of it because Ferguson had, at one time, "placed a reward of $2,000 on President Andrew Johnson's head." The president responded, "since Champ had threatened his life, he would let the law take its course."[59] Although dramatic, it is unlikely that President Johnson's full motivation for refusing Ferguson's pardon was derived from his personal feelings about the man.

Apart from President Johnson's dismissal of the various requests for clemency, one should not assume that Ferguson's cause was widely popular. Many people certainly celebrated his conviction, particularly those who had witnessed much of his wartime work in the Cumberland region. Parson Brownlow's son, John, wrote a letter eight months after Ferguson's execution giving his thoughts on the guerrilla. John had attended several days of the trial and had read the full transcript. He encouraged his friend to read the transcript and could not see how "any respectable rebel could sympathize with him or petition for his pardon[,] yet in this City the rebel population sympathized with him and those boasting of their *chivalry* and aristocratic position petitioned the President to pardon him."[60]

While it is unknown if Ferguson saw the irony of asking for compassion from a man whom he might well have killed if he had met him under favorable circumstances during the war, President Andrew Johnson surely did. Johnson had no intention of allowing his home state's greatest Confederate guerrilla to escape the noose and refused to answer the various letters requesting clemency. During wartime, Ferguson could use his wits to place himself in an advantageous position, but in the end, his techniques were painfully shortsighted. Andrew Johnson, the politician, would ultimately play the game better than Ferguson. Rising from congressman, to military governor, then to the vice presidency and presidency during the war, this man of wartime words, not physical actions, would have a hand in killing one of his most disturbing nemeses.

As Ferguson sat in his cell awaiting a reprieve that would never come, he granted an in-depth interview with local reporters. During his "confession," Ferguson outlined his motives in the various killings, alternately accepting responsibility for some deaths and denying culpability in others. The value of these interviews is questionable because of the often contradictory nature of his statements. While Ferguson's words were not released to the public before his death, Nashville newspapers published the interview transcript in the days following his execution.[61]

During these last days, Ferguson was given an unexpected, but welcome, reprieve by James Johnson, deputy commandant of the prison and nephew of President Johnson. Recalling his time at the penitentiary many years after the event, he remembered Ferguson as a well-behaved prisoner. In the last weeks of Ferguson's life, the weather in Nashville had turned quite cold. Inside of the cells, the biting temperatures were particularly uncomfortable. Johnson, in an attempt to make Ferguson's final days as comfortable as possible, gave the prisoner a choice. He could either remain locked in his cell or submit to a ball and chain, which would allow him access to his entire wing. Ferguson chose the latter and spent his last days carrying his iron ball through the prison halls. Growing close to the condemned man in these final days, Johnson frequently asked questions about Ferguson's wartime killings. Cryptically, Ferguson always responded, "When they kill Champ Ferguson, he will have killed as many of them as they can of him."[62]

As the end neared, Ferguson took comfort in his wife and daughter. While most of his closest wartime friends had abandoned him out of pragmatic necessity and his mother, brothers, and sisters had not spoken to him in years, his wife and daughter never wavered in their support. In what had to be a torturous time for Ferguson, he spent his last days either talking with visitors or alone with his thoughts. On October 17, he wrote a rambling and emotional final letter to his wife. "My Dear Wife, this is Long Lomson [lonesome] Day. I have bin Looking for you now Ever Sense Saturday. The time Seems Longe to mee. I Wante to see you and my poor childe. My trouble is mostly a aboute you and my poor Baby."

Apparently overcome by emotion white drafting the letter, Ferguson wrote "Martha Ferguson Martha Ferguson Martha Ferguson Ann Elizabeth Ferguson Ann Miss Ann Elizabeth Ferguson 17 [her age]." Regaining his composure, he continued,

> Martha if it was note [not] For you and Ann Elizabeth I good [could] take things very Well But to think of the condition thate you are Lefte in the condition thate you are Lefe in ite troubles me very much. I now [know] that you have nothing to helpe your self to and my poor childe thate we

wonste [once] had I good [could] take thinks Beter. I am Riting to Bidding
to pass the time off as easy as posable. Martha Ferguson this will Doo for a
them paper to Look at to Riccolecte champ.

In Faulknerian fashion, he closed the letter rambling, "Champ Ferguson Martha Martha Ferguson My Dear Wife Ann Elizabeth Ferguson."[63] (Punctuation
added to letter.)

The letter likely shocked Martha, who probably had never thought her
husband could be so fragile. She hurried to Nashville to be at his side and
comfort him. Arriving the day before his execution and being given liberal
permission to stay with her husband for much of that day and all night, a visibly distraught Mrs. Ferguson sought to hold herself together for the sake of
her husband. That day, a reporter visited Ferguson and attested to the calming
effect of his wife. The two also discussed the important question of what to do
with Ferguson's body after his death. They agreed that she should take him for
burial to his adopted home in White County.[64]

The reporter was impressed by the condemned man's clarity of conscience
on that, his last, full day. Describing him as "mild, pleasant and cheerful,"
Ferguson conversed "freely regarding his fate." As Ferguson, his family, and
the reporter alternated between the formal interview and family matters, the
journalist noted that Champ, "cheered his wife and daughter at intervals by a
few words lightly spoken, as though he never thought of his doom." When a
Presbyterian minister visited him in his cell, he "appeared pleased to turn his
attention on his spiritual welfare, and firmly believes in a future world and
merciful God."[65]

At 10:00 on the morning of October 20, while Ferguson spent his last moments with his wife and daughter inside his cell, journalists entered the yard of
the penitentiary where a scaffold had been erected. Apart from the newspaper
writers and the prison officials, a company of Federal soldiers who would be
used as guards and three hundred citizens had been issued passes to witness
the execution. Outside the prison walls, throngs of people hoped to push
their way inside to see Ferguson meet his fate. For an hour after the reporters
and other witnesses arrived in the yard, prison officials checked and double-
checked the trap door, rope, and slipknot.[66]

As the prison prepared for the execution, several reporters asked Colonel
William R. Shafter, the prison's commandant, to allow them one last visit with
Ferguson. Acquiescing, Shafter led them to Ferguson's cell where they found

him with his wife and daughter, who had scarcely left his side since their arrival the day before. As they left the cell, Shafter asked them to say their goodbyes. Struggling to remain composed, his wife, saying nothing, squeezed his hand and turned away, while his daughter rushed her father and hugged him for a minute, before screaming, "farewell, my poor, poor, papa!"[67] Upon their parting, Ferguson's wife and daughter exited the prison and waited at Johnson's house across the street for the dreadful business to conclude.[68]

After a brief meeting, during which Ferguson clarified a couple of points regarding the previous day's interview, the condemned man was led outside. Ironically, black soldiers had been detailed as guards that day, and as Ferguson stepped into the fresh air for the last time, he "held his head up, and deliberately surveyed the audience." Nearing the scaffold, "he cast his eyes upward . . . and then mounted the stairs with a firm step." Once on the platform, he turned toward the crowd and recognized a handful of familiar faces. Bowing to several friendly faces in the audience, Ferguson "appeared like a man who was about to make a speech on some leading topic."[69]

Standing on the scaffold with the rope around his neck, Ferguson remained still and straight as the charges and sentence was read. Acknowledging that he "could tell it better than that" regarding one of the charges, he remained subdued, only offering the statement, "I am ready to die." After a touching prayer, a visibly moved Ferguson whispered to Colonel Shafter, asking him to take a handkerchief and wipe the tears from his face. While Shafter dried Ferguson's eyes, he spoke quietly. It is unknown what he said, but whatever it was lifted Ferguson's spirits. As the cherry coffin was brought to the front of the gallows, Ferguson spoke his final words. He asked that his body be quickly put inside and given over to his wife and daughter to be taken back to White County. "I do not want to be buried in such soil as this." Finally, a white hood was drawn over his head to obscure the facial expressions of death. Through it, the crowd heard Ferguson shout, "Good Lord have mercy on my soul!"[70] Within seconds, at 11:40 a.m., the hatchet was raised, the trap door's rope cut, and Champ Ferguson, likely the most notorious single Confederate guerrilla of the American Civil War, fell to his death.

Falling only two feet, Ferguson's body weight did not quite do its job. There he hanged, still alive, but "insensible to suffering." The press, which had been placed nearby, saw the clenching of his fists as the only obvious movement. After five minutes, Ferguson's shoulders heaved slightly two or three times. The three doctors on hand that day affirmed that Ferguson maintained a slight pulse for seventeen minutes, and soon blood began seeping into the white hood in the area of the nose. After hanging for thirty minutes, he was declared dead by the doctors.[71]

Immediately after the confirmation of death, Ferguson's body was cut down, his wrists unbound, and he was neatly laid in the coffin. Once the casket was loaded onto a hearse stationed at the front gate of the prison, widow Ferguson and her daughter took charge of Ferguson's remains. Slowly they returned home to their land on the Calfkiller, where they laid Ferguson to rest in a small cemetery next to a church.[72] Just as Ferguson had taken "time by the forelock" during the war, his enemies had done the same afterward and ultimately defeated him.

Four days later, a similar court in Washington, D.C., found Hartman Heinrich Wirz guilty on eleven charges of murdering prisoners in his care at Andersonville, Georgia. Although the United States Army had arrested Wirz shortly before Ferguson, it had waited until the Ferguson trial was all but over before beginning the proceedings against Wirz. On November 10, Wirz, in a scene reminiscent of Ferguson's execution in Nashville, strode out into the yard of the Old Capitol Prison in Washington, where he was hanged surrounded by Federal soldiers.[73] With the deaths of Ferguson and Wirz, America had exacted its revenge.[74]

10

QUIET RESURRECTIONS OF
AN UNLIKELY HERO

Well, I believe that there is a God, who governs and rules the universe, and that we are all held responsible for our acts in this world. I think, in fact, that the "Old Man" has been on my side this far in life, and I believe he will stay with me, and bring me out of this trouble all right.
—CHAMP FERGUSON on religion

Even before Champ Ferguson's body dropped through the trap door of the gallows, his legend was growing. A man who epitomized the fierce brutality of upcountry guerrilla warfare was evolving into a tragic figure among a sizable contingent of sympathetic southerners even before the conflict drew to a close. Unlike raiders such as William Clarke Quantrill and Jesse James, who often advertised their successes, Ferguson tended to maintain a generally quiet air, going about his business with steely determination and little fanfare. Ferguson left little in the way of personal recollections, although others either perpetuated his self-invented myths or created a veil of legend on his behalf. The result has been the elevation of an irregular warrior for whom no one volunteered to take responsibility to a Lost Cause hero, not within the realm of the Jacksons or Lees, but more akin to the Forrests and Morgans.

The mythology of Champ Ferguson mainly revolves around establishing his motives for joining the Confederate cause and justifying the level of brutality that he practiced. His fans tell an assault story about an event during which his family was harassed and harmed by Union soldiers. Out of this tale grew the story of Ferguson's son's death, in which his child was shot dead by enemy soldiers. As the assault legend grew, it was expanded by those sympathetic to Ferguson's cause and legacy, thereby creating a twisted form of moral justification for a troublesome Confederate hero.

The assault tale was rooted in the story of an attack on his wife and daughter by Federal troops during the conflict's infancy. In this story, Ferguson was away from home when a group of soldiers came to his house and assaulted his wife and daughter. The oft-repeated tale described the purported assailants in a variety of ways from regular Union soldiers to Jayhawkers. Whatever their identity, the story continued with the men, numbering from eleven to sixteen, entering the home and, in some order, forcing Ferguson's wife and daughter to undress, cook a meal, and parade up and down the road.[1] In another version, the men killed both the wife and daughter and "burned the house to better conceal their damnable crimes."[2]

The result of this outrage, the story goes, was Ferguson's returning home, learning of the events, and, in the version in which his family lives, finding out the names of each perpetrator from his distraught wife and daughter. In response, he swore revenge upon the men who had violated his family. The vengeance motive gave numerous authors an opportunity to justify Ferguson's killings as defensive acts. In various accounts, these retributive killings are credited to a protective husband's anger, usually with the killing of Lieutenant Smith at Emory and Henry College completing the list.[3]

The story apparently grew spontaneously in the earliest days of the war. Throughout the conflict, fellow soldiers told the tale in an effort to explain Ferguson's behavior. Basil Duke first put the wife-and-daughter story to paper when he reported in 1867, "ill-treatment of his wife and daughter, by some soldiers and Home-guards enlisted in his own neighborhood, made him relentless in this hatred of all Union men."[4] Almost forty-five years later, Duke, writing his reminiscences, expanded the harassment story by describing how "his Union neighbors . . . visited his [Ferguson's] house during his absence and brutally whipped the women."[5]

If John Weatherred, a Confederate soldier who rode with Morgan and was along when Ferguson killed one of his archenemies, is to be believed, Ferguson himself knew the story and retold it as early as New Year's Day 1863. On the night that he roused Elam Huddleston from his sleep and killed him, the regular soldiers who had ridden with Ferguson apparently voiced displeasure at the guerrilla style of warfare Ferguson practiced. In order to calm their objections and to cast his actions in an honorable light, he told them the story of the harassment of his wife and daughter. In his diary, Weatherred claimed he and the other soldiers objected to Ferguson's cutting the throat of a severely wounded Huddleston. "We were very mad that he did this; but he explained that Capt. Elam Huddleston had burned his house and outraged his wife and daughter a few months before this and he had sworn revenge against him and his men who were there at the outrage."[6]

Although Weatherred offers the earliest confirmed example of the use of the story and the only instance of Ferguson's personally telling it, there are significant problems with his recollection. First, his diary is undated. While his memory is strong concerning many events, his lack of consistency in dealing with specific events suggests that he wrote his account many years after the war, possibly during the early twentieth century. Second, the postwar writing of the diary was probably tinged with the Lost Cause literature of the struggle, which Weatherred most assuredly read. One of the main propagators of the pro-Confederate interpretation of Ferguson's actions that sprang up during the last part of the nineteenth and early twentieth centuries was Basil Duke, one of the first interpreters of the war in the Cumberland region. With Duke's postwar writings telling the tale of Ferguson's life and motivations, Weatherred may have unconsciously adopted that secondary information as primary knowledge and used it to help explain away the killing as the reasonable reaction of a tragic figure. The third, and most damning, of the problems with Weatherred's account is that while he claimed Ferguson told the heart-rending story to the men, Ferguson indirectly refuted the validity of the family assault tale shortly before his death by addressing and dismissing the legend in regard to his killing of Lieutenant Smith and by failing to revisit the story during his final interview.[7] To be fair to Weatherred, Ferguson may have used the story for his own benefit, but his discounting of the tale at such a late point in his life almost assures its lack of truth. The condemned man had nothing to gain by disavowing the story; in fact, his bolstering of it might have served him much better in death.

A second popular legend concerning Champ's motivation for joining the war also centered on the dual themes of familial protection and vengeance, this time involving the death of a son. Of two accepted variations, the most popular is the tale of Ferguson's three-year-old son waving a Confederate flag when a group of Federal soldiers passed on the main road. The little boy, seeing soldiers, unknowingly responded by waving the enemy's flag, at which point the men drew their guns and killed him on his own front porch.[8] Bromfield Ridley told it best in a biographical article on Ferguson for the *Confederate Veteran*:

> Champ was at his home, a citizen, when a tocsin was sounded, and stayed there until his own precincts were invaded. A rabid fire eater passed his house with a troop of Blues. Champ Ferguson's little three-year-old child came into the porch waving a Confederate flag. One of the men in blue leveled his gun and killed the child. O anguish! how that father's heart bled! His spirit welled up like the indomitable will of the primitive Norseman. In a moment of frenzy he said that the death of his baby would cost the "bluecoats" a hundred lives. And it did. One hundred and twenty is believed to be the number he put to death.[9]

The second story removed the deliberation from the boy's death by placing him in the line of fire when Federal soldiers shot at Ferguson. Missing the father, they hit the son, thereby earning Ferguson's everlasting hatred.

These two compelling stories present a single significant problem: Ferguson did not have a three-year-old son at that time. As the event was purported to have happened before Ferguson became an active participant in the war, which would have been summer 1861, the boy would have shown up on the 1860 census with his father, mother, and older sister. Although unlikely, it is possible, of course, that the census taker missed recording the child.

Unlike the sexual assault tale, the son story is rooted in verifiable reality. Although Ferguson did not have a son with his second wife, he did with his first wife, during the early 1840s. He and his first wife were married in 1842 and had the boy soon afterward. Although impossible to confirm, many early writers noted the child died in the epidemic of 1845, as a three-year-old. This story is interesting in that Ferguson's defenders combined the political crisis of the 1860s with a tragic family event that happened twenty years earlier in his first family.

Many early writers created the defense of family as a primary motive for Ferguson's bloody career and some also augmented it with other, more dramatic, imagery. Ferguson, seeking an answer to his quandary of whether or not he would go to war, "went to a cave to think it over while trying to make up his mind." While he was inside contemplating his future, Union soldiers perpetrated the infamous harassment of his wife and daughter. The writer even added a final piece of irony to the story by placing Ferguson's arch nemesis, Tinker Dave Beatty, as the mastermind behind the crime.[10] Thematically similar was J. P. Austin's story about Ferguson's response to the mythical murder of his wife and daughter at the hands of Union guerrillas. A grief-stricken Ferguson sat down on a log, and after a period of mourning, he rose, "and with uplifted hands in the presence of his God and over the ashes of his loved ones," he vowed revenge. Austin's account even suggested Ferguson's possession of a rustic chivalry, as he reportedly "conducted the famous female spy, Belle Boyd, from Louisville, Kentucky, across the country on horse-back safely inside of our own lines."[11] As one might expect, the story is unverifiable.

Despite the highly organic nature of the familial protection stories, much of Ferguson's wartime legend was invented. Much of the credit for wrapping Ferguson's legend in the flag of the Confederacy can be credited to one of his former superiors. Upon the close of the conflict, Basil Duke returned home to Lexington, Kentucky, with the intention of never allowing the story of the rebellion to fade. To that end, he became one of the South's most prolific historical authors as he told and retold tales of the Confederate cause. In 1867, he released his *History of Morgan's Cavalry*, which first introduced Ferguson, and numerous other colorful characters who rode with Morgan, to a wide audience. One of the founders of the Filson Club, a premier historical society in Kentucky, he spent two years during the middle 1880s editing the *Southern Bivouac*, focusing the magazine on the southern experience during the Civil War. Nearly thirty years later, he published his reminiscences, which added to the Ferguson mystique.[12]

In *A History of Morgan's Cavalry*, Duke gave what is probably a fair description of Ferguson. Noting that his legend had preceded him to Morgan's command, Duke described how Ferguson behaved responsibly while working with an official command but never gave quarter "when upon his own private expeditions." Seeing him as a man of considerable natural intelligence, Duke added that the guerrilla could be ferocious with little provocation, but he sincerely appreciated kindness and valued his friendships. The former Confederate commander only guessed that by the end of the war, Ferguson had killed more men than he could remember.[13]

By the time Duke wrote his reminiscences, the Lost Cause had propelled such men as Ferguson into a positive light, providing their actions could be remotely justified. By 1911, Ferguson's motives had been fully developed, and Duke added to the lore. Apart from the general physical description, the old man revealed a mystical detail that had escaped him previously: "He had one peculiarity of feature which I remember to have seen in only two or three other men, and each of these was, like himself, a man of despotic will and fearless, ferocious temper. The pupil and iris on the eye were of nearly the same colour, and, except to the closest inspection, seemed perfectly blended." Although it is quite possible Ferguson's eyes were exceptionally dark, Duke's tracing that unique trait to the man's very nature was probably influenced by the nineteenth-century interest in phrenology.[14]

In the years that immediately followed the war, many groups used Champ Ferguson's legend for their own purposes. In an 1868 letter to Ferguson's nemesis J. D. Hale, one unidentified character wrote, "This is to notify you that the *Spirit* of Champ Ferguson still lives and there are men living that are determined to avenge his death and you are also aware that your *oppressive* and *wicked* acts towards the best Citizens of Overton County stand recorded against you. Our motto "Sic Semper Tyrannis" Prepare to meet your God."[15] Although not attributed to a specific person or organization, the symbols and language used in the letter suggest that it originated from the Ku Klux Klan or a similar organization.

Certainly, the pivotal question concerning Champ Ferguson, both then and now, regards the nature of his service. He claimed to hold a commission in the Confederate army, but had no documentation and no Confederate commander came forward with concrete evidence. As one writer put it, "he was such a cut-throat that the Confederate army would not let him join."[16] This may have been true, but that did not prevent the further development of his legend. When asked if Ferguson had been "received and recognized as a captain in the Confederate service," Joe Wheeler could not corroborate the story. He responded, "I heard him always spoken of as Captain," but he never verified Ferguson's status. Wheeler noted that when Ferguson was ordered to jail in Virginia in early 1865, J. Stoddard Johnston wrote asking for verification of the commission. In investigating Ferguson's legitimacy, Wheeler believed, and informed Johnston, that Ferguson had been granted a captaincy along with permission to raise an independent company to operate along the Tennessee-Kentucky border. As far as Wheeler could tell, Edmund Kirby Smith had given the commission in 1862.[17]

If Wheeler is to be believed, the real problem lay deep within the Confederate army. Noting, "It was customary when a man was authorized to raise a company and did so to regard them as officers upon producing their muster rolls." In Ferguson's case, this habit of assuming any man with a muster roll and a company of men to be a legitimate Confederate officer would have serious consequences. Wheeler elaborated, "I don't know of a single instance of the war department issuing commissions to live officers in the cavalry service . . . their muster rolls were sufficient."[18]

Although Ferguson never produced proof of a commission, Wheeler placed the responsibility on Edmund Kirby Smith, and Smith never spoke on the matter. Many remained convinced that Ferguson formally had been part of the Confederate army. After his death, the legend grew, with some maintaining that none other than Nathan Bedford Forrest had offered enlistment and legitimacy to the mountaineer. While the story fits well into the Lost Cause lore, corroboration has not been found nor does evidence exist that Ferguson ever met Forrest.[19]

The question of enlistment and commission is not the only point where the Ferguson legend meets Lost Cause military heroes. Perhaps in an attempt to build a more detailed circumstantial history of Ferguson's Confederate service, many stories were constructed during the war years, showing more traditional and accepted military heroes reaching out to Ferguson and his irregular practices. The most popular story line involves the gift of a knife. Numerous contemporaries told tales of famous Confederates, most notably Braxton Bragg, giving the guerrilla a knife with an inspirational message suggesting possible uses. Despite the number of stories about luminaries offering such a gift, at his trial, Ferguson confessed that he only received one knife as a gift and that came from his old friend and associate, James McHenry.[20]

Interestingly, Ferguson's legend may have also made the transition into early twentieth-century local-color literature. In *The Little Shepherd of Kingdom Come*, John Fox, Jr., presented readers with the Dillon brothers. Fox, a world-renowned journalist and famous writer of local-color fiction, may have been exposed to Ferguson's story from an early age. A native of Bourbon County, Kentucky, and young scholar in Basil Duke's Lexington, Fox witnessed much of the creation of Kentucky's Lost Cause legacy.[21]

In *Little Shepherd*, Fox introduced Jake and Jerry Dillon. Because "Jake was drapped when he was a baby" and "didn't have good sense," Jerry grew into the more forceful brother, being sometimes manipulative and the more violent of the two. In one of their many fights, which coincided with the earliest days of the Civil War, Jerry hit Jake in the head with a fence rail, knocking him unconscious. After several minutes, Jake came to and "had just as good sense as anybody." As a result of his violent enlightenment and his memory of his mis-treatment at the hands of his brother, Jake swore revenge on his brother "and now he hates Jerry like pizen, an' Jerry's half afeared of him."[22] The story of Jerry and Jake reminds readers of Champ and Jim; reportedly, the two broth-ers had never gotten along very well.

Fox continued by explaining that the Dillon family was a strong unionist clan. The only exception was Jerry. When he struck Jake, the rebellious Jerry had awakened Jake's intelligence and loyalty, which resulted in the split be-tween the two. While Jerry supported the South, Jake and the rest of the family remained steadfastly loyal to the Union.[23] Here, the vagaries of Fox's story, as applied to the Fergusons, become clearer. Champ, or as Fox renamed him, Jerry, became the predator, while Jim, or Yankee Jake, was the loyal victim. Just as Jerry and Jake had sworn to kill each other during the war, Champ and Jim were ready to take a brother's life if the opportunity presented itself.

Fox goes further in his apparent mirroring of the Fergusons and the Dil-lons. Fox tells the story of Morgan's men riding along the border of Virginia and Kentucky with Rebel Jerry Dillon leading the column.[24] Morgan did pass through this region of eastern Kentucky and southwestern Virginia late in the war, shortly before his death at Greeneville, Tennessee, but Fox apparently transferred the action of Middle Tennessee and south-central Kentucky east-ward for literary purposes and because eastern Kentucky was a region Fox knew well. While Fox used the image of Jerry riding in the advance guard to set up an unrelated story, here, too, striking similarities can be seen. Fergu-son's early operations were in the company of Morgan as a scout to lead the raider's column through the hills of Tennessee and Kentucky.

In Fox's story, Rebel Jerry confesses, "I got a brother on t'other side." Just like Champ's brother Jim, Jerry's brother Jake served with Frank Wolford's cav-alry unit. Jerry confides in a friend, "We've been lookin' fer each other sence the war broke out. I reckon he went on t'other side to keep me from killin' him." Also of interest is Fox's tale of Rebel Jerry's capture by Federals, which smacks of Champ's arrest by Union Home Guards.[25]

While Jim Ferguson was killed before he and his brother ever met on the field, Jerry and Jake did meet. In a vicious fight, Jake nearly killed Jerry with a knife, leaving his brother with "a half a dozen rents in his uniform and a fearful slash under his chin." In a way that is both fitting and surprising, the brothers' feud ended peacefully in a military hospital at Abingdon, Virginia. A fearful and wounded Jerry was terrified when his brother entered his room after Lee's surrender. Suspecting that the end was upon him, Jerry grabbed his pistol, which was immediately taken away by Jake. The next day, the two brothers, former enemies, started their long journey home with two others who had also stood on opposite sides of the conflict.[26] Curiously, John Fox, Jr.'s, fictional hospital lies only ten miles from Emory and Henry College, where Ferguson killed Lieutenant Smith, a kinsman, in his bed.

Whereas Fox's use of Ferguson's story in his own writing is fairly clear, less so, but still compelling, is the story of Ferguson's possible transition to the big screen. Born in 1925 in northern Alabama, Asa Earl Carter grew into one of the state's most virulent racists. After serving in the navy during World War II and attending college in Colorado, he returned to his home state, where he established himself as one of the leading protectors of whiteness in an era filled with such men. In 1962, Asa, or Ace, as he was commonly called, began working for gubernatorial candidate George Wallace. Ultimately, he would write some of Wallace's most memorable speeches, including the famous passage, "In the name of the greatest people that ever tread the earth, I draw the line in the dust and toss the gauntlet before the feet of tyranny. And I say: Segregation now! Segregation tomorrow! Segregation forever!" Although he stayed on during Lurleen Wallace's administration, the ultra-inflammatory Ace Carter was cast aside in 1968 when the governor's husband decided to run for the presidency. Feeling used and abandoned by his political patron, Carter challenged George Wallace for the governor's seat in 1970 and suffered a humiliating loss. His political career was over.[27]

In the years following his defeat, Carter, whom few had really known even though he was ostensibly a public figure, reinvented himself. He changed his name from Asa Earl to Bedford Forrest Carter, in homage to the famous Confederate cavalryman, and moved away from Alabama. Splitting time between St. George's Island, Florida, and Sweetwater, Texas, Carter transitioned away from writing racist venom to penning thoughtful fiction with successes like *The Education of Little Tree*. In 1973, *The Rebel Outlaw Josey Wales*, later renamed *Gone to Texas*, was published and its film rights quickly sold to Clint Eastwood's Malpaso Productions. Released as *The Outlaw Josey Wales* in 1976, Eastwood's title character became instantly identified as the guerrilla ideal of the Civil War.[28]

The character of Josey Wales was likely a composite of several personalities, Jesse James and "Bloody Bill" Anderson being the most pronounced, and the film combined various circumstances of the conflict. Setting his tale in the

Missouri borderland, Carter used historical events loosely as a base for his story of a man versus the government he distrusts. In the first pages, Kansas Redlegs make an 1858 raid into Josey's community, burning his cabin with his wife and young son inside.[29] Like Wales, Ferguson claimed to have been driven to fight by his enemies rather than entering the fray on his own volition. The various stories about the atrocities committed against Ferguson's family were similar to those perpetrated on the fictional Wales clan, including the killing of a son. A second parallel between the Wales and Ferguson stories concerns the question of surrender. In *Josey Wales,* Dave Pool rode into camp and announced, "All a feller has to do is ride in to the Union post, raise his right hand, and swear sich as he'll be loyal to the United States. Then . . . he kin taken up his hoss . . . and go home." As he watched his comrades shuffle off preparing to take the loyalty oath, Josey bade them farewell, stubbornly remaining a rebel.[30] Similarly, Ferguson was not allowed to turn over his arms nor take the oath of allegiance. In the movie, those men who fought with Wales were killed in the process of surrendering.[31]

Politically, the connection of Wales and Ferguson might be strongest. As a leader in the segregation fight in the South and a supposed descendant of a Confederate soldier who rode with John Hunt Morgan in Kentucky and Tennessee, Asa Carter likely knew and respected Ferguson's biographer, Thurman Sensing. A contemporary of Carter's in the fight against civil rights, Sensing was a leader in the Southern States Industrial Council where he opposed integration, public housing initiatives, and the expansion of the power of the federal government.[32] When taken together, Sensing's and Carter's politics agreed as much as their love of Civil War lore. Despite the absence of confirming evidence, the potential link between Thurman Sensing and Asa Carter cannot be dismissed.

Death is the point where one might naturally see life's legends subside, but upon Champ Ferguson's death, the legends blossomed, with his escape of fate as the central theme. In an 1886 issue of the *Nashville Banner,* a reporter "who knew and loved Champ Ferguson" revealed a mysterious story told to him by "a man from the mountains, who positively affirms that the hanging of Champ Ferguson was all a hoax." In the tale, another condemned man was substituted for the guerrilla and Ferguson was freed and sent to Canada where his wife and daughter later joined him. The reporter placed the cost of such a hoax at $15,000, which Ferguson paid to save his life.[33]

This bizarre story even made the reporter suspicious. He searched several months trying but failing to find someone to corroborate it. As for the possibility of Ferguson having $15,000 with which to purchase his life, the journalist was also doubtful. Ferguson had lost his prewar wealth because of the conflict, and what money he did accumulate during the war would have been in worthless Confederate currency. There is the possibility that sympathetic citizens could have quietly hoarded the cash, but Middle Tennessee's economy in the immediate postwar period was suffering mightily. The tale of Ferguson reuniting with his family in Canada only serves to reinforce the patent falsehood of the claim. As the reporter himself thought, the hoax was not perpetuated by the government, but by a free-talking visitor to Nashville.

Stories continued to develop even into the twentieth century. A 1909 article in the Fentress County *Gazette* claimed that Champ Ferguson was alive and well. The paper's correspondent, G. A. Smith, claimed to have spoken with Henry Deeds, a White County man who had helped bury the Confederate guerrilla in late 1865. Deeds was convinced that there was no body in the coffin. Clementine Dowdy, a member of the formerly unionist Dowdy family, provided Smith with more evidence. Alleging that he took Ms. Dowdy to the insane asylum near Knoxville where she met the institution's superintendent, Dowdy supposedly found the man to look much like Ferguson and blurted out, "I know you, Champ Ferguson! My father helped make a doll and hung it in your stead, and saved your life!" Smith's final fragment of evidence was his introduction to a man in Oklahoma, T. C. Ferguson, who claimed to be Ferguson's son.[34]

In December 1909, Smith returned with further evidence of Champ Ferguson's continued survival. In his letter, he presented more of his correspondence with T. C. Ferguson. The son told Smith that since childhood his parents had taught him that his father had been hanged in Nashville shortly after the war. Smith revealed that Ferguson was living in Hazlehurst, Mississippi, but readers should not intrude on his privacy because "if Champ Ferguson of [the] civil war [sic] is really at Hazlehurst, and if a man was to go to nosing around there about the matter, he would be in safer business trying to kill a grizzly bear with a pea shooter."[35]

In 1942, Ferguson's ghost reappeared with the publication of a newspaper article. A woman from Cookeville, Tennessee, told the story of a supposed rescue attempt on the eve of Ferguson's hanging. She recalled, "Fifty ragged, war weary men procured the best horses available, and heavily armed, started on the perilous trip." Traveling at night in small groups, they met outside of the city of Nashville. They sent one man into the city to scout the area and confirm the location of Ferguson's cell, the number of guards, and the general state of security, but when the scout returned to the group after dark, he carried with him the news that Ferguson had been hanged that day, one day before the scheduled execution.[36] Despite the apparent logic of the story, the execution date did not change from the original schedule of October 20.

One of the more recent stories appears in the afterword of the 1995 reprint of *Champ Ferguson: Confederate Guerrilla.* Thurman Sensing, Jr., relayed a story he had read in an unspecified Cookeville, Tennessee, newspaper. The conspiracy theory held that military officials sympathized with Ferguson, despite the wishes of Commander in Chief and President Andrew Johnson. Believing that Ferguson had done no worse than many others who escaped prosecution, the story goes, the Federals in Nashville began constructing a scaffold that would allow Ferguson's getaway. With the underside of the scaffold enclosed and ringed by soldiers in formation, Ferguson fell through the trap door and had help untying the knot. Lying down in the casket, he was carried out to the waiting wagon and turned over to his wife and daughter. Outside of the city, he exited the casket and left Tennessee for a new life and a new name in Oklahoma with his wife and daughter.[37] Again, this type of story makes for interesting reading but is demonstrably false, considering that Martha and Ann returned home to White County, Tennessee.

Back in White County, young Ann married George T. Metcalfe. A well-to-do farmer, particularly in the aftermath of the Civil War, Metcalfe was quite a catch. The 1870 census recorded George as a twenty-five-year-old farmer who owned $1,500 in real estate and another $500 in personal wealth. In addition to land and cash, the young Metcalfes employed a housekeeper and a farm laborer. Most interestingly, they had a forty-three-year-old housekeeper living with them named Martha Bohannan.[38] Although no firm evidence exists as to the mysterious woman's true identity, the first name, one-year age difference, and residence with the family suggests that she was Ann's mother, the former Martha Ferguson. If true, her new surname presents several possibilities. It is possible that Martha remarried a man named Bohannon, but no affirming documentation has been found. More likely, Martha found that being Champ Ferguson's widow, even in a pro-Confederate area like White County, Tennessee, was difficult. Possibly hoping to blend into society in Reconstruction-era Tennessee, Martha may have adopted the new last name in an attempt to obscure her past, particularly since she might have played a more active role in some of Champ's endeavors than documented.

In 1871, the family moved to Kansas, where Martha would live out her days. She remained in her daughter's household at Louisburg Township, in Montgomery County. While in Kansas, George became an auctioneer and then a businessman, and Ann gave birth to a total of eight children. In the early 1890s, Martha suffered a stroke that left her paralyzed to the point that she could no longer attend church. In October 1901, she was stricken with a second stroke that resulted in her death. She died on November 10, 1901, the seventy-five-year-old widow of one of the Civil War's most notorious figures.[39]

To be sure, Champ Ferguson was a polarizing character in both life and death. Perhaps the best example of the varying interpretations of his legacy can be seen at the two geographic bookends of his existence. Standing on the courthouse square in Albany, Kentucky, not far from Ferguson's birthplace, is a state historical marker, erected in 1964:

CIVIL WAR TERRORIST

Champ Ferguson born here in 1821. Guerrilla leader with Confederate leaning, but attacked supporters of both sides thruout Civil War in southern Ky., Tenn. Over 100 murders ascribed to Ferguson alone. Hunted by both CSA and USA. Taken after end of war, convicted by US Army Court, Nashville, and hanged Oct. 20, 1865. Buried at home in White County, Tennessee.

Sixty miles south of Albany, along Tennessee Highway 84, lies the small but distinguished France Cemetery and, within it, Champ Ferguson's remains. Standing above the unique comb graves and Gothic headstones is a lone historical marker placed there by the Sons of Confederate Veterans.[40] Just as Albany, Kentucky, earned its unionist reputation during the war, White County, Tennessee, exemplified Confederate patriotism, with both places still maintaining some of their respective traditions. Almost as if in response to the sign near Ferguson's birthplace, the one unveiled in 1975 at his final resting place reads:

CAP'T CHAMP FERGUSON
(Confederate Guerilla)

Gen'l Morgan's Cavalry was joined at Sparta, June 1862, by Champ Ferguson, as guide for Morgan's invasion into Kentucky.
Cap't Ferguson, and his co-fighters, were the only protection the people of

the Cumberland and Hickory Valley area had against the Federal guerillas during the Civil War.

Ferguson was hanged by the Federals, in Nashville, but by his request, buried here in White County.

The historian's jaundiced eye falls on the misconceptions and interpretive errors presented on each of the large, heavy, and impersonal metal plates, but, as wisdom teaches us, the real story—the real truth—probably lies somewhere in between. Maybe the truth lies at the site of the old jail in Jamestown, about thirty miles north of the cemetery and an equal distance south of the birthplace, where Champ Ferguson was held for the killing of a constable, met and befriended by his lawyer and later commander Scott Bledsoe, and unknowingly started on his violent journey to the gallows in Nashville.

NOTES

INTRODUCTION

1. In comparison, the famous Confederate cavalryman Nathan Bedford Forrest claimed to have killed thirty men during the war. See Brian Steel Wills, *A Battle from the Start: The Life of Nathan Bedford Forrest* (New York: HarperPerennial, 1992), 1–2.

2. Ferguson always denied killing twelve black soldiers in the aftermath of the Battle of Saltville in early October 1864.

3. *Nashville Dispatch,* October 22, 1865.

4. Clyde C. Walton, ed., *Private Smith's Journal: Recollections of the Late War* (Chicago: R. R. Donnelley and Sons, 1963), 228.

5. Abraham Lincoln to Charles D. Drake and Others, October 5, 1863, *Abraham Lincoln: Speeches and Writings, 1859–1865* (New York: Library of America, 1989), 523.

6. J. D. Hale, *The Bloody Shirt* (Unknown, 1888), 3.

7. Unfortunately, my contention that Ferguson's worldview was shaped in part by his understanding of religion was misunderstood by another biographer. As a result, Thomas D. Mays built a straw man of Ferguson as a committed Christian and erroneously attributed it to my earlier work. See Thomas D. Mays, *Cumberland Blood: Champ Ferguson's Civil War* (Carbondale: Southern Illinois University Press, 2008), 10.

8. Hale, *The Bloody Shirt*; J. D. Hale, *Champ Furguson: The Border Rebel, and Thief, Robber, and Murderer* (Cincinnati, OH: Privately printed, 1864); J. D. Hale, *Champ Furguson: A Sketch of the War in East Tennessee Detailing Some of the Leading Spirits of the Rebellion* (Cincinnati, OH: Privately printed, 1862); and J. D. Hale, *Sketches of Scenes in the Career of Champ Ferguson and His Lieutenant* (Unknown, 1870).

9. J. A. Brents, *The Patriots and Guerillas of East Tennessee and Kentucky* (New York: J. A. Brents, 1863; reprint, Danville, KY: Kentucky Jayhawker Press, 2001).

10. Thurman Sensing, *Champ Ferguson: Confederate Guerilla* (Nashville: Vanderbilt University Press, 1942). Sensing's treatment is generally sympathetic to Ferguson and somewhat incomplete because of its dependence on newspaper coverage. Many of its weaknesses can be traced to its age and the changes in interpretation that have taken place during the intervening more than six decades.

11. Mays, *Cumberland Blood,* 7–10, 149. Mays's work on Ferguson also spans several other tangential and direct treatments including Thomas Davidson Mays, "Cumberland Blood: Champ Ferguson's Civil War" (Ph.D. diss., Texas Christian University, 1996); and Thomas D. Mays, *The*

Saltville Massacre (Abilene, TX: McWhiney Foundation Press, 1998). The dissertation "Cumberland Blood" provided readers with the first modern narrative of Ferguson's story, but with only two hundred pages of text and a surprisingly brief bibliography of three pages, it added little in the way of interpretation or historiography. *The Saltville Massacre* suffers from a complete absence of citation, an issue pointed out by William Marvel in the last paragraph of William Marvel to Dear Mr. Brown, August 21, 2000, online at http://mywebpages.comcast.net/5thuscc/marvelresponse.htm. Thankfully, Mays's recent book seeks to rectify one of the aforementioned weaknesses by providing citations and a bibliography.

12. "Irregular Warfare, 1861–1865," *North & South*, vol. 11, no. 3 (June 2009): 22. Virtually all books on the Appalachian Civil War preach the significance of localized warfare. The following titles offer more expansive and nuanced discussions of this phenomenon than that presented by Mays in his introduction: Victoria E. Bynum, *The Free State of Jones: Mississippi's Longest Civil War* (Chapel Hill: University of North Carolina Press, 2001); Noel C. Fisher, *War at Every Door: Partisan Politics and Guerrilla Violence in East Tennessee, 1860–1869* (Chapel Hill: University of North Carolina Press, 1997); Barton A. Myers, *Executing Daniel Bright: Race, Loyalty, and Guerrilla Violence in a Coastal Carolina Community, 1861–1865* (Baton Rouge: Louisiana State University Press, 2009); and Jonathan Dean Sarris, *A Separate Civil War: Communities in Conflict in the Mountain South* (Charlottesville: University of Virginia Press, 2007).

13. Nicholas Stayton Miles, "I Do Not Want to Be Buried in Such Soil as This: The Life and Times of Confederate Guerrilla Champ Ferguson" (M.A. thesis, University of Kentucky, 2005).

14. Mark Grimsley, *The Hard Hand of War: Union Military Policy Toward Southern Civilians, 1861–1865* (Cambridge, UK: Cambridge University Press, 1995); Clay Mountcastle, *Punitive War: Confederate Guerrillas and Union Reprisals* (Lawrence: University of Kansas Press, 2009); and David Williams, *A People's History of the Civil War: Struggles for the Meaning of Freedom* (New York: New Press, 2005).

15. Robert R. Mackey, *The Uncivil War: Irregular Warfare in the Upper South, 1861–1865* (Norman: University of Oklahoma Press, 2004). The comments concerning Mackey's attempts to clarify the categories of irregular participation should not be taken as condemnation of his work. It is the opinion of this author that when dealing with men of Ferguson's ilk, official military and legal definitions obscure much more than they clarify. Mackey, who is an army officer trained in the more strategic and tactical elements of military history, seems more accurate in his characterizations the closer those parties are to official service; however, the closer to criminal gangs, the less certain his conclusions appear.

16. Daniel E. Sutherland, *A Savage Conflict: The Decisive Role of Guerrillas in the American Civil War* (Chapel Hill: University of North Carolina Press, 2009), xi–xii.

17. Michael Fellman, *Inside War: The Guerrilla Conflict in Missouri During the American Civil War* (New York: Oxford University Press, 1989); Thomas Goodrich, *Black Flag: Guerrilla Warfare on the Western Border, 1861–1865* (Bloomington: Indiana University Press, 1995); Kirby Ross, ed., *Autobiography of Samuel S. Hildebrand* (Fayetteville: University of Arkansas Press, 2005); Albert Castel and Tom Goodrich, *Bloody Bill Anderson: The Short, Savage Life of a Civil War Guerrilla* (Lawrence: University of Kansas Press, 1998); Albert Castel, *William Clarke Quantrill: His Life and Times* (Columbus, OH: The General's Books, 1992); and T. J. Stiles, *Jesse James: Last Rebel of the Civil War* (New York: Knopf, 2002).

18. Adam Rankin Johnson, *The Partisan Rangers of the Confederate States Army* (Austin, TX: State House Press, 1995); Phillip Shaw Paludan, *Victims: A True Story of the Civil War* (Knoxville: University of Tennessee Press, 1981); John Sickles, *The Legends of Sue Mundy and*

One Armed Berry: Confederate Guerrillas in Kentucky (Merrillville, IN: Heritage Press, 1999); Virgil Carrington Jones, *Gray Ghosts and Rebel Raiders: The Daring Exploits of the Confederate Guerillas* (New York: Galahad Books, 1956); Richard R. Duncan, *Beleaguered Winchester: A Virginia Community at War, 1861–1865* (Baton Rouge: Louisiana State University Press, 2007); Brian Steel Wills, *The War Hits Home: The Civil War in Southeastern Virginia* (Charlottesville: University Press of Virginia, 2001); and Brian D. McKnight, *Contested Borderland: The Civil War in Appalachian Kentucky and Virginia* (Lexington: University Press of Kentucky, 2006).

19. Myers, *Executing Daniel Bright.*

20. Daniel S. Sutherland, ed., *Guerrillas, Unionists, and Violence on the Confederate Home Front* (Fayetteville: University of Arkansas Press, 1999); Kenneth W. Noe and Shannon H. Wilson, eds., *The Civil War in Appalachia* (Knoxville: University of Tennessee Press, 1997); and John C. Inscoe and Robert C. Kenzer, eds., *Enemies of the Country: New Perspectives on Unionists in the Civil War South* (Athens: University of Georgia Press, 2001).

21. Patsy (Keel) Boggs, September 28, 1941, in Elihu Jasper Sutherland, ed., *Pioneer Recollections of Southwest Virginia* (Clintwood, VA: H. S. Sutherland, 1984), 38.

22. Newton Sutherland Reminiscence, December 27, 1924, in Sutherland, *Pioneer Recollections,* 393; and George W. Fleming Reminiscence, July 17, 1937, in Sutherland, *Pioneer Recollections,* 141.

23. L. Thomas to Hon. Simon Cameron, September 23, 1861, *Official Records,* IV, 269; and John F. Marszalek, *Sherman: A Soldier's Passion for Order* (New York: Free Press, 1993), 159.

24. Esther Ann Frogg Testimony, August 2, 1865, Proceedings of the Trial of Champ Ferguson, RG 153, Records of the Office of the Judge Advocate General (Army), 1792–1981, Court Martial Case Files, Textual Archives Services Division, National Archives and Records Administration, Washington, D.C., hereinafter cited as NARA-Trial; and Isaac T. Reneau to Gov. A. Johnson, March 31, 1861, Military Governor Andrew Johnson Papers, 1862–1865, Manuscripts and Archives Section, Tennessee State Library and Archives, Nashville, Tennessee, hereinafter cited as TSLA-Johnson.

25. J. M. McCrary to Dear Mollie, January 25, 1863, John M. McCrary Papers, Atlanta History Center, Atlanta, GA, hereinafter cited as AHC-McCrary.

26. *Abingdon Virginian,* March 18, 1864.

27. Mays, *Cumberland Blood,* 14. Mays refers to Fisher, *War at Every Door,* and Kenneth W. Noe, "Who Were the Bushwhackers? Age, Class, Kin, and Western Virginia's Confederate Guerrillas, 1861–1862," *Civil War History* 49: 1 (2003): 5–31.

28. T. H. Breen, *Tobacco Culture: The Mentality of the Great Tidewater Planters on the Eve of Revolution* (Princeton, NJ: Princeton University Press, 1985); Altina L. Waller, *Feud: Hatfields, McCoys, and Social Change in Appalachia, 1860–1900* (Chapel Hill: University of North Carolina Press, 1988); and Pete Daniel, *Lost Revolutions: The South in the 1950s* (Chapel Hill: University of North Carolina Press for the Smithsonian National Museum of American History, 2000).

1. THE "NATURAL MAN"

1. Although most sources note Ferguson's place of birth as two miles outside of Albany in Clinton County, Kentucky, that county was not formed at the time of his birth. Prior to February 1835, Cumberland and Wayne counties shared the area that would become Clinton County.

2. *Nashville Dispatch,* August 19, 1865. Zilpha's name is phonetically spelled *Zilphy* in the 1850 census.

3. J. D. Hale, *Champ Furguson: The Border Rebel,* 3. It will be noticed that the spelling of Ferguson varies in the primary sources. Assuming *Ferguson* is correct, as it was noted in census records, even his tombstone is misspelled. Additionally, in many cases, the name *Champ* has been erroneously extended to the more formal *Champion* and he has even been mistakenly identified as Samuel Ferguson.

4. *Nashville Dispatch,* August 19, 1865. Although it is possible that Champ Ferguson's given name was *Champion,* as is sometimes recorded, censuses and other official records use *Champ.*

5. For further analysis of the family dynamic of farm life, see John Mack Faragher, *Sugar Creek: Life on the Illinois Prairie* (New Haven: Yale University Press, 1986), 96–109, and Stephanie McCurry, *Masters of Small Worlds: Yeoman Households, Gender Relations, and the Political Culture of the Antebellum South Carolina Low Country* (New York: Oxford University Press, 1995), 59–60.

6. Lewis Collins, *History of Kentucky* (Cincinnati, OH: Lewis Collins, J. A. James, and U. P. James, 1847), 246–47; and Robert M. Rennick, *Kentucky Place Names* (Lexington: University Press of Kentucky, 1984), 3, 61–62.

7. Collins, *History of Kentucky,* 246–47; and Rennick, *Kentucky Place Names,* 267–68.

8. *Nashville Dispatch,* August 19, 1865; and Bill Cecil-Fronsman, *Common Whites: Class and Culture in Antebellum North Carolina* (Lexington: University Press of Kentucky, 1992), 38.

9. Thomas D. Clark, *A History of Kentucky* (New York: Prentice-Hall, 1937), 303–33.

10. *Nashville Dispatch,* August 19, 1865.

11. Ibid.; 1850 Census, Clinton County, Kentucky; and 1860 Census, Clinton County, Kentucky.

12. Collins, *History of Kentucky,* 110; and Mark A. Noll, *A History of Christianity in the United States and Canada* (Grand Rapids, MI: Eerdmans, 1992), 178–81.

13. For more on the political reorganizations during this contentious era, see William J. Cooper, Jr., *Liberty and Slavery: Southern Politics to 1860* (New York: Knopf, 1983), 249–85; Arthur Charles Cole, *The Whig Party in the South* (Gloucester, MA: Peter Smith, 1962), 309–343; Michael F. Holt, *The Rise and Fall of the American Whig Party: Jacksonian Politics and the Onset of the Civil War* (New York: Oxford University Press, 1999), 836–985; and William E. Gienapp, *The Origins of the Republican Party, 1852–1856* (New York: Oxford University Press, 1987), 37–68.

14. J. A. Brents, *The Patriots and Guerillas of East Tennessee and Kentucky* (Danville: Kentucky Jayhawker Press, 2001), 28.

15. In 1840, Ferguson's father would have been forty years old, his brother Benjamin seventeen, and brother James fifteen.

16. 1840 Census. Population Schedule. Clinton County, Kentucky.

17. Brents, *Patriots and Guerillas,* 20.

18. Sutherland, *A Savage Conflict,* 10–11, 28; Mays, *Cumberland Blood,* 7–10.

19. Maude Z. McGlasson, ed., *Jackson County, Tennessee, Bible and Family Records* (Unknown, 1938), 62, handwritten notations; Bill Cecil-Fronsman, *Common Whites: Class and Culture in Antebellum North Carolina* (Lexington: University Press of Kentucky, 1992), 150–51; and *Nashville Dispatch,* August 19, 1865. Unfortunately, no census information on Ann Eliza Smith has been located, suggesting that she moved into the Clinton County area between 1840 and 1844.

20. *Nashville Dispatch,* August 19, 1865; Tombstone of Capt. C. Furguson, French Cemetery, White County, Tennessee; 1850 Census, Population Schedule, Clinton County, Kentucky, and 1900 Census, Population Schedule, Montgomery County, Kansas.

21. 1850 Census, Population Schedule, Clinton County, Kentucky.

22. For further examination of farm inheritance, see Steven Hahn and Jonathan Prude, eds., *The Countryside in the Age of Capitalist Transformation: Essays in the Social History of Rural America* (Chapel Hill: University of North Carolina Press, 1985), 276–77, 332–35. As the Hahn and Prude essays illustrate, inheritance rules often varied by culture, locality, and even family. In Champ Ferguson's case, his status as oldest son was the determining factor. See also, Cecil-Fronsman, *Common Whites,* 140, 150–52; Steven Hahn, *The Roots of Southern Populism: Yeoman Farmers and the Transformation of the Georgia Upcountry, 1850–1890* (New York: Oxford University Press, 1983), 77–84; and Willard Rouse Jillson, *The Kentucky Land Grants* (Baltimore: Genealogical Publishing, 1971), 1244. The 1850 census was recorded prior to William Ferguson's death and lists Zilphy, 48, female; Jemima A., 21, female; William, 17, male; Sarah, 14, female; Elizabeth, 12, female; Mary, 9, female; and Margarett, 5, female, as members of the William R. Ferguson household.

23. General census data taken from The United States Historical Census Data Browser at http://fisher.lib.virginia.edu/census/.

24. Mays, *Cumberland Blood,* 13; 1850 Census, Population Schedule, Clinton County, Kentucky; and 1860 Census, Population Schedule, Clinton County, Kentucky.

25. http://fisher.lib.virginia.edu/census/.

26. Mary Jean DeLozier, "The Civil War and Its Aftermath in Putnam County," *Tennessee Historical Quarterly* 38 (1979): 438.

27. Mays, *Cumberland Blood,* 14.

28. 1850 Census. Population Schedule. Clinton County, Kentucky.

29. Mays, *Cumberland Blood,* 15.

30. Brents, *Patriots and Guerillas,* 21.

31. Hale, *Champ Furguson, the Border Rebel,* 3; Brents, *Patriots and Guerillas,* 20; and Grady McWhiney, *Cracker Culture: Celtic Ways in the Old South* (Tuscaloosa: University of Alabama Press, 1988), 106–108.

32. Brents, *Patriots and Guerillas,* 20.

33. The date can only be estimated based on the fact that the Clinton County, Kentucky, court dismissed Ferguson's case against the Evans brothers in early July 1858.

34. *Nashville Dispatch,* August 19, 1865.

35. Ibid.; and Brents, *Patriots and Guerillas,* 21.

36. Ibid.

37. For more on the social aspect of the camp meeting see Thomas D. Clark, *Agrarian Kentucky,* The Kentucky Bicentennial Bookshelf (Lexington: University Press of Kentucky, 1977), 68–70; and John B. Boles, *The Great Revival, 1787–1805* (Lexington: University Press of Kentucky, 1972), 83–95.

38. Hale, *Champ Furguson, the Border Rebel* 3–4. Hale claimed that the meeting in question took place in the fall of 1857. That estimation is incorrect since at that time, Ferguson was still pursuing legal means to recoup his losses. The warrant for his arrest that the Evanses swore out came as a result of his taking their stock in satisfaction of the debt and followed his filing suit against them in Overton County, Tennessee, probably in late 1857. Rev. A. B. Wright, *Autobi-*

ography of Rev. A. B. Wright (Cincinnati, OH: Cranston and Curts, 1896), 37, places the date in August 1858.

39. *Nashville Dispatch,* August 19, 1865.

40. Ibid.

41. Hale, *Champ Furguson, the Border Rebel* 4.

42. Brents, *Patriots and Guerillas,* 22.

43. *Nashville Dispatch,* August 19, 1865.

44. Ibid.; and Brents, *Patriots and Guerillas,* 22.

45. *Nashville Dispatch,* August 19, 1865.

46. "The Man Who Once Did Sell the Lion's Skin While the Beast Lived, was Killed While Hunting Him," Number Two, 9, HSCC-Hale.

47. *Nashville Dispatch,* August 19, 1865.

48. Brents, *Patriots and Guerillas,* 22.

49. Albert R. Hogue, *Mark Twain's Obedstown and Knobs of Tennessee: A History of Jamestown and Fentress County, Tennessee* (Jamestown, TN: Cumberland Print Company, 1950), 58; and Mays, "Cumberland Blood," 23.

50. Hale, *Champ Furguson, the Border Rebel* 4; Brents, *Patriots and Guerillas,* 22; *Nashville Daily Press and Times* (TN), July 13, 1865; 1870 Census. Population Schedule. Johnson County, Texas; and Donna Brand, *Cleburne Memorial Cemetery of Johnson County, Texas* (Joshua, TX: The Author, 1999), 131.

51. Brents, *Patriots and Guerillas,* 22.

52. *Nashville Daily Press and Times,* July 13, 1865; and *Nashville Dispatch,* August 19, 1865. The theory that Ferguson escaped prosecution by joining the Confederate army can also found in the arguments of Brents and Hale.

53. Albert R. Hogue, *History of Fentress County, Tennessee* (Baltimore: Regional, 1975), 35.

54. Hale, *Champ Furguson, the Border Rebel* 4; and *Nashville Dispatch,* August 19, 1865.

55. Circuit Court Office Minutes, Fentress County, Tennessee, vol. A, June 1854–July 1866, Fentress County Public Library, Jamestown, Tennessee, 449–54, hereinafter cited as FCPL-CCOM.

56. Like the famous case, *Dred Scott v. Sandford,* a court also misspelled Ferguson's name. Although the court, like many others, assumed his proper name to be Champion, no evidence supports this conclusion.

57. Circuit Court Office Minutes, Fentress County, Tennessee, vol. A, June 1854–July 1866, FCPL-CCOM.

2. EXILED TO TENNESSEE

1. David M. Potter, *The Impending Crisis, 1848–1861,* ed. Don E. Fehrenbacher (New York: Harper and Row, 1976), 407–415; and James M. McPherson, *Battle Cry of Freedom: The Civil War Era* (New York: Oxford University Press, 1988), 214.

2. Ibid., 413; and William C. Davis, *Breckinridge: Statesman, Soldier, Symbol* (Baton Rouge: Louisiana State University Press, 1974), 223–25.

3. Potter, *The Impending Crisis,* 416–17.

4. Ibid., 418–29; David Herbert Donald, *Lincoln* (London, UK: Jonathan Cape, 1995), 246–

51; and James McPherson, *Ordeal by Fire: The Civil War and Reconstruction,* 3d ed. (Boston: McGraw-Hill, 1982), 131-32.

5. McPherson, *Ordeal by Fire,* 138.

6. E. Merton Coulter, *The Civil War and Readjustment in Kentucky* (Gloucester, MA: Peter Smith, 1966), 24.

7. Dwight Lowell Dumond, *The Secession Movement, 1860-1861* (New York: Octagon, 1963), 189-212.

8. Michael T. Dues, "The Pro-Secessionist Governor of Kentucky: Beriah Magoffin's Credibility Gap," *Register of the Kentucky Historical Society* 67 (1969): 221; Wallace B. Turner, "The Secession Movement in Kentucky," *Register of the Kentucky Historical Society* 66 (1968): 267; Coulter, *Civil War and Readjustment in Kentucky,* 38; Lowell H. Harrison, "Governor Magoffin and the Secession Crisis," *Register of the Kentucky Historical Society* 72 (1974): 106-107.

9. *Journal of the Senate of the Commonwealth of Kentucky,* May 2, 1861, quoted in Dues, "The Pro-Secessionist Governor of Kentucky," 221; Turner, "The Secession Movement in Kentucky," 267; Coulter, *Civil War and Readjustment in Kentucky,* 38; Harrison, "Governor Magoffin and the Secession Crisis," 105-107; and James M. Pritchard, "Champion of the Union: George D. Prentice and the Secession Crisis in Kentucky," *Cincinnati Historical Society Bulletin* 39 (1981): 123.

10. Coulter, *Civil War and Readjustment in Kentucky,* 142-44; and John E. Kleber, ed., *The Kentucky Encyclopedia* (Lexington: University Press of Kentucky, 1992), 108.

11. DeLozier, "The Civil War and Its Aftermath in Putnam County," 436-37, 441-42.

12. Lela McDowell Blankenship, ed., *Fiddles in the Cumberlands* (New York: Richard R. Smith, 1943), 47.

13. "Continued Lifting of the Masks," Number Four, 5, 6, J. D. Hale Papers, Wright Room Research Library, Historical Society of Cheshire County, Keene, New Hampshire, hereinafter cited as HSCC-Hale.

14. J D Hale to Dear Sir [Horace Maynard], June 25, 1864, Series I, General Correspondence, 1833-1916, Abraham Lincoln Papers, Library of Congress, Washington, D.C., hereinafter cited as LC-Lincoln.

15. *Nashville Union and American,* June 25, 1861, Mary Jean DeLozier, "The Civil War and Its Aftermath in Putnam County," 436-37, 441-42; Robert L. Mason, *Cannon County* (Memphis, TN: Memphis State University Press, 1982), 49-50; Robert L. Eldridge and Mary Eldridge, *Bicentennial Echoes of the History of Overton County, Tennessee, 1776-1976* (Livingston, TN: Enterprise, 1976), 50-51; and Tim Huddleston, *History of Pickett County, Tennessee* (Collegedale, TN: College Press, 1973), 26-27.

16. Carroll Van West, *The Tennessee Encyclopedia of History and Culture* (Nashville: Rutledge Hill Press, 1998), 831.

17. *New York Times,* May 4, 1986.

18. DeLozier, "The Civil War and Its Aftermath in Putnam County," 443-44.

19. Gladys Inez Williams, "The Life of Horace Maynard" (M.A. thesis, University of Tennessee, 1931), 24-25. See also Thomas B. Alexander, *Thomas A. R. Nelson of East Tennessee* (Nashville: Tennessee Historical Commission, 1956), 79.

20. Albert W. Schroeder, Jr., "Writings of a Tennessee Unionist," *Tennessee Historical Quarterly* 9 (September 1950): 246-47.

21. Ibid., 246.

22. Blankenship, *Fiddles in the Cumberlands,* 49-50.

23. Hale, *Bloody Shirt,* 22.

24. McKnight, *Contested Borderland,* 122–23.

25. "No Sir, I Can't Tell You, But I Can Go and Show You," Number Nine, HSCC-Hale.

26. "Continued Lifting of Masks," Number Four, 7, HSCC-Hale; and History Committee of the Stoddard Historical Society, *The History of the Town of Stoddard, New Hampshire* (Stoddard, NH: N. P., 1974), 309–10.

27. "No Sir, I Can't Tell You, But I Can Go and Show You," Number Nine, HSCC-Hale.

28. Tho. E. Bramblette to Mrs. F. Hale, July 12, 1861, HSCC-Hale.

29. John C. Smith to Dear bro. Reneau, August 23, 1861, Papers of Isaac Tipton Reneau, Special Collections, Bosworth Memorial Library, Lexington Theological Seminary, Lexington, Kentucky, hereinafter cited as LTS-Reneau.

30. C. B. Ryan to Hon Andrew Johnson, July 9, 1861, Leroy P. Graf and Ralph W. Haskins, eds., *The Papers of Andrew Johnson,* vol. 4, *1860–1861* (Knoxville: University of Tennessee Press, 1976), 553–54.

31. George W. Keith to Hon Andrew Johnson Sen. Tennessee, July 12, 1861, Graf and Haskins, eds., *The Papers of Andrew Johnson,* 560–61.

32. Benjamin T. Staples to Hon Andrew Johnson, August 16, 1861, Graf and Haskins, eds., *The Papers of Andrew Johnson,* 681–82.

33. Hambleton Tapp and James C. Klotter, eds., *The Union, the Civil War, and John W. Tuttle: A Kentucky Captain's Account* (Frankfort: Kentucky Historical Society, 1980), 22.

34. Ibid., 1–2.

35. G. Glenn Clift, *Governors of Kentucky, 1792–1942* (Cynthiana, KY: Hobson Press, 1942), 77–79; Lowell H. Harrison, ed., *Kentucky's Governors, 1792–1985* (Lexington: University Press of Kentucky, 1985), 77–81; David S. Heidler and Jeanne T. Heidler, eds., *Encyclopedia of the American Civil War: A Political, Social, and Military History* (Santa Barbara, CA: ABC-CLIO, 2000), 269–70; and Kleber, ed., *Kentucky Encyclopedia,* 112–13.

36. Tapp and Klotter, *John W. Tuttle,* 22–23.

37. *Nashville Union,* October 21, 1865.

38. *Nashville Dispatch,* October 21, 1865.

39. *Nashville Daily Press,* September 19, 1865.

40. Tapp and Klotter, *John W. Tuttle,* 23; Thomas D. Mays's doctoral dissertation, "Cumberland Blood," alleges in footnote 25 of chapter 2 that "Captain John W. Tuttle recorded 2 July 1861 in his diary that 'Snowden Worhsam went out alone to meet Champ Ferguson's Bushwhackers and dispersed them. Noted for bravery.'" However, no such quote can be found in the cited source.

41. James E. Copeland, "Where Were the Kentucky Unionists and Secessionists?" *Register of the Kentucky Historical Society* 71 (1973), 350, 358–59.

42. Ibid., 357.

43. Ibid., 353–54, 362.

44. Ibid., 354–55, 363.

45. Ferguson exhibited some inconsistency in regard to his early loyalties. He claimed to have been a "Union man in the beginning" in interviews for the *Nashville Dispatch,* August 15, 1865, and the *Nashville Union,* October 21, 1865. However, in an interview with the *Nashville Dispatch,* October 21, 1865, he claimed that he "was a Southern man at the start."

46. *Nashville Daily Press,* September 19, 1865.

47. John C. Smith to Dear bro. Reneau, August 23, 1861, LTS-Reneau.

48. Brents, *Patriots and Guerillas,* 22.

49. *Nashville Daily Press,* September 19, 1865; Schroeder, "Writings of a Tennessee Unionist," 250; and R. R. Hancock, *Hancock's Diary: or, A History of the Second Tennessee Confederate Cavalry* (Nashville: Brandon, 1887), 36–37. Hancock's unit was encamped in the vicinity of Jamestown, Tennessee, and may have been the one frequented by Ferguson in the summer of 1861.

50. At the time of Ferguson's arrest, he was heading from the general direction of the Confederate camp, although it is not known if he had in fact been there. An alternate story exists, however, that the arresting group was moving southward into Tennessee for the purpose of impressing stock and captured Ferguson to keep him from informing the nearby Federals of their motives. Both stories are logical and collaborated, but neither emerges as more likely than the other.

51. Probably John Denton, who frequently rode with Ferguson during the war.

52. L. W. Duvall Testimony, August 7, 1865, NARA-Trial. A slightly, but not substantially, different version of the trial transcript is located in the Manuscripts and Folklife Archives, Kentucky Library and Museum, Western Kentucky University, Bowling Green, Kentucky; and Brents, *Patriots and Guerillas,* 23. Brents recorded the story of Ferguson's capture in a more deliberate tone. He wrote, "About the last of August four Union citizens planned his capture, and succeeded." In reality, it appears that the meeting between the two groups was chance and took both parties off guard.

53. L. W. Duvall Testimony, August 7, 1865, NARA-Trial; Brents, *Patriots and Guerillas,* 23; and Thomas D. Mays, "Cumberland Blood: Champ Ferguson's Civil War" (Ph.D. diss., Texas Christian University, 1996), 41. The events surrounding Ferguson's arrest and subsequent escape have always been shrouded in confusion. Mays offers that Ferguson's captors had two options: to turn him over to Confederate authorities to face justice on his murder indictment, or to send him to Federal authorities at Camp Dick Robinson. It is unrealistic to expect that these obviously unionist men would do anything other than seek justice for Ferguson from the United States military. Though Mays claims Ferguson "slipped off in the middle of the night as his captors dozed," no evidence supports this assertion.

54. Alvin C. Piles Testimony, July 26, 1865, NARA-Trial. In his dissertation, Mays reversed the sequence of Ferguson's arrest and the incident at the blacksmith's shop. Though he may be correct, it is more likely that Ferguson, who was lightly armed when arrested by the Duvalls, turned to arming himself heavily as a response to this recent threat on his freedom.

55. *Nashville Daily Press,* September 19, 1865. Ferguson's memory on the chronology cannot be fully trusted since he claimed that he joined Bledsoe in November 1862. He was certainly operating as part of Bledsoe's company by the end of the year 1861.

56. D. P. Wright Testimony, August 21, 1865, NARA-Trial; and Brents, *Patriots and Guerillas,* 18. Wright is misidentified on several occasions as D. P. and D. O. Wright. In fact, Jack Ferguson, in *Early Times in Clinton County* (Albany, KY: J. Ferguson, 2003), identifies him correctly as Daniel B. Wright.

57. *New York Times,* September 26, 1861.

58. Ferguson, *Early Times in Clinton County,* vol. 3, 37; Frederick H. Dyer, *A Compendium of the War of the Rebellion* (Des Moines, IA: Dyer, 1908), vol. 2, 595.

59. F. K. Zollicoffer to Lieutenant-Colonel Mackall, October 2, 1861, *Official Records,* IV, 200–201; and Ferguson, *Early Times in Clinton County,* vol. 3, 37.

60. Hoskins to Thomas, September 29, 1861, *Official Records,* IV, 203.

61. F. K. Zollicoffer to Lieutenant-Colonel Mackall, October 2, 1861, *The War of the Rebellion: A Compilation of the Official Records of the Union and Confederate Armies* (Washington, D.C.: Government Printing Office, 1880–1901), Ser. I, vol. IV, 200–201, hereinafter cited as *Official Records* (unless otherwise indicated, all citations are to Series I).

62. W. A. Hoskins to General George H. Thomas, September 29, 1861, *Official Records,* IV, 203.

63. Geo. H. Thomas to Capt. Oliver D. Greene, October 1, 1861, *Official Records,* IV, 203; Dyer, *Compendium,* vol. 2, 595; and E. B. Long, *The Civil War Day by Day: An Almanac, 1861–1865* (New York: Da Capo, 1971), 121.

64. Ferguson, *Early Times in Clinton County,* vol. 3, 38.

65. *Nashville Union,* October 21, 1865; and Brents, *Patriots and Guerillas,* 28; for a more in-depth examination of brother versus brother warfare, see chapter 3, Amy Murrell Taylor, *The Divided Family in Civil War America* (Chapel Hill: University of North Carolina Press, 2005). Unfortunately, Taylor's study avoids the Appalachian borderland where, perhaps, the most frequent and overtly violent familial divisions occurred.

66. John C. Inscoe and Gordon B. McKinney, "Highland Households Divided: Familial Deceptions, Diversions, and Divisions in Southern Appalachia's Inner Civil War," in John C. Inscoe, *Race, War, and Remembrance in the Appalachian South* (Lexington: University Press of Kentucky, 2008), 125.

67. Long, *The Civil War Day by Day,* 122.

68. Wright, *Autobiography,* 42. Inscription from tombstone of James M. Saulfey, Travisville Cemetery, Travisville, Tennessee. In the Adjutant General's Report, James Ferguson's enrollment is dated July 27, 1861. It notes that he was mustered into Federal service at Camp Dick Robinson on October 28, 1861, nearly a month after his first fight.

69. James W. McHenry to General A. Sidney Johnston, October 10, 1861, *Official Records,* IV, 442–43.

70. W. T. Gass to Brig. Gen. W. R. Caswell, October 14, 1861, *Official Records,* IV, 447–48.

71. Brents, *Patriots and Guerillas,* 28.

72. Ibid., 28–29.

73. Ibid., 29. Brents, an ardent unionist, may have been attempting to protect a fellow unionist's reputation when he wrote that "Beasly was the only citizen killed by [Jim] Ferguson, so far as my knowledge extends."

74. Wright, *Autobiography,* 44; Esther Ann Frogg Testimony, August 2, 1865, NARA-Trial; and Isaac T. Reneau to Gov. A. Johnson, March 31, 1861, Military Governor Andrew Johnson Papers, 1862–1865, Manuscripts and Archives Section, Tennessee State Library and Archives, Nashville, Tennessee, hereinafter cited as TSLA-Johnson.

75. A. J. Mace Testimony, August 2, 1865, NARA-Trial.

76. Esther Ann Frogg Testimony, August 2, 1865, NARA-Trial; and Brents, *Patriots and Guerillas,* 23.

77. Esther Ann Frogg Testimony, August 2, 1865, NARA-Trial.

78. *Daily Press and Times* (Nashville, TN), September 19, 1865; and *Nashville Union,* October 21, 1865.

79. *Nashville Dispatch,* October 21, 1865.

80. *Nashville Union,* October 21, 1865.

81. Ibid.

82. P. A. Hale testimony, August 12, 1865, NARA-Trial, and Thos. L. Wilson, *Sufferings Endured for a Free Government: A History of the Cruelties and Atrocities of the Rebellion* (Washington, D.C.: The Author, 1864), 110–11.

83. "The Man Who Once Did Sell the Lion's Skin," Number Two, 9, HSCC-Hale.

84. Miss Elizabeth Wood Testimony, August 4, 1865, NARA-Trial; Robert W. Wood Testimony, August 5, 1865, NARA-Trial; Hale, *Bloody Shirt*, 5; and Brents, *Patriots and Guerillas*, 23.

85. Wright, *Autobiography*, 44; Miss Elizabeth Wood Testimony, August 4, 1865, NARA-Trial; Robert W. Wood Testimony, August 5, 1865, NARA-Trial; and Isaac T. Reneau to Gov. A. Johnson, March 31, 1861, TSLA-Johnson.

86. Miss Elizabeth Wood Testimony, August 4, 1865, NARA-Trial; Robert W. Wood Testimony, August 5, 1865, NARA-Trial; and Wilson, *Sufferings Endured for a Free Government*, 111.

87. *Nashville Daily Press*, August 6, 1865.

88. Lucinda Hatfield statement, undated; and Rufus Dowdy statement, undated, J. D. Hale, *Sketches of Scenes*, 18–19.

89. *Nashville Dispatch*, October 21, 1865; and *Nashville Union*, October 21, 1865.

90. Robert Wood Testimony, August 5, 1865, NARA-Trial.

91. Mays, *Cumberland Blood*, 45.

3. FIGHT ON THE CUMBERLAND

1. Mark M. Boatner III, *The Civil War Dictionary* (New York: David McKay, 1959), 954; *Biographical Dictionary of the American Congresses, 1774–1989* (Washington, D.C.: Government Printing Office, 1989), 2104; Dumas Malone, ed., *Dictionary of American Biography*, vol. 20 (New York: Charles Scribner's Sons, 1936), 659–60; Heidler and Heidler, eds., *Encyclopedia of the American Civil War*, 2171–72; and Kenneth A. Hafendorfer, *Mill Springs: Campaign and Battle of Mill Springs, Kentucky* (Louisville, KY: KH Press, 2001), 23–24, 60–73. Hafendorfer erroneously placed Zollicoffer in the U.S. Senate.

2. Raymond E. Myers, *The Zollie Tree* (Louisville, KY: Filson Club Press, 1964), 61.

3. Brents, *Patriots and Guerillas*, 30; and Eastham Tarrant, *The Wild Riders of the First Kentucky Cavalry: A History of the Regiment, in the Great War of the Rebellion, 1861–1865* (Lexington: Henry Clay Press, 1969), 57.

4. Brents, *Patriots and Guerillas*, 31; and Mays, *Cumberland Blood*, 48.

5. Brents, *Patriots and Guerillas*, 33.

6. Ferguson, *Early Times in Clinton County*, vol. III, 83.

7. Myers, *The Zollie Tree*, 78.

8. Marion Johnson Testimony, August 8, 1865, NARA-Trial.

9. Preston Huff Testimony, July 24, 1865, NARA-Trial; and Marion Johnson Testimony, August 8, 1865, NARA-Trial. Johnson confused Preston and William Huff. He stated that William Huff was released by Zollicoffer's headquarters and then threatened by Champ Ferguson on the road, but Preston Huff later placed himself at the center of that altercation.

10. Cordell Hull, *The Memoirs of Cordell Hull*, vol. 1 (New York: Macmillan, 1948), 3–4; Harold B. Hinton, *Cordell Hull: A Biography* (Garden City, NY: Doubleday, Doran, 1942), 22; and Eldridge and Eldridge, *Bicentennial Echoes of the History of Overton County*, , 58.

11. Cordell Hull, *Memoirs*, vol. 1, 4.

12. Fisher, *War at Every Door*, 52–53, 122–23; Robert W. Winston, *Andrew Johnson: Plebeian and Patriot* (New York: Barnes and Noble, 1969), 217–19; Lately Thomas, *The First President Johnson: The Three Lives of the Seventeenth President of the United States of America* (New York: William Morrow, 1968), 215, 230; and Myers, *The Zollie Tree*, 64.

13. Kenneth W. Noe, *Southwest Virginia's Railroad: Modernization and the Sectional Crisis* (Urbana: University of Illinois Press, 1994), 112–13.

14. John F. Marszalek, *Sherman: A Soldier's Passion for Order* (New York: Free Press, 1993), 160–61; Boatner, *The Civil War Dictionary*, 15, 750–51; Frank J. Welcher, *The Union Army, 1861–1865*, vol. II, *The Western Theater* (Bloomington: Indiana University Press, 1993), 157–58; and Gerald J. Prokopowicz, *All for the Regiment: The Army of the Ohio, 1861–1862* (Chapel Hill: University of North Carolina Press, 2001), 66–67.

15. Marszalek, *Sherman*, 163; and Stephen D. Engle, *Don Carlos Buell: Most Promising of All* (Chapel Hill: University of North Carolina Press, 1999), 88.

16. Francis F. McKinney, *Education in Violence: The Life of George H. Thomas and the History of the Army of the Cumberland* (Detroit, MI: Wayne State University Press, 1961), 81.

17. Engle, *Don Carlos Buell*, 89, 142–44; Freeman Cleaves, *Rock of Chickamauga: The Life of General George H. Thomas* (Norman: University of Oklahoma Press, 1948), 94–95; McKinney, *Education in Violence*, 124–25; and Wilbur Thomas, *General George H. Thomas: The Indomitable Warrior* (New York: Exposition Press, 1964), 174.

18. John C. Duval, *The Adventures of Big-Foot Wallace* (Lincoln: University of Nebraska Press, 1966), 171–85; T. R. Fehrenbach, *Lone Star: A History of Texas and the Texans* (Toronto, Ontario, Canada: Macmillan, 1968), 478–80; and Sam W. Haynes, *Soldiers of Misfortune: The Somervell and Mier Expeditions* (Austin: University of Texas Press, 1990), 36–47.

19. Hafendorfer, *Mill Springs*, 132–33; Jefferson Davis, *The Rise and Fall of the Confederate Government*, vol. II (New York: D. Appleton, 1881), 19–20; Myers, *The Zollie Tree*, 78; C. David Dalton, "Zollicoffer, Crittenden, and the Mill Springs Campaign: Some Persistent Questions," *Filson Club History Quarterly* 60 (October 1986), 464–46; and Thomas Lawrence Connelly, *Army of the Heartland: The Army of Tennessee, 1861–1862* (Baton Rouge: Louisiana State University Press, 1967), 95. Although Hafendorfer contends that "the river had not risen. No measurable amount of rain had fallen in the region between the 26th of December and the 2nd of January," Crittenden, in his report dated two weeks after his arrival on the field (*O.R.* VII, 105), described the river as "(greatly swollen), with high muddy banks."

20. Frank A. Palumbo, *George Henry Thomas: The Dependable General* (Dayton, OH: Morningside House, 1983), 90–94; Myers, *The Zollie Tree*, 88–94; Engle, *Don Carlos Buell*, 142–43; Davis, *The Rise and Fall*, 20–21; and Larry J. Daniel, *Days of Glory: The Army of the Cumberland, 1861–1865* (Baton Rouge: Louisiana State University Press, 2004), 51.

21. Myers, *The Zollie Tree*, 95–97; Engle, *Don Carlos Buell*, 143–44; Davis, *The Rise and Fall*, 21; and Hafendorfer, *Mill Springs*, 287–90.

22. Engle, *Don Carlos Buell*, 144–45; Davis, *The Rise and Fall*, 20–23; Palumbo, *George Henry Thomas*, 90–94; Richard J. Reid, *The Rock Riseth: George H. Thomas at Logan's Crossroads* (Central City: Western Kentucky Printing and Office Supply, 1988), 25–32; Charles P. Rowland, *Albert Sidney Johnston: Soldier of Three Republics* (Lexington: University Press of Kentucky, 2001), 282; and Daniel, *Days of Glory*, 53.

23. James M. Beatty Testimony, August 9, 1865, NARA-Trial.

24. David Beatty Testimony, July 21, 1865, NARA-Trial; and Sean Michael O'Brien, *Mountain Partisans: Guerrilla Warfare in the Southern Appalachians, 1861–1865* (Westport, CT: Praeger, 1999), 55.

25. *Nashville Dispatch*, July 21, 1865.

26. *Louisville Journal* (KY), February 26, 1862.

27. Rufus Dowdy Testimony, August 26, 1862, NARA-Trial.

28. Ibid.

29. Tarrant, *Wild Riders*, 68.

30. Isaac T. Reneau to Gov. A. Johnson, March 31, 1861, TSLA-Johnson.

31. H. Leo Boles, *Biographical Sketches of Gospel Preachers* (Nashville: Gospel Advocate Company, 1932), 116–17.

32. Isaac T. Reneau to Gov. A. Johnson, March 31, 1861, TSLA-Johnson.

33. "The Man Who Once Did Sell the Lion's Skin," Number Two, 4–5, HSCC-Hale.

34. Winburne W. Goodpasture Testimony, August 22, 1865, NARA-Trial.

35. Undated statement signed by John J. McDonald, John Boles, Sen., H. Stover, and John Winingham, in J. D. Hale, *Sketches of Scenes*, 7–8; and James Alex Baggett, *Homegrown Yankees: Tennessee's Union Cavalry in the Civil War* (Baton Rouge: Louisiana State University Press, 2009), 28.

36. Winburne W. Goodpasture Testimony, August 22, 1865, NARA-Trial; James Beatty Testimony, August 9, 1865, NARA-Trial; Marion Johnson Testimony, August 9, 1865, NARA-Trial; and Hale, *Champ Furguson: A Sketch of the War*, 1862), 8.

37. Goodpasture in his August 22, 1865, testimony and Rufus Dowdy on August 26, 1865, confirmed that McHenry broke the accord within days of its adoption. Other interesting statements regarding the compromise effort can be found in Hale, *Sketches of Scenes*, 7–10.

38. John A. Capps Testimony, August 21, 1865, NARA-Trial.

39. Brents, *Patriots and Guerillas;* and Tarrant, *Wild Riders*, 21.

40. Hale, *Champ Furguson: A Sketch of the War;* Hale, *Champ Furguson: The Border Rebel;* and Brents, *Patriots and Guerillas*, 12–14.

41. Jonathan D. Hale to Honerable Andrew Johnson, December 16, 1861, Graf and Haskins, eds., *Papers of Andrew Johnson*, vol. 5, 61.

42. Speech to Davidson County Citizens, March 22, 1862, Graf and Haskins, eds., *Papers of Andrew Johnson*, vol. 5, 237.

43. Isaac T. Reneau to Gov. A. Johnson, March 31, 1862, Graf and Haskins, eds., *Papers of Andrew Johnson*, vol. 5, 257–58.

44. Ibid.

45. Leroy S. Clements to Hon Andrew Johnson Gov, April 9, 1862, Graf and Haskins, eds., *Papers of Andrew Johnson*, vol. 5, 286–87.

4. THE TENSIONS OF THE BORDERLAND

1. Hale, *Sketches of Scenes in the Career of Ferguson Ferguson and His Lieutenant* (Unknown, 1870), 7.

2. *Nashville Union*, October 21, 1865; and *Nashville Dispatch*, October 21, 1865.

3. *Nashville Dispatch*, October 22, 1865; and John A. Capps testimony, August 21, 1865.

4. *Nashville Union,* October 21, 1865; and Wilson, *Sufferings Endured for a Free Government,* 187–88.

5. *Nashville Union,* October 21, 1865.

6. Mays, *Cumberland Blood,* 62.

7. A. F. Capps testimony, August 2, 1865, NARA-Trial.

8. *Nashville Union,* October 21, 1865; and Wilson, *Sufferings Endured for a Free Government,* 194.

9. A. F. Capps testimony, August 2, 1865, NARA-Trial; and John A. Capps, August 21, 1865, NARA-Trial.

10. Mays, *Cumberland Blood,* 62–63.

11. P. A. Hale testimony, August 12, 1865, NARA-Trial.

12. Ibid.

13. Esther A. Jackson testimony, July 28, 1865, NARA-Trial; Rufus Dowdy testimony, August 24, 1865, NARA-Trial; A. F. Capps testimony, August 2, 1865, NARA-Trial; and Brents, *Patriots and Guerillas,* 25.

14. Hale, *Bloody Shirt,* 17.

15. *Nashville Dispatch,* October 22, 1865.

16. Schroeder, "Writings of a Tennessee Unionist," 257.

17. *Daily Nashville Union,* April 19, 1862.

18. Brents, *Patriots and Guerillas,* 25.

19. Schroeder, "Writings of a Tennessee Unionist," 257.

20. Ibid.

21. Blankenship, *Fiddles in the Cumberlands,* 168–69.

22. Schroeder, "Writings of a Tennessee Unionist," 257.

23. Ibid.

24. Oliver D. Greene to Col. E. C. Williams, April 17, 1862, *Official Records,* X/2, 110.

25. Tarrant, *Wild Riders,* 76–77.

26. Ibid., 77–79.

27. Hogue, *History of Fentress County, Tennessee,* 35.

28. William B. Williams testimony, July 25, 1865, NARA-Trial; and Mays, *Cumberland Blood,* 66–67.

29. Ibid.

30. Ibid.; and Wright, *Autobiography,* 44.

31. Nancy Brooks testimony, August 17, 1865, NARA-Trial. Williams estimated thirty minutes passed between the first shots and final shot.

32. William B. Williams testimony, July 25, 1865, NARA-Trial.

33. *Nashville Dispatch,* October 22, 1865.

34. William B. Williams testimony, July 25, 1865, NARA-Trial; Nancy Brooks testimony, August 17, 1865, NARA-Trial; and *Nashville Union,* October 21, 1865.

35. Nancy Brooks testimony, August 17, 1865, NARA-Trial.

36. Preston Huff Testimony, July 24, 1865, NARA-Trial.

37. Davis and Swentor, eds., *Bluegrass Confederate,* 41–42.

38. Marion Johnson testimony, August 8, 1865, NARA-Trial.

39. *Daily Nashville Union,* April 19, 1862.

40. James A. Ramage, *Rebel Raider: The Life of General John Hunt Morgan* (Lexington: University Press of Kentucky, 1986), 84.

41. Ibid.

42. Report of Brig. Gen. Ebenezer Dumont, U.S. Army, May 5, 1862, *Official Records*, X/1, 884; Report of Col. William W. Duffield, Ninth Michigan Infantry, May 5, 1862, *Official Records*, X/1, 884–85; Report of Col. William W. Duffield, Ninth Michigan Infantry, May 6, 1862, *Official Records*, X/1, 885–86; *Biographical Dictionary of the American Congresses*, 935; Boatner, *The Civil War Dictionary*, 251; Ramage, *Rebel Raider*, 84–85; Tarrant, *Wild Riders*, 83; and John Fitch, *Annals of the Army of the Cumberland* (Mechanicsburg, PA: Stackpole, 2003), 377–78.

43. Report of Brig. Gen. Ebenezer Dumont, U.S. Army, May 5, 1862, *Official Records*, X/1, 884; Report of Col. William W. Duffield, Ninth Michigan Infantry, May 5, 1862, *Official Records*, X/1, 884–85; Report of Col. William W. Duffield, Ninth Michigan Infantry, May 6, 1862, *Official Records*, X/1, 885–86; Tarrant, *Wild Riders*, 84–85; Ramage, *Rebel Raider*, 85; and Fitch, *Annals*, 377–78.

44. Ramage, *Rebel Raider*, 85.

45. Gary Robert Matthews, *Basil Wilson Duke, C.S.A.: The Right Man in the Right Place* (Lexington: University Press of Kentucky, 2005), 60. For more on Duke, see Lowell H. Harrison, "General Basil W. Duke, C.S.A.," *Filson Club History Quarterly* 54:1 (January 1980): 5–36.

46. Basil W. Duke, *A History of Morgan's Cavalry* (Cincinnati, OH: Miami, 1867), 163–64; and Howard Swiggett, *The Rebel Raider: A Life of John Hunt Morgan* (Indianapolis, IN: Bobbs-Merrill, 1934), 60.

47. Duke, *Morgan's Cavalry*, 165–66; Ramage, *Rebel Raider*, 85–87; and *Richmond Enquirer* (VA), May 22, 1862.

48. John W. Rowell, *Yankee Cavalrymen: Through the Civil War with the Ninth Pennsylvania Cavalry* (Knoxville: University of Tennessee Press, 1971), 55–56.

49. James Haggard to Dear Sir, June 2, 1862, Graf and Haskins, eds., *Papers of Andrew Johnson*, vol. 5, 433–34.

50. Nancy Kogier testimony, August 5, 1865, NARA-Trial; and Jane Walker testimony, August 5, 1865, NARA-Trial.

51. Nancy Kogier testimony, August 5, 1865, NARA-Trial.

52. Preston Huff testimony, July 24, 1865, NARA-Trial; and Jane Walker testimony, August 5, 1865, NARA-Trial.

53. Jane Walker testimony, August 5, 1865, NARA-Trial.

54. *Nashville Dispatch*, October 22, 1865; and *Weekly Press and Times* (Nashville, TN), October 22, 1865.

55. Hale, *Bloody Shirt*, 16; and Mays, *Cumberland Blood*, 73.

56. Esther A. Jackson testimony, July 28, 1865, NARA-Trial.

57. Ibid.

58. Mays, *Cumberland Blood*, 74.

59. *Nashville Dispatch*, October 21, 1865; and *Weekly Press and Times* (Nashville, TN), October 22, 1865.

60. Rowell, *Yankee Cavalrymen*, 55–57; and J. T. Boyle to Hon. E. M. Stanton, June 7, 1862, *Official Records*, X/2, 272.

61. Report of Col. Edward C. Williams, Ninth Pennsylvania Cavalry, June 13, 1862, *Official Records*, X/1, 914–15; and Report of Maj. Thomas J. Jordan, Ninth Pennsylvania Cavalry, June 11, 1865, *Official Records*, X/1, 916–17.

62. Rowell, *Yankee Cavalrymen*, 57–58.

63. Report of Col. Edward C. Williams, Ninth Pennsylvania Cavalry, June 13, 1862, *Official*

Records, X/1, 914–15; and Report of Maj. Thomas J. Jordan, Ninth Pennsylvania Cavalry, June 11, 1865, *Official Records,* X/1, 916–17.

64. Andrew J. Hall to Gov. Andrew Johnson, June 15, 1862, Graf and Haskins, eds., *Papers of Andrew Johnson,* vol. 5, 478–79; and James Johnson Statement, James Knox Polk Papers, Manuscripts and Archives Section, Tennessee State Library and Archives, Nashville, Tennessee, hereinafter cited as TSLA-Johnson. James Johnson, recalling Ferguson's final days many years after the guerrilla's death, suggested Ferguson had placed a $2,000 reward on Andrew Johnson's head. Considering Ferguson's continual financial problems throughout the war and his virtual insolvency upon its close, the report is likely false. It may also be a poorly told variation of the Gardenhire story.

65. Duke, *Morgan's Cavalry,* 182.

66. Ibid.

67. R. C. M. to Dr Johny, May 4, 1863, John Hunt Morgan Papers, Southern Historical Collection, Manuscripts Department, Wilson Library, University of North Carolina at Chapel Hill, hereinafter cited as SHC-Morgan.

68. Basil W. Duke, *The Civil War Reminiscences of General Basil W. Duke, C.S.A.* (New York: Cooper Square Press, 2001), 123–24; and Matthews, *Basil Wilson Duke, C.S.A.,* 62.

69. Ramage, *Rebel Raider,* 93.

70. Ibid., 98–105.

71. Nancy Kogier testimony, August 5, 1865, NARA-Trial.

5. STABILITY AND PARTITION

1. Duke, *Reminiscences,* 123.

2. Nancy Kogier testimony, August 5, 1865, NARA-Trial; and Jane Walker testimony, August 5, 1865, NARA-Trial.

3. *Nashville Union,* October 21, 1865.

4. *Louisville Courier Journal* (KY), September 27, 1862; and *Columbus Gazette* (OH), October 3, 1864.

5. Isham G. Harris, November 14, 1861, *Official Records,* IV, 243; and O'Brien, *Mountain Partisans,* 54.

6. F. K. Zollicoffer to Lieutenant-Colonel Mackall, November 17, 1861, *Official Records,* IV, 244.

7. S. A. M. Wood to Hon. J. P. Benjamin, November 17, 1861, *Official Records,* IV, 247.

8. George W. Morgan to Hon. E. M. Stanton, May 24, 1862, *Official Records,* X/2, 213.

9. Report of Col. William Clift, October 28, 1862, *Official Records,* XVI/2, 858.

10. Grady McWhiney, *Braxton Bragg and Confederate Defeat,* vol. I, Field Command (New York: Columbia University Press, 1969), 271–73; James Lee McDonough, *War in Kentucky: From Shiloh to Perryville* (Knoxville: University of Tennessee Press, 1994), 77–79; Earl J. Hess, *Banners to the Breeze: The Kentucky Campaign, Corinth, and Stones River* (Lincoln: University of Nebraska Press, 2000), 22–24; Joseph Howard Parks, *General Edmund Kirby Smith, C.S.A.* (Baton Rouge: Louisiana State University Press, 1954), 198–202; and Prokopowicz, *All for the Regiment,* 136–44.

11. Engle, *Don Carlos Buell,* 282–83, 287.

12. Ibid., 286; Parks, *Edmund Kirby Smith, C.S.A.,* 212–16; and Craig L. Symonds, *Stonewall*

of the West: Patrick Cleburne and the Civil War (Lawrence: University Press of Kansas, 1997), 89–92.

13. Heidler and Heidler, eds., *Encyclopedia of the American Civil War*, 1642–43; and Parks, *Edmund Kirby Smith, C.S.A.*, 218.

14. Engle, *Don Carlos Buell*, 288–90.

15. Ibid., 290; and McWhiney, *Braxton Bragg and Confederate Defeat*, 288–89.

16. Engle, *Don Carlos Buell*, 291.

17. Ibid., 306–310; and McWhiney, *Braxton Bragg and Confederate Defeat*, 311–20. For the best full treatment of the Battle of Perryville, see Kenneth W. Noe, *Perryville: This Grand Havoc of Battle* (Lexington: University Press of Kentucky, 2001).

18. Bennett Mearger to Mr. D. E. Downing, August 14, 1862, Governor Beriah Magoffin Papers, Military Correspondence, Public Records Division, Kentucky Department for Libraries and Archives, Frankfort, Kentucky, hereinafter cited as KDLA-Magoffin.

19. J. B. Alexander, R. Cross, Mr. Ryan, and Mr. Long to Honerable J. F. Robinson, August 25, 1862, Governor James F. Robinson Papers, Military Correspondence, Public Records Division, Kentucky Department for Libraries and Archives, Frankfort, Kentucky, hereinafter cited as KDLA-Robinson.

20. "Continued Lifting of Masks," Number Four, 2–11, HSCC-Hale.

21. Report of Col. William Clift, October 28, 1862, *Official Records*, XVI/2, 858.

22. Mays, *Cumberland Blood*, 83.

23. Boatner, *The Civil War Dictionary*, 520; Heidler and Heidler, eds., *Encyclopedia of the American Civil War*, 1267–68; John C. Waugh, *The Class of 1846: From West Point to Appomattox: Stonewall Jackson, George McClellan, and Their Brothers* (New York: Warner Books, 1994), xiv–xvi; Louise Horton, *Samuel Bell Maxey: A Biography* (Austin: University of Texas Press, 1974), 7–18; and W. C. Nunn, *Ten More Texans in Gray* (Hillsboro, TX: Hill Junior College Press, 1980), 59–71.

24. Maxey to My dearest Marilda, October 10, 1862, Samuel Bell Maxey Papers, Archives and Information Services Division, Texas State Library and Archives Commission, Austin, Texas.

25. Preston Huff testimony, July 24, 1865, NARA-Trial. The date is taken from the testimony of Vina Piles, July 24, 1865, NARA-Trial.

26. John Huff testimony, August 10, 1865, NARA-Trial.

27. Ibid.

28. Ibid.

29. Vina Piles testimony, July 24, 1865, NARA-Trial; John Huff testimony, August 10, 1865, NARA-Trial; and Preston Huff testimony, July 24, 1865, NARA-Trial.

30. Colonel William B. Stokes of DeKalb County, Tennessee, organized the 5th Tennessee Cavalry (U.S.A.) in late 1861 or early 1862.

31. *Nashville Union*, October 21, 1865.

32. *Nashville Dispatch*, August 10, 1865.

33. John Huff testimony, August 10, 1865, NARA-Trial.

34. Nancy Upchurch set the timing of Ferguson's meeting with her family. In her testimony, August 18, 1865, she claimed to overhear one of Ferguson's band say that they had already killed three men that morning.

35. Silas Upchurch testimony, August 18, 1865, NARA-Trial.

36. *Nashville Dispatch*, October 22, 1865.

37. *Nashville Union,* October 21, 1865.

38. Mays, *Cumberland Blood,* 85–86.

39. *Louisville Daily Journal* (KY), November 19, 1862.

40. Ibid., 116.

41. William Thrasher testimony, July 31, 1865, NARA-Trial; and George D. Thrasher testimony, July 29, 1865, NARA-Trial.

42. Ibid., and Wilson, *Sufferings Endured for a Free Government,* 159. Wilson identified Grimes as Durham Graham.

43. Ibid.

44. George D. Thrasher testimony, July 29, 1865, NARA-Trial.

45. *Nashville Dispatch,* October 21, 1865.

46. Brents, *Patriots and Guerillas,* 14–16.

47. Moses Huddleston testimony, July 27, 1865, NARA-Trial.

48. Duke, *Reminiscences,* 124.

49. William Thrasher testimony, July 31, 1865, NARA-Trial; and George D. Thrasher testimony, July 29, 1865, NARA-Trial.

50. J. T. Boyle to Major-General Wright, November 12, 1862, *Official Records,* XX/2, 40.

51. *Nashville Daily Press and Times,* October 11, 1865.

52. Wilson, *Sufferings Endured for a Free Government,* 147.

53. *Nashville Union,* October 21, 1865

54. *Nashville Dispatch,* October 21, 1865.

55. Ramage, *Rebel Raider,* 123–26.

56. J. A. Morrison to Dear Sir, December 3, 1865, Guerrilla Letters, Archives, Kentucky Military History Museum, Frankfort, Kentucky, hereinafter cited as KMHM-Guerrilla.

6. LESSONS OF PERSEVERANCE

1. Geo. H. Thomas to Col. J. P. Garesche, December 15, 1862, *Official Records,* XX/2, 184–85, and Wartime Diary of John Weatherred, copy held privately by Mr. Jack Masters, Gallatin, Tennessee.

2. Chas. R. Thompson to Major-General Thomas, December 15, 1862, *Official Records,* XX/2, 185; and Geo. H. Thomas to Col. J. P. Garesche, December 16, 1862, *Official Records,* XX/2, 190.

3. William M. Lamers, *The Edge of Glory: A Biography of General William S. Rosecrans, U.S.A.* (1961; Baton Rouge: Louisiana State University Press, 1999), 196.

4. Ramage, *Rebel Raider,* 137.

5. Ibid.; McWhiney, *Braxton Bragg and Confederate Defeat,* 341; Duke, *History of Morgan's Cavalry,* 325–42; Thomas Lawrence Connelly, *Autumn of Glory: The Army of Tennessee, 1863–1865* (Baton Rouge: Louisiana State University Press, 1971), 29.

6. Confederates referred to Stones River as the Battle of Murfreesboro.

7. Wartime Diary of John Weatherred, copy held privately by Mr. Jack Masters, Gallatin, Tennessee.

8. Ibid.; Matthews, *Basil Wilson Duke, C.S.A.,* 120; and Moses Huddleston testimony, July 27, 1865, NARA-Trial.

9. Moses Huddleston testimony, July 27, 1865, NARA-Trial; *Louisville Daily Journal* (KY), January 8, 1863; and Matthews, *Basil Wilson Duke, C.S.A.,* 120.

10. Wartime Diary of John Weatherred; and Matthews, *Basil Wilson Duke, C.S.A.,* 120.

11. Moses Huddleston testimony, July 27, 1865, NARA-Trial; and *Louisville Daily Journal* (KY), January 8, 1863.

12. Moses Huddleston testimony, July 27, 1865Ibid.

13. Ibid.

14. Sarah Dowdy testimony, July 28, 1865, NARA-Trial.

15. Ibid.

16. Wartime Diary of John Weatherred.

17. Moses Huddleston testimony, July 27, 1865, NARA-Trial; and *Louisville Daily Journal* (KY), January 12, 1863.

18. Moses Huddleston testimony, July 28, 1865.

19. Duke, *Reminiscences,* 125.

20. *Nashville Union,* October 21, 1865.

21. *Nashville Dispatch,* October 21, 1865.

22. Ramage, *Rebel Raider,* 108–111, 208–225

23. Davis and Swentor, eds., *Bluegrass Confederate,* 464.

24. *Louisville Daily Journal* (KY), April 16, 1863.

25. Report of Capt. Wendell D. Wiltsie, May 11, 1863, *Official Records,* XXIII/1, 307–309.

26. Report of Capt. Wendell D. Wiltsie, May 11, 1863, *Official Records,* XXIII/1, 307–309; Report of Lieut. Col. W. Huntington Smith, May 12, 1863, *Official Records,* XXIII/1, 304–306; Report of Col. Richard T. Jacob, May 12, 1863, *Official Records,* XXIII/1, 299–303; and Ramage, *Rebel Raider,* 157.

27. Ramage, *Rebel Raider,* 170–78.

28. *Nashville Dispatch,* August 19, 1865.

29. Duke, *History of Morgan's Cavalry,* 417.

30. S. P. Carter to Brig. Gen. O. B. Willcox, May 23, 1863, *Official Records,* XXIII/2, 359.

31. Ibid.

32. Report of Col. George G. Dibrell, August 18, 1865, *Official Records,* XXIII/1, 847.

33. George Gibbs Dibrell Statistical Sketch, July 17, 1875, Civil War Collection: Confederate and Federal, 1861–1865, Confederate Collection, Tennessee State Library and Archives, Nashville, Tennessee; Clement A. Evans, Jr., *Confederate Military History,* Vol. 8, Tennessee (Atlanta, GA, 1899), 305–306; and Eric J. Wittenberg, *The Battle of Monroe's Crossroads and the Civil War's Final Campaign* (New York: Savas Beatie, 2006), 49–50.

34. Fitch, *Annals,* 205.

35. The fight is also sometimes called the Battle of Meredith's Mill.

36. Report of Col. George G. Dibrell, August 18, 1865, *Official Records,* XXIII/1, 847–48; and Report of Col. Robert H. G. Minty, August 11, 1863, *Official Records,* XXIII/1, 846–47.

37. Report of Col. George G. Dibrell, August 18, 1865, *Official Records,* XXIII/1, 848; and Evans, *Confederate Military History,* volume 8, 306.

38. James T. Siburt, "Colonel John M. Hughs: Brigade Commander and Confederate Guerrilla," *Tennessee Historical Quarterly* 51:2 (Summer 1992): 87–88.

39. H. P. Van Cleve to Brigadier-General Garfield, August 13, 1863, *Official Records,* XXX/3, 21.

40. Thos. E. Bremlette Statement, April 28, 1864, Jonathan D. Hale Collection, Special Collections Library, Hodges Library, University of Tennessee, Knoxville, Tennessee, hereinafter cited as UT-Hale.

41. Geo. H. Thomas to Brig. Gen. James A. Garfield, August 1, 1863, *Official Records,* XXIII/2, 586.

42. Julia Ann Williams testimony, August 21, 1865, NARA-Trial.

43. Ibid.

44. *Louisville Daily Journal* (KY), October 27, 1863; and October 29, 1863.

45. Ibid., October 27, 1863.

46. Gilbert's reference to Muncy appears erroneous. Graf and Haskins correct the name to Thomas B. Murray.

47. H C Gilbert Col 19th to Gov. Andrew Johnson, November 7, 1863, Graf and Haskins, eds., *Papers of Andrew Johnson,* vol. 6, 459.

48. E. H. Hobson, October 17, 1863, *Official Records,* XXX/4, 450; and E. H. Hobson, October 17, 1863, *Official Records,* XXX/4, 450 (two separate dispatches).

49. Report of Col. John M. Hughs, April 28, 1864, *Official Records,* XXXI/1, 575.

50. H. W. Tuttle to Governor, April 13, 1865, KMHM-Guerrilla.

51. Parson Brownlow was Knoxville newspaperman William Ganaway Brownlow. An outspoken unionist, Brownlow traveled throughout Federal territory building support for the plight of southern unionists.

52. Report of Lieut. Col. James P. Brownlow, November 25, 1863, *Official Records,* XXXI/1, 573; Fisher, *War at Every Door,* 81–82; and Rowell, *Yankee Cavalrymen,* 158–59.

53. Report of Col. John M. Hughs, April 28, 1864, *Official Records,* XXXI/1, 575; and Fisher, *War at Every Door,* 81–82.

54. Report of Col. John M. Hughs, April 28, 1864, *Official Records,* XXXI/1, 575.

55. E. H. Hobson to Capt. A. C. Semple, December 22, 1863, *Official Records,* XXXI/3, 469.

7. THE BORDERLAND GUERRILLA LIFESTYLE

1. John M. Hughs.

2. A. J. Cropsey to Gov. Andrew Johnson, January 6, 1864, Graf and Haskins, eds., *Papers of Andrew Johnson,* vol. 6, 538–39.

3. Geo. H. Thomas to Governor Andrew Johnson, January 10, 1864, *Official Records,* XXXII/2, 64–65; reprinted in Graf and Haskins, eds., *Papers of Andrew Johnson,* vol. 6, 553.

4. U S Grant to Gov A Johnson, January 24, 1864, Graf and Haskins, eds., *Papers of Andrew Johnson,* vol. 6, 591.

5. "Notable Tennesseans . . . Living and Dead," unknown newspaper, Stokes and Tubb Papers, Manuscripts Division, Tennessee State Library and Archives, Nashville, Tennessee, hereinafter cited as TSLA-Stokes and Tubb.

6. Colonel John P. Murray began his service with the 28th Tennessee Infantry Regiment in 1861. Not reelected to the colonelcy, he raised the 4th (Murray's) Tennessee Cavalry Regiment in August 1862. That same year, he was elected to the Confederate Congress as representative of Tennessee's Fourth District. Although Harrison mentioned Colonel Murray as an active guerrilla leader, by early 1864, Murray may have already curtailed his guerrilla activities or even left active service in preparation for his political career. Kenneth C. Martis, *The Historical Atlas of the Congresses of the Confederate States of America: 1861–1865* (New York: Simon and Schuster, 1994), 34.

7. Report of Col. Thomas J. Harrison, January 14, 1864, *Official Records,* XXXII/1, 65; and Fisher, *War at Every Door,* 89.

8. Report of Col. Thomas J. Harrison, January 14, 1864, *Official Records,* XXXII/1, 65–66.

9. Report of Col. William B. Stokes, February 2, 1864, *Official Records,* XXXII/1, 162–63.

10. *Louisville Daily Journal* (KY), February 12, 1864.

11. Report of Col. Henry K. McConnell, February 10, 1864, *Official Records,* XXXII/1, 155–56.

12. Ibid.

13. Ibid.

14. Daniel W. Garrett testimony, July 22, 1865, NARA-Trial; Isham Richards testimony, July 22, 1865, NARA-Trial; and Captain Rufus Dowdy testimony, August 24, 1865, NARA-Trial.

15. Daniel W. Garrett testimony, July 22, 1865, NARA-Trial.

16. Ibid.; Isham Richards testimony, July 22, 1865, NARA-Trial; and Captain Rufus Dowdy testimony, August 24, 1865, NARA-Trial.

17. Confession of Columbus German, July 3, 1866, HSCC-Hale.

18. Report of Col. William B. Stokes, February 24, 1864, *Official Records,* XXXII/1, 416.

19. W. B. Hyder Recollections, Special Collections, Angelo and Jennette Volpe Library and Media Center, Tennessee Technological University, Cookeville, Tennessee, hereinafter cited as TTU-Hyder.

20. The Battle of Dug Hill is sometimes called the Battle of the Calfkiller or Battle of Calfkiller River.

21. Betty Jane Dudney, "Civil War in White County, Tennessee, 1861–1865," M.A. thesis, Tennessee Technological University, 1985, 35–36; Monroe Seals, *History of White County, Tennessee* (Spartanburg, SC: The Reprint Company, 1982), 71–72; and Lewis A. Lawson, *Wheeler's Last Raid* (Greenwood, FL: Penkevill, 1986), 248–49.

22. Siburt, "Colonel John M. Hughs," 90.

23. Report of Col. William B. Stokes, February 24, 1864, *Official Records,* XXXII/1, 416.

24. W. B. Hyder Recollections, TTU-Hyder.

25. Compiled Service Record of Jacob H. Davis, 8th Tennessee Cavalry Regiment (C.S.A.), National Archives and Records Administration, Washington, D.C., hereinafter cited as NARA-CSR; and Compiled Service Record of G. W. Franklin, 8th Tennessee Cavalry Regiment (C.S.A.), NARA-CSR.

26. Compiled Service Record of Martin Eldridge, 8th Tennessee Cavalry Regiment (C.S.A.), NARA-CSR.

27. Compiled Service Record of John Farris, 8th Tennessee Cavalry Regiment (C.S.A.), NARA-CSR.

28. Compiled Service Record of L. S. Poston, 8th Tennessee Cavalry Regiment (C.S.A.), NARA-CSR.

29. Compiled Service Record of John Newton Vance, 8th Tennessee Cavalry Regiment (C.S.A.), NARA-CSR.

30. Alvan C Gillem to Governor, March 11, 1864, Graf and Haskins, eds., *Papers of Andrew Johnson,* vol. 6, 643–44.

31. If those statements are to be believed, they provide a precedent for Ferguson's battlefield behavior at Saltville, Virginia, in October 1864.

32. *Nashville Union,* October 21, 1865; W. B. Hyder Recollections, TTU-Hyder.

33. Report of Col. William B. Stokes, February 24, 1864, *Official Records,* XXXII/1, 416.

34. Ibid.

35. *Nashville Daily Union,* March 13, 1864.

36. Confession of Columbus German, July 3, 1866, HSCC-Hale.

37. Ibid.

38. William S. Jones, "The Civil War in Van Buren County, 1861–1865," *Tennessee Historical Quarterly* 67 (Spring 2008), 61.

39. G. Granger to Major-General Thomas, February 20, 1864, *Official Records,* XXXII/1, 485; *Nashville Daily Union,* March 13, 1864; and Confession of Columbus German, July 3, 1866, HSCC-Hale.

40. Report of Col. William B. Stokes, March 28, 1865, *Official Records,* XXXII/1, 494; Siburt, "Colonel John M. Hughs, 91; and *Louisville Daily Journal* (KY), March 21, 1864.

41. *Louisville Daily Journal* (KY), March 21, 1865.

42. W. B. Hyder Recollections, TTU-Hyder.

43. *Nashville Daily Union,* March 29, 1864.

44. Ibid., March 27, 1864.

45. Ibid., April 1, 1864. The *Louisville Daily Journal* (KY), March 26, 1864, originated the story affirming Ferguson's death and further confirmation of Ferguson's death was offered by the *Louisville Daily Journal* (KY), April 4, 1864, and the *Memphis Daily Appeal* (TN), April 7, 1864.

46. *Nashville Union,* October 21, 1865.

47. *Confederate Veteran,* vol. III, no. 10 (October 1895), 301.

48. Report of Col. William B. Stokes, March 28, 1864, *Official Records,* XXXII/1, 494; and Siburt, "Colonel John M. Hughs," 91.

49. Ibid.

50. Report of Col. William B. Stokes, March 28, 1864, *Official Records,* XXXII/1, 494.

51. Siburt, "Colonel John M. Hughs," 91.

52. Ibid.; and Report of Col. William B. Stokes, March 28, 1865, *Official Records,* XXXII/1, 494–95.

53. Capt. David Beity to Gov. Johnson, April 10, 1864, Graf and Haskins, eds., *The Papers of Andrew Johnson,* vol. 6, 666–67.

54. F. H. Mason, *The Twelfth Ohio Cavalry* (Cleveland, OH: Nevins' Steam Printing House, 1871), 22–23.

55. Report of Maj. Thomas H. Reeves, July 9, 1864, *Official Records,* XXXIX/1, 351–52.

56. Ibid.; and Fisher, *War at Every Door,* 82.

57. Report of Maj. Thomas H. Reeves, July 20, 1864, *Official Records,* XXXIX/1, 353.

58. Ibid.

59. Ibid.

60. Order re Governor's Guard, August 1, 1864, Leroy P. Graf, ed., *The Papers of Andrew Johnson,* vol. 7, *1864–1865* (Knoxville: University of Tennessee Press, 1986), 70.

61. Alvan C Gillem to Governor, August 9, 1864, Graf, *Papers of Andrew Johnson,* vol. 7, 86–87.

62. Ibid., 92.

63. Ibid., 86–87.

64. Joseph H. Blackburn to Governor, Johnson, August 5, 1864, Graf, *Papers of Andrew Johnson,* vol. 7, 76–77.

65. *Nashville Dispatch,* August 25, 1865; August 27, 1865.

66. John P. Dyer, *From Shiloh to San Juan: The Life of "Fightin' Joe" Wheeler* (Baton Rouge: Louisiana State University Press, 1989), 100–102, 146–47; John Randolph Poole, *Cracker Cava-*

liers: The 2nd Georgia Under Wheeler and Forrest (Macon, GA: Mercer University Press, 2000), 90–92; Richard M. McMurry, *John Bell Hood and the War for Southern Independence* (Lexington: University Press of Kentucky, 1982), 144–46; Judith Lee Hallock, *Braxton Bragg and Confederate Defeat*, vol. II (Tuscaloosa: University of Alabama Press, 1991), 111–12; Thomas Lawrence Connelly, *Autumn of Glory: The Army of Tennessee, 1863–1865* (Baton Rouge: Louisiana State University Press, 1971), 269–70; and Hogue, *History of Fentress County, Tennessee,* 25–26.

67. Dyer, *From Shiloh to San Juan,* 147–52; Poole, *Cracker Cavaliers,* 151–58; Steven E. Woodworth, *Jefferson Davis and His Generals: The Failure of Confederate Command in the West* (Lawrence: University Press of Kansas, 1990), 288–89; *Confederate Veteran,* vol. XXIII (January 1915), 30; J. C. Williamson, ed., "The Civil War Diary of John Coffee Williamson," *Tennessee Historical Quarterly* XV (March 1956), 62–68; and John Witherspoon DuBose, *General Joseph Wheeler and the Army of Tennessee* (New York: Neale, 1912), 383–89.

68. Dyer, *From Shiloh to San Juan,* 150–51; W. B. Stokes to His Excellency Gov. Johnson, September 12, 1864, in Graf, *The Papers of Andrew Johnson,* vol. 7, 153–54; Connelly, *Autumn of Glory,* 435–36, 457–58; DuBose, *General Joseph Wheeler and the Army of Tennessee,* 385, 387–88; and Lawson, *Wheeler's Last Raid,* 161.

69. General Joseph Wheeler testimony, August 28, 1865, NARA-Trial.

70. Ibid.

8. A TERRIBLE CAREER'S GRAND CLIMAX

1. Dyer, *From Shiloh to San Juan,* 150–51.

2. Thomas D. Mays, *The Saltville Massacre,* Civil War Campaigns and Commanders, ed. Grady McWhiney (Abilene, TX: McWhiney Foundation Press, 1998), 19; Heidler and Heidler, eds., *Encyclopedia of the American Civil War,* 323–24; and Boatner, *The Civil War Dictionary,* 106.

3. William C. Davis, "The Massacre at Saltville," *Civil War Times Illustrated,* February 1971, 4, 5.

4. Kleber, ed., *Kentucky Encyclopedia,* 142; Davis, "The Massacre at Saltville," 4, 5; Mays, *The Saltville Massacre,* 15–19; William Marvel, The Battles for Saltville: *Southwest Virginia in the Civil War* (Lynchburg, VA: H. E. Howard, 1992), 100–102; James S. Brisbin to Brig. Gen. L. Thomas, October 20, 1864, *Official Records,* XXXIX/1, 557.

5. Davis, "Massacre at Saltville," 7; A. E. Jackson to Capt. H. T. Stanton, October 1, 1864, *Official Records,* XXXIX/1, 560; and Report of Bvt. Maj. Gen. Stephen G. Burbridge, October 7, 1864, *Official Records,* XXXIX/1, 552.

6. Davis, "Massacre at Saltville," 5–6, 8.

7. William Marvel, "The Battle of Saltville: Massacre or Myth?" *Blue and Gray Magazine* 8:6 (August 1991), 18–19.

8. John S. Wise, *The End of an Era* (Boston: Houghton, Mifflin, 1899), 379.

9. Marcus J. Wright, *Texas in the War: 1861–1865,* compiled by Harold B. Simpson (Hillsboro, TX: Hill Junior College Press, 1965), 89–90; and Ralph A. Wooster, *Lone Star Generals in Gray* (Austin, TX: Eakin, 2000), 203–207.

10. Davis, "Massacre at Saltville," 9.

11. Ibid., 10–11, 44.

12. Ibid., 9.

13. Ibid., 10–11.

14. Ibid., 11.

15. Ibid.

16. Ibid.; and *Richmond Daily Dispatch* (VA), October 6, 1864; October 12, 1864; October 30, 1864.

17. George Dallas Mosgrove, *Kentucky Cavaliers in Dixie: Reminiscences of a Confederate Cavalryman* (Jackson, TN: McCowat-Mercer, 1957), 206.

18. Ibid., 208.

19. Davis and Swentor, eds., *Bluegrass Confederate*, 546–47.

20. *Nashville Dispatch*, August 2, 1865. Crawford Henselwood, as Shocker pronounced his name and court recorders and news reporters recorded it, was likely George C. Hinshillwood, a private in company B of the 12th Ohio, from Cleveland. Hinshillwood enlisted for a three-year term on October 23, 1863.

21. Ibid.; and George S. Burkhardt, *Confederate Rage, Yankee Wrath: No Quarter in the Civil War* (Carbondale: Southern Illinois University Press, 2007), 198–99.

22. Davis, "Massacre at Saltville," 45. Lieutenant George Cutler has historically been misidentified as Lieutenant George Carter. Bryce Suderow, Phyllis Brown, and David Brown discovered the error during the process of reexamining the controversy surrounding the Battle of Saltville, October 1864. Suderow's, Brown's, and Brown's findings can be examined at http://mywebpages.comcast.net/5thuscc/massacr.htm. An examination of the current state of the study of the aftermath of the Battle of Saltville can be found in Brian D. McKnight, "The Winnowing of Saltville: Remembering a Civil War Atrocity," *Journal for the Liberal Arts and Sciences* 14 (Fall 2009), 34–51.

23. Report of Surg. William H. Gardner, October 26, 1864, *Official Records*, series I, volume XXXIX/1, 554–55.

24. Marvel, *Saltville*, 144–45.

25. Orange Sells testimony, August 12, 1865, NARA-Trial.

26. Report of Surg. William H. Gardner, October 26, 1864, *Official Records*, series I, volume XXXIX/1, 554–55; and Milton P. Jarrigan, November 8, 1864, MIAC Endorsements on Letters, Department of East Tennessee, 1862–1864, chapter 8, volume 357, War Department Collection of Confederate States of America Records, National Archives and Records Administration, Washington, D.C., hereinafter cited as NARA-MIAC Endorsements.

27. "Dr. Murfree Meets Champ Ferguson," *Rutherford County Historical Society* (Winter 1973): 15–19. The 1860 census listed Elza Smith as a twenty-four-year-old farmer and single father, with two sons: H. D., three years, and Hiram R., eleven months.

28. W. W. Stringfield, "The Champ Ferguson Affair," *The Emory and Henry Era* 17:6 (May 1914), 300–302; R. N. Price, *Holston Methodism: From Its Origin to the Present Time* (Nashville: Publishing House of the Methodist Episcopal Church, South, 1913), 396–99; Orange Sells testimony, August 12, 1865, NARA-Trial; and Milton P. Jarrigan, November 8, 1865, NARA-MIAC Endorsements. Smith's record of service can be found in *Report of the Adjutant General of the State of Kentucky*, vol I, Union, 1861–1865 (Frankfort: Kentucky Yeoman Office, 1866), 12–13, 361, 363.

29. Mason, *The Twelfth Ohio Cavalry*, 70.

30. *Nashville Union*, October 21, 1865.

31. *Nashville Dispatch*, October 21, 1865.

32. *Nashville Union*, October 21, 1865.

33. Ibid.

34. *Nashville Dispatch*, October 21, 1865.

35. History of Hamilton's and Shaw's 4th Battallion Tennessee Cavalry, Leroy Moncure Nutt Papers, Southern Historical Collection, University of North Carolina, Chapel Hill, hereinafter cited as UNC-Nutt; and Duke, *Reminiscences,* 124. Duke's *Reminiscences* erroneously identify Bledsoe as the man killed while in Federal captivity, but he lived through the war and settled in Texas at the end of the conflict.

36. Davis, "Massacre at Saltville," 47.

37. Mosgrove, *Kentucky Cavaliers in Dixie,* 207; and Davis, *Breckinridge,* 459.

38. Douglas Southall Freeman, ed., *Lee's Dispatches* (New York: G. P. Putnam's Sons, 1957), 299–300; and John B. Jones, *A Rebel War Clerk's Diary,* ed. Earl Schenck Miers (Baton Rouge: Louisiana State University Press, 1993), 431.

39. *Daily Dispatch* (Richmond, VA), October 12, 1864; and *Lynchburg Daily Virginian,* October 7, 1864.

40. Charles Marshall to Maj. Gen. J. C. Breckinridge, October 21, 1864, *Official Records,* ser. II, VII, 1020.

41. Davis, "Massacre at Saltville," 47.

42. Felix Robertson did not leave very much in the way of correspondence, but of those letters that survive, only one reference is made to the Battle of Saltville and there is no mention of the controversy surrounding the behavior of the Confederates on the field the morning following the fight. The letter from Robertson to George Knox Miller, June 10, 1895, is printed in Richard M. McMurry, ed., *An Uncompromising Secessionist: The Civil War of George Knox Miller, Eighth (Wade's) Confederate Cavalry* (Tuscaloosa: University of Alabama Press, 2007), 282–83.

43. Compiled Service Record of Thomas D. Burris, 8th Tennessee Cavalry Regiment (C.S.A.), NARA-CSR.

44. Milton P. Jarrigan, November 8, 1865, NARA-MIAC Endorsements.

45. Document O, NARA-Trial.

46. Joseph Wheeler testimony, August 28, 1865, NARA-Trial.

9. REVELATION OF A CLEAR CONSCIENCE

1. Long, *The Civil War Day By Day,* 670–90; and Sensing, *Champ Ferguson,* 17.

2. Compiled Service Record of Thomas Ferris, 8th Tennessee Cavalry Regiment, NARA-CSR.

3. Compiled Service Record of William L. Sliger, 8th Tennessee Cavalry Regiment, NARA-CSR.

4. *Nashville Dispatch,* July 21, 1865; Mays, *Cumberland Blood,* 127; Sensing, *Champ Ferguson,* 76; and David Beatty testimony, July 20, 1865, NARA-Trial.

5. *Nashville Dispatch,* July 21, 1865; Mays, *Cumberland Blood,* 127; Sensing, *Champ Ferguson,* 76; and David Beatty testimony, July 20, 1865, NARA-Trial.

6. L. W. Duvall Testimony, August 7, 1865, NARA-Trial.

7. Ibid.; and Martin Hurt testimony, August 8, 1865, NARA-Trial.

8. L. W. Duvall Testimony, August 7, 1865, NARA-Trial; and Martin Hurt testimony, August 8, 1865, NARA-Trial; and *Louisville Daily Journal* (KY), May 6, 1865.

9. Document H, NARA-Trial; and Mays, *Cumberland Blood,* 129.

10. H. C. Whittemore to Major-General Milroy, May 16, 1865, *Official Records,* XLIX/2, 806; Mays, *Cumberland Blood,* 129–30; and *New York Herald,* May 19, 1865.

11. *Louisville Daily Journal* (KY), May 13, 1865, and May 19, 1865.

12. Jno. O. Cravens to Capt. Henry Shook, May 19, 1865, *Official Records,* XLIX/2, 843.

13. Document N, NARA-Trial; and Col. Joseph Blackburn testimony, August 23, 1865, NARA-Trial.

14. Wilburn W. Goodpasture testimony, August 23, 1865, NARA-Trial; Col. Joseph Blackburn testimony, August 23, 1865, NARA-Trial; Captain Rufus Dowdy testimony, August 24, 1865, NARA-Trial; and Document T, NARA-Trial.

15. Ibid.

16. Ibid.

17. Mays, *Cumberland Blood,* 131.

18. Ibid., 180.

19. Wilburn W. Goodpasture testimony, August 23, 1865, NARA-Trial; Col. Joseph Blackburn testimony, August 23, 1865, NARA-Trial; and Captain Rufus Dowdy testimony, August 24, 1865, NARA-Trial.

20. Mays, *Cumberland Blood,* 132; *New York Herald,* May 31, 1865; and *The Daily Picayune* (New Orleans, LA), June 10, 1865.

21. Your Son Robert Johnson to Dear Father, May 31, 1865, in Paul H. Bergeron, ed., *The Papers of Andrew Johnson,* vol. 8, May–August 1865 (Knoxville: University of Tennessee Press, 1989), 155–56; and Larry D. Gossett, "The Keepers and the Kept: The First Hundred Years of the Tennessee State Prison System, 1830–1930," vol. 1 (Ph.D. diss., Louisiana State University and Agricultural and Mechanical College, 1992), 64.

22. Wm. D. Whipple to General George H. Thomas, May 30, 1865, *Official Records,* XLIX/2, 931; and Wm. D. Whipple to Major-General Stoneman, May 30, 1865, *Official Records,* XLIX/2, 933.

23. *Nashville Union,* July 12, 1865.

24. Heidler and Heidler, eds., *Encyclopedia of the American Civil War,* 2138–39; and Elizabeth D. Leonard, *Lincoln's Avengers: Justice, Revenge, and Reunion after the Civil War* (New York: W. W. Norton, 2004), 157–58. Leonard notes that the language of the Wirz Court Martial Order was similar to that used to charge the Lincoln conspirators. As Lincoln's killers were charged with "maliciously, unlawfully, and traitorously . . . combining, confederating, and conspiring together" to kill Lincoln, Andrew Johnson, William Henry Seward, and Ulysses S. Grant, Wirz was charged with "maliciously, willfully, and traitorously . . . combining, confederating, and conspiring, together with John H. Winder . . . and others unknown, to injure the health and destroy the lives of soldiers in the military service of the United States, then held and being prisoners of war within the lines of the so-called Confederate States . . . to the end that the armies of the United States might be weakened and impaired, in violation of the laws and customs of war."

25. Leonard, *Lincoln's Avengers,* 133–34; and Benjamin P. Thomas and Harold M. Hyman, *Stanton: The Life and Times of Lincoln's Secretary of War* (New York: Knopf, 1962), 434–35.

26. Mays, *Cumberland Blood,* 132–33; Sensing, *Champ Ferguson,* 27–28; and Walter T. Durham, *Josephus Conn Guild and Rose Mont: Politics and Plantation in Nineteenth Century Tennessee* (Franklin, TN: Hillsboro Press, 2002), 125–26.

27. Marvel, *Battles for Saltville,* 146.

28. Mays, *Cumberland Blood,* 134.

29. Ibid., 184; and Sensing, *Champ Ferguson*, 29.

30. Mays, *Cumberland Blood*, 135.

31. Sensing, *Champ Ferguson*, 16–18, 29–30, 40–41.

32. Ibid., 41–42.

33. Durham, *Josephus Conn Guild and Rose Mont*, 19–20; and Sensing, *Champ Ferguson*, 45.

34. Ibid., 51–53; and *Daily Press and Times* (Nashville, TN), July 15, 1865.

35. *Frank Leslie's Illustrated Weekly,* September 23, 1865.

36. *Harper's Weekly,* September 23, 1865, and November 11, 1865.

37. *Nashville Union,* September 3, 1865.

38. Mays, *Cumberland Blood*, 139.

39. *Nashville Dispatch,* August 19, 1865.

40. Ibid.

41. Ibid.

42. David Beatty testimony, July 21, 1865, NARA-Trial; Nancy Kogier testimony, August 5, 1865, NARA-Trial; A. F. Capps testimony, August 2, 1865, NARA-Trial; John A. Capps testimony, August 21, 1865, NARA-Trial; and Winburn Goodpasture testimony, August 22, 1865, NARA-Trial.

43. Mays, *Cumberland Blood*, 141.

44. *Nashville Dispatch,* August 23, 1865; *Louisville Daily Journal* (KY), September 1, 1865; and J. Wheeler to Maj. Gen. G. H. Thomas, August 23, 1865, *Official Records,* ser. II, VIII, 726–27.

45. *Nashville Dispatch,* August 25, 1865, and August 26, 1865.

46. Sensing, *Champ Ferguson*, 216–26.

47. Martha Ferguson contract, August 29, 1865, Champ Ferguson Biography File, Kentucky Historical Society, Frankfort, Kentucky, hereinafter cited as KHS-CFBF.

48. Mays, *Cumberland Blood*, 143. Although Tinker Dave Beatty's band likely fought a similar style of war as that of Ferguson, his unit was officially recognized within the Union army. Beatty started his unit with ninety-nine men and by the end of the war, he had lost twelve, including his son. Ten of those deaths occurred in battle. See A. R. Hogue to Hon. John Trotwood Moore, June 28, 1923, Civil War Collection: Federal Collection, Casualty Lists, Manuscripts Division, Tennessee State Library and Archives, Nashville, Tennessee.

49. Ibid., 197.

50. *Daily Press and Times* (Nashville, TN), September 19, 1865.

51. Ibid., October 11, 1865.

52. Ibid.

53. Champ Ferguson to Sir [Andrew Johnson], October 11, 1865, Bergeron, *Papers of Andrew Johnson,* vol. 9, 225.

54. Jno McClelland to Dear Sir & Friend, October 15, 1865, Bergeron, *Papers of Andrew Johnson,* vol. 9, 243–44.

55. M. Winbourne, Lyle Preston, and others to Prest. Johnson (telegram), October 16, 1865, Andrew Johnson Papers, Manuscripts Division, Library of Congress, Washington, D.C., hereinafter cited as LC-Johnson.

56. R. M. Goodwin to Hon. A. Johnson, October 9, 1865, LC-Johnson.

57. Maclain L. J. DeVillia, October 14, 1865, LC-Johnson.

58. John W. James, Jr., October 14, 1865, LC-Johnson.

59. James Johnson Statement, TSLA-Johnson.

60. John B. Brownlow to My dear Sir, June 3, 1866, John Bell Brownlow Letter, 1866, Special Collections Library, University of Tennessee, Knoxville, Tennessee, hereinafter cited as UT-Brownlow.

61. *Nashville Union,* October 21, 1865; and *Nashville Dispatch,* October 22, 1865.

62. James Johnson Statement, TSLA-Johnson.

63. Mis Martha Ferguson from Champ, October 17, 1865, Frazier International History Museum, Louisville, Kentucky.

64. *Nashville Dispatch,* October 20, 1865; and James Johnson Statement, TSLA-Johnson.

65. *Nashville Dispatch,* October 20, 1865, and October 21, 1865.

66. Ibid., October 21, 1865.

67. Ibid.; and *New York Times,* October 20, 1865.

68. James Johnson Statement, TSLA-Johnson.

69. *Nashville Dispatch,* October 21, 1865; Clyde C. Walton, ed., *Private Smith's Journal: Recollections of the Late War* (Chicago: R. R. Donnelley and Sons, 1963), 228.

70. *Nashville Dispatch,* October 21, 1865; *Louisville Daily Journal* (KY), October 24, 1865; and James Johnson Statement, TSLA-Johnson.

71. *Nashville Dispatch,* October 21, 1865; and Walton, *Private Smith's Journal,* 228-29.

72. History has not recorded any details of the meetinghouse that sat near Ferguson's White County home. It is quite possible, however, that the congregation was Disciples of Christ since that denomination was very popular in the county and region during that era.

73. William Marvel, *Andersonville: The Last Depot* (Chapel Hill: University of North Carolina Press, 1994), 243-47; Heidler and Heidler, eds., *Encyclopedia of the American Civil War,* 2139; and Leonard, *Lincoln's Avengers,* 161-63.

74. Historically, Wirz has been identified as the only Confederate to be executed for war crimes. This work, along with several others, contends that Champ Ferguson qualifies to be listed alongside Wirz. Lonnie Speer argues that a third man, Captain John Beall, who planned to stage a massive prisoner break at Johnson's Island, Ohio, should be included with Ferguson and Wirz.

10. QUIET RESURRECTIONS OF AN UNLIKELY HERO

1. For a variety of these wife and daughter stories, see Sensing, *Champ Ferguson,* 36-37, 131-32, 141; Duke, *History of Morgan's Cavalry,* 182-83; Duke, *Reminiscences,* 124; Linda C. White, "Champ Ferguson: A Legacy of Blood," *Tennessee Folklore Society Bulletin* 44 (June 1978), 68; Anne Klebenow, *200 Years through 200 Stories: A Tennessee Bicentennial Collection* (Knoxville: University of Tennessee Press, 1996), 102; Paul Roy, *Scott County in the Civil War* (Huntsville, TN: Scott County Historical Society, 2001), 365; Seals, *History of White County,* 101; *Echoes From the Foothills* (Nashville: A. L. Young, 1952), 78; William Lynwood Montell, *Don't Go Up Kettle Creek: Verbal Legacy of the Upper Cumberland* (Knoxville: University of Tennessee Press, 1983), 66; E. G. Rogers, *Memorable Historical Accounts of White County and Area* (Collegedale, TN: The College Press, 1972), 53-54; Arthur McDade, "The Civil War: Champ Ferguson, Guerrilla of the Upper Cumberland Plateau," *Tennessee Conservationist* 63:5 (September/October 1997), 12; *The Sparta Expositor,* March 6, 1975; Unidentified Newspaper Clipping, August 16, 1942, Vertical File, Manuscripts Section, Tennessee State Library and Archives, Nashville, Tennessee, hereinafter cited as TSLA-VF; and Price, *Holston Methodism,* 395.

2. J. P. Austin, *The Blue and the Gray: Sketches of a Portion of the Unwritten History of the Great American Civil War* (Atlanta, GA: Franklin Printing and Publishing, 1899), 90.

3. Roy, *Scott County in the Civil War*, 365; White, "Champ Ferguson," 68.

4. Duke, *History of Morgan's Cavalry*, 182–83.

5. Duke, *Reminiscences*, 124.

6. Diary of John Weatherred.

7. *Nashville Dispatch*, October 21, 1865.

8. For the story of Federal soldiers shooting Ferguson's son, see "120 Yankees Died to Pay Champ Ferguson for His Child's Life," unidentified newspaper, August 7, 1932, James Knox Polk Papers, Manuscript Division, Tennessee State Library and Archives, Nashville, Tennessee; Roy, *Scott County in the Civil War*, 365; White, "Champ Ferguson," 68; Seals, *History of White County Tennessee*, 101; Montell, *Don't Go Up Kettle Creek*, 66; Sensing, *Champ Ferguson*, 35; *Confederate Veteran*, vol. 7, no. 10, 442; *Nashville Tennessean*, August 7, 1932, TSLA-VF; Champ Ferguson Information Sheet, Civil War Collection: Confederate and Federal, 1861–1865, Confederate Collection, Manuscripts Section, Tennessee State Library and Archives, Nashville, Tennessee, hereinafter cited as TSLA-CWC; Swiggett, *The Rebel Raider*, 60; and Rogers, *Memorable Historical Accounts of White County and Area*, 53–54.

9. *Confederate Veteran*, vol. 7, no. 10, 442; and Bromfield L. Ridley, *Battles and Sketches of the Army of Tennessee* (Mexico, MO: Missouri Printing and Publishing, 1906), 522.

10. Rogers, *Memorable Historical Accounts of White County and Area*, 53.

11. Austin, *The Blue and the Gray*, 90.

12. Heidler and Heidler, eds., *Encyclopedia of the American Civil War*, 625; and Ezra J. Warner, *Generals in Gray: Lives of the Confederate Commanders* (Baton Rouge: Louisiana State University Press, 1959), 76–77.

13. Duke, *History of Morgan's Cavalry*, 182–83.

14. Duke, *Reminiscences*, 124.

15. High Chief to John D. Hale, April 12, 1868, HSCC-Hale.

16. Seals, *History of White County, Tennessee*, 101.

17. General Joseph Wheeler testimony, August 28, 1865, NARA-Trial.

18. Ibid.

19. Seals, *History of White County, Tennessee*, 101.

20. Sensing, *Champ Ferguson*, 97.

21. Warren I. Titus, *John Fox, Jr.* (New York: Twayne, 1971), 17–19; Arthur Newman Kruger, "The Life and Works of John Fox, Jr." (Ph.D. diss., Louisiana State University and Agricultural and Mechanical College, 1941), 9–19; Harold Everett Green, *Towering Pines: The Life of John Fox, Jr.* (Boston: Meador, 1943), 13–22; and Swiggett, *The Rebel Raider*, 60.

22. John Fox, Jr., *The Little Shepherd of Kingdom Come* (Lexington: University Press of Kentucky, 1987), 206.

23. Ibid., 208.

24. Ibid., 208, 232.

25. Ibid., 233, 247.

26. Ibid., 286–88, 291, 293–94.

27. Allen Barra, "The Education of Little Fraud: How Did a Racist Speechwriter for George Wallace Turn into a 'Cherokee' Sage and Author of a Revered Multicultural Text? The Weird Tale of Asa ('Forrest') Carter," *Salon*, December 20, 2001; John Leland and Marc Peyser, "New

Age Fable From an Old School Bigot? The Murky History of the Best-Selling 'Little Tree,'" *Newsweek,* October 14, 1991, 62; *New York Times,* October 4, 1991; Dana Rubin, "The Real *Education of Little Tree," Texas Monthly* 20, no. 2, February 1992, 79–81, 93–96; Dan T. Carter, *From George Wallace to Newt Gingrich: Race in the Conservative Counterrevolution, 1963–1994* (Baton Rouge: Louisiana State University Press, 1996), 2–4; Dan T. Carter, "Southern History, American Fiction: The Secret Life of Southwestern Novelist Forrest Carter," in Lothar Honninghausen and Valeria Gennaro Lerda, eds., *Rewriting the South: History and Fiction,* Transatlantic Perspectives (Tubingen, GE: A. Francke Verlag, 1993), 286–304; Handbook of Texas Online, s.v., http://www .tsha.utexas.edu/handbook/online/articles/CC/fcaak.html; Amy Kallio Bollman, "Dangerous Eloquence: Hate Speech Tactics in the Discourse of Asa/Forrest Carter From 1954–74" (Ph.D. diss., University of Oklahoma, 2004), 10–11, 38–39; and Glenn T. Eskew, *But for Birmingham: The Local and National Movements in the Civil Rights Struggle* (Chapel Hill: University of North Carolina Press, 1997), 114–18.

28. Ibid. Bedford Forrest Carter's demise came in a way that both Champ Ferguson and Josey Wales could have respected. On June 7, 1979, he was involved in a fistfight in Abilene, Texas, and died after choking on food and blood.

29. Bedford Forrest Carter, *Gone to Texas* (Albuquerque: University of New Mexico Press, 1989), 5–6.

30. Ibid., 9–13.

31. *The Outlaw Josey Wales,* videocassette, prod. Robert Daley, dir. Clint Eastwood, 136 min. (1976; Warner Brothers); and Brian Steel Wills, *Gone With the Glory: The Civil War in Cinema* (Lanham, MD: Rowman & Littlefield, 2006), 74–75.

32. *Commercial Appeal* (Memphis, TN), March 23, 1998.

33. *Nashville Banner,* October 16, 1886.

34. Fentress County *Gazette,* March 4, 1909; and Miles, "I Do Not Want," 89–90.

35. Miles, "I Do Not Want," 90.

36. Unidentified Newspaper Clipping, August 16, 1942, TSLA-VF.

37. Sensing, *Champ Ferguson,* 257.

38. 1870 Census, Population Schedules, White County, Tennessee.

39. 1900 Census, Population Schedules, Montgomery County, Kansas. Martha Ferguson is buried in Elk City, Kansas; and undated newspaper article, Champ Ferguson Collection, Frazier International History Museum, Louisville, Kentucky.

40. *Herald-Citizen* (Cookeville, TN), undated.

BIBLIOGRAPHY

PRIMARY AND CONTEMPORARY SOURCES

Manuscript Collections and Government Documents

Atlanta, Georgia
    Atlanta History Center. Archives Division.
        John M. McCrary Papers
Austin, Texas
    Texas State Library and Archives Commission. Archives and Information
        Services Division.
        Samuel Bell Maxey Papers
Bowling Green, Kentucky
    Western Kentucky University. Kentucky Library and Museum, Manuscripts and
        Folklife Archives.
        Proceedings of the Trial of Champ Ferguson
Chapel Hill, North Carolina
    University of North Carolina, Chapel Hill. Wilson Library, Southern Historical
        Collection.
        George Hovey Cadman Papers
        John Hunt Morgan Papers
        Leroy Moncure Nutt Papers
Cookeville, Tennessee
    Tennessee Technological University. Angelo and Jennette Volpe Library and
        Media Center, Special Collections.
        Vertical File
        W. B. Hyder Recollections
Frankfort, Kentucky
    Kentucky Department for Libraries and Archives. Public Records Division.
        Governor Beriah Magoffin Papers

Kentucky Historical Society. Library.
    Champ Ferguson Biography File
    James Ferguson Biography File
Kentucky Military History Museum. Archives.
    Guerrilla Letters, 1861–1866
Gallatin, Tennessee
    Private Collection of Mr. Jack Masters.
        Wartime Diary of John Weatherred, copy.
Jamestown, Tennessee
    Fentress County Public Library.
        Fentress County, Circuit Court Office Minutes, Volume A, June 1854–
            July 1866.
Keene, New Hampshire
    Historical Society of Cheshire County. Wright Room Research Library.
        J. D. Hale Papers.
Knoxville, Tennessee
    University of Tennessee, Knoxville. Hodges Library, Special Collections Library.
        John Bell Brownlow Letter
        Jonathan D. Hale Collection, 1863–1885
Lexington, Kentucky
    Lexington Theological Seminary. Bosworth Memorial Library, Special
      Collections.
        Papers of Isaac Tipton Reneau
Louisville, Kentucky
    Frazier International History Museum.
        Champ Ferguson letter
        Undated newspaper article
Nashville, Tennessee
    Tennessee State Library and Archives. Manuscripts and Archives Section.
        Civil War Collection: Confederate and Federal, 1861–1865, Confederate
            Collection
        James Knox Polk Papers
        Military Governor Andrew Johnson Papers, 1862–1865
        Stokes and Tubb Papers
        Talbot-Fentress Family Papers
        Vertical File
Washington, D.C.
    Library of Congress. Manuscripts Division.
        Abraham Lincoln Papers
        Andrew Johnson Papers

National Archives and Records Administration. Washington, D.C.

    Compiled Service Records, 8th Tennessee Cavalry Regiment (C.S.A.)

    MIAC Endorsements on Letters, Department of East Tennessee, 1862–
        1864, Chapter 8, Volume 357, War Department Collection of Confed-
        erate States of America Records

    RG 153, Proceedings of the Trial of Champ Ferguson, of the Office of the
        Judge Advocate General (Army), 1792–1981, Court Martial Case Files

    United States Census. 1840, 1850, 1860, 1870, 1880, 1890, 1900.

Books and Articles

Axford, Faye Acton. *"To Lochaber Na Mair": Southerners View the Civil War.* Athens,
    AL: Athens Publishing, 1986.

Bergeron, Paul H., ed. *The Papers of Andrew Johnson.* Vol. 8, May–August 1865. Knox-
    ville: University of Tennessee Press, 1989.

Blankenship, Lela McDowell, ed. *Fiddles in the Cumberlands.* New York: Richard R.
    Smith, 1943.

Brand, Donna. *Cleburne Memorial Cemetery of Johnson County, Texas.* Joshua, TX:
    The Author, 1999.

Brents, J. A. *The Patriots and Guerillas of East Tennessee and Kentucky.* New York: J. A.
    Brents, 1863; reprint, Danville, KY: Kentucky Jayhawker Press, 2001.

Davis, Jefferson. *The Rise and Fall of the Confederate Government.* 2 vols. New York:
    D. Appleton, 1881.

Davis, William C., and Meredith L. Swentor, eds. *Bluegrass Confederate: The Head-
    quarters Diary of Edward O. Guerrant.* Baton Rouge: Louisiana State University
    Press, 1999.

"Dr. Murfree Meets Champ Ferguson." *Rutherford County Historical Society* (Winter
    1973): 15–19.

Duke, Basil W. *A History of Morgan's Cavalry.* Cincinnati, OH: Miami, 1867.

———. *The Civil War Reminiscences of General Basil W. Duke, C.S.A.* New York: Coo-
    per Square Press, 2001.

Duval, John C. *The Adventures of Big-Foot Wallace.* Lincoln: University of Nebraska
    Press, 1966.

Dyer, Frederick H. *A Compendium of the War of the Rebellion.* 3 vols. Des Moines, IA:
    Dyer, 1908.

Fitch, John. *Annals of the Army of the Cumberland.* Mechanicsburg, PA: Stackpole,
    2003.

Freeman, Douglas Southall. *Lee's Dispatches: Unpublished Letters of General Robert E.
    Lee, C.S.A. to Jefferson Davis and the War Department of the Confederate States of
    America.* New York: G. P. Putnam's Sons, 1957.

Goodpasture, Albert V. *Overton County.* Nashville: B. C. Goodpasture, 1954.

Graf, Leroy P., ed. *The Papers of Andrew Johnson.* Vol. 7, 1864–1865. Knoxville: University of Tennessee Press, 1986.

Hale, J. D. *Champ Furguson: The Border Rebel, and Thief, Robber, and Murderer.* Cincinnati, OH: Privately printed, 1864.

———. *Champ Furguson: A Sketch of the War in East Tennessee Detailing Some of the Leading Spirits of the Rebellion.* Cincinnati, OH: Privately printed, 1862.

———. *Sketches of Scenes in the Career of Champ Ferguson and His Lieutenant.* Unknown, 1870.

———. *The Bloody Shirt.* Unknown, 1888.

Hancock, R. R. *Hancock's Diary: or, A History of the Second Tennessee Confederate Cavalry.* Nashville: Brandon Printing, 1887.

Hull, Cordell. *The Memoirs of Cordell Hull.* 2 vols. New York: Macmillan, 1948.

Jillson, Willard Rouse. *The Kentucky Land Grants.* Baltimore, MD: Genealogical Publishing, 1971.

Johnson, Adam Rankin. *The Partisan Rangers of the Confederate States Army.* Louisville, KY: G. G. Fetter, 1904; reprint Austin, TX: State House Press, 1995.

Johnson, Andrew. *The Papers of Andrew Johnson.* Ed. Leroy P. Graf and Ralph W. Haskins. 16 vols. Knoxville: University of Tennessee Press, 1967–2000.

Jones, John J. *A Rebel War Clerk's Diary.* Ed. Earl Schenck Miers. Baton Rouge: Louisiana State University Press, 1993.

Lincoln, Abraham. Abraham Lincoln: Speeches and Writings, 1859–1865. New York: Library of America, 1989.

Mason, F. H. *The Twelfth Ohio Cavalry.* Cleveland, OH: Nevins' Steam Printing House, 1871.

McGlasson, Maude Z. *Jackson County, Tennessee, Bible and Family Records.* Unknown, 1938.

McMurry, Richard M. *An Uncompromising Secessionist: The Civil War of George Knox Miller, Eighth (Wade's) Confederate Cavalry.* Tuscaloosa: University of Alabama Press, 2007.

Mosgrove, George Dallas. *Kentucky Cavaliers in Dixie: Reminiscences of a Confederate Cavalryman.* Jackson, TN: McCowat-Mercer, 1957.

Quisenberry, Anderson Chenault. "The Eleventh Kentucky Cavalry, C.S.A." *Southern Historical Society Papers* 35 (1907): 259–89.

Report of the Adjutant General of the State of Kentucky. Volume I, 1861–1865 (Union). Frankfort: Kentucky Yeoman Office, 1866.

Ridley, Bromfield L. *Battles and Sketches of the Army of Tennessee.* Mexico, MO: Missouri Printing and Publishing, 1906.

Rosenburg, R. B. *"For the Sake of My Country": The Diary of Col. W. W. Ward, 9th Tennessee Cavalry, Morgan's Brigade, C.S.A.* Murfreesboro, TN: Southern Historical Press, 1992.

Ross, Kirby, ed. *Autobiography of Samuel S. Hildebrand.* Fayetteville: University of Arkansas Press, 2005.

Schroeder, Albert W., Jr., ed. "Writings of a Tennessee Unionist." *Tennessee Historical Quarterly* 9 (September 1950): 244–72.

Strickland, W. P., ed. *Autobiography of Peter Cartwright: The Backwoods Preacher.* New York: Carlton and Porter, 1856.

Stringfield, W. W. "The Champ Ferguson Affair." *The Emory and Henry Era* 17:6 (May 1914): 300–302.

Sutherland, Elihu Jasper, ed. *Pioneer Recollections of Southwest Virginia.* Clintwood, VA: H. S. Sutherland, 1984.

Tapp, Hambleton, and James C. Klotter, eds. *The Union, The Civil War, and John W. Tuttle: A Kentucky Captain's Account.* Frankfort: Kentucky Historical Society, 1980.

Tarrant, Eastham. *The Wild Riders of the First Kentucky Cavalry: A History of the Regiment, in the Great War of the Rebellion, 1861–1865.* Lexington, KY: Henry Clay Press, 1969.

Twain, Mark. *The Autobiography of Mark Twain.* New York: HarperPerennial, 1990.

Walton, Clyde C., ed. *Private Smith's Journal: Recollections of the Late War.* Chicago: R. R. Donnelley and Sons, 1963.

The War of the Rebellion: A Compilation of the Official Records of the Union and Confederate Armies. 129 vols. Washington, D.C.: Government Printing Office, 1880–1901.

Williamson, J. C., ed. "The Civil War Diary of John Coffee Williamson," *Tennessee Historical Quarterly* XV (March 1956): 61–74.

Wilson, Thos. L. *Sufferings Endured for a Free Government: A History of the Cruelties and Atrocities of the Rebellion.* Washington, D.C.: The Author, 1864.

Wise, John S. *The End of an Era.* Boston: Houghton, Mifflin, 1899.

Wright, Rev. A. B. *Autobiography of Rev. A. B. Wright.* Cincinnati, OH: Cranston and Curts, 1896.

SECONDARY SOURCES

Books

Abbott, Geoffrey. *The Executioner Always Chops Twice: Ghastly Blunders on the Scaffold.* New York: St. Martin's Press, 2004.

Abrahamson, James L. *The Men of Secession and Civil War, 1859–1861.* Wilmington, DE: Scholarly Resources, 2000.

Alexander, Thomas B. *Thomas A. R. Nelson of East Tennessee.* Nashville: Tennessee Historical Commission, 1956.

Allardice, Bruce S., and Lawrence Lee Hewitt. *Kentuckians in Gray: Confederate Generals and Field Officers of the Bluegrass State.* Lexington: University Press of Kentucky, 2008.

Armstrong, Joan Tracy. *History of Smyth County, Virginia.* 2 vols. Marion, VA: Smyth County Historical and Museum Society, 1986.

Arnow, Harriette Simpson. *Seedtime on the Cumberland.* New York: Macmillan, 1960.

Ash, Stephen V. *Middle Tennessee Society Transformed, 1860–1870: War and Peace in the Upper South.* Baton Rouge: Louisiana State University Press, 1988.

———. "Poor Whites in the Occupied South, 1861–1865." *Journal of Southern History* 57 (February 1991): 39–62.

———. *When the Yankees Came: Conflict and Chaos in the Occupied South, 1861–1865.* Chapel Hill: University of North Carolina Press, 1995.

Asprey, Robert B. *War in the Shadows: The Guerrilla in History.* 2 vols. Garden City, NY: Doubleday, 1975.

Austin, J. P. *The Blue and the Gray: Sketches of a Portion of the Unwritten History of the Great American Civil War.* Atlanta, GA: Franklin Printing and Publishing, 1899.

Baggett, James Alex. *Homegrown Yankees: Tennessee's Union Cavalry in the Civil War.* Baton Rouge: Louisiana State University Press, 2009.

Barber, Allene H., and Joniece M. Nichols. *Ancestors, Family, and Descendants of Champion Ferguson and Rachel Duckett Ferguson.* Plano, TX: A. H. Barber, 1994.

Beard, William E. *Nashville: The Home of History Makers.* Nashville: Civitan Club of Nashville, Tennessee, 1929.

Beckett, Ian F. W. *Modern Insurgencies and Counter-Insurgencies: Guerrillas and Their Opponents since 1750.* Warfare and History. Ed. Jeremy Black. London, UK: Routledge, 2001.

Billings, Dwight B., Gurney Norman, and Katherine Ledford, eds. *Confronting Appalachian Stereotypes: Back Talk from an American Region.* Lexington: University Press of Kentucky, 1999.

Biographical Directory of the American Congress, 1774–1989. Washington, D.C.: Government Printing Office, 1989.

Birdwell, Michael E., and W. Calvin Dickinson. *Rural Life and Culture in the Upper Cumberland.* Lexington: University Press of Kentucky, 2004.

Boatner, Mark M., III. *The Civil War Dictionary.* New York: David McKay, 1959.

Boles, John B. *The Great Revival, 1787–1805.* Lexington: University Press of Kentucky, 1972.

———. *Religion in Antebellum Kentucky.* Lexington: University Press of Kentucky, 1976.

Boles, H. Leo. *Biographical Sketches of Gospel Preachers.* Nashville: Gospel Advocate, 1932.

Bolton, Charles C. *Poor Whites of the Antebellum South: Tenants and Laborers in Central North Carolina and Northeast Mississippi.* Durham, NC: Duke University Press, 1994.

Boyd, Ernest Houston. *Nuggets of Putnam County History.* Vol. 1. N.p., 1985.

Bradley, Michael R. *With Blood and Fire: Life Behind Union Lines in Middle Tennessee, 1863–65.* Shippensburg, PA: Burd Street Press, 2003.

Breen, T. H. *Tobacco Culture: The Mentality of the Great Tidewater Planters on the Eve of Revolution*. Princeton, NJ: Princeton University Press, 1985.

Brown, Dee Alexander. *The Bold Cavaliers: Morgan's 2nd Kentucky Cavalry Raiders*. Philadelphia, PA: J. B. Lippincott, 1959.

Brown, Sterling Spurlock. *History of Woodbury and Cannon County, Tennessee*. Manchester, TN: Doak, 1936.

Burkhardt, George S. *Confederate Rage, Yankee Wrath: No Quarter in the Civil War*. Carbondale: Southern Illinois University Press, 2007.

Bynum, Victoria E. *The Free State of Jones: Mississippi's Longest Civil War*. Chapel Hill: University of North Carolina Press, 2001.

Carlson, Paul H. *"Pecos Bill": A Military Biography of William R. Shafter*. College Station: Texas A&M University Press, 1989.

Carter, Bedford Forrest. *Gone to Texas*. Albuquerque: University of New Mexico Press, 1989.

Carter, Dan T. *From George Wallace to Newt Gingrich: Race in the Conservative Counterrevolution, 1963–1994*. Walter Lynwood Fleming Lectures in Southern History. Baton Rouge: Louisiana State University Press, 1996.

Castel, Albert. *William Clarke Quantrill: His Life and Times*. Columbus, OH: The General's Books, 1992.

Castel, Albert, and Thomas Goodrich. *Bloody Bill Anderson: The Short, Savage Life of a Civil War Guerrilla*. Lawrence: University of Kansas Press, 1998.

Cecil-Fronsman, Bill. *Common Whites: Class and Culture in Antebellum North Carolina*. Lexington: University Press of Kentucky, 1992.

Clark, Thomas D. *Agrarian Kentucky*. The Kentucky Bicentennial Bookshelf. Lexington: University Press of Kentucky, 1977.

———. *A History of Kentucky*. New York: Prentice-Hall, 1937.

Cleaves, Freeman. *Rock of Chickamauga: The Life of General George H. Thomas*. Norman: University of Oklahoma Press, 1948.

Clift, G. Glenn. *Governors of Kentucky, 1792–1942*. Kentucky Sesquicentennial Edition. Cynthiana, KY: Hobson Press, 1942.

Cole, Arthur Charles. *The Whig Party in the South*. Gloucester, MA: Peter Smith, 1962.

Collins, Lewis. *History of Kentucky*. Cincinnati, OH: Lewis Collins, J. A. James, and U. P. James, 1847.

Connelly, Thomas Lawrence. *Army of the Heartland: The Army of Tennessee, 1861–1862*. Baton Rouge: Louisiana State University Press, 1967.

———. *Autumn of Glory: The Army of Tennessee, 1863–1865*. Baton Rouge: Louisiana State University Press, 1971.

Cooling, Benjamin Franklin. *Fort Donelson's Legacy: War and Society in Kentucky and Tennessee, 1862–1863*. Knoxville: University of Tennessee Press, 1997.

Cooper, William J., Jr. *Liberty and Slavery: Southern Politics to 1860*. New York: Knopf, 1983.

Corlew, Robert E. *Tennessee: A Short History*, 2d ed. Knoxville: University of Tennessee Press, 1981.

Coulter, E. Merton. *The Civil War and Readjustment in Kentucky*. Gloucester, MA: Peter Smith, 1966.

Crofts, Daniel W. *Reluctant Confederates: Upper South Unionists in the Secession Crisis*. Chapel Hill: University of North Carolina Press, 1989.

Daniel, Larry J. *Days of Glory: The Army of the Cumberland, 1861–1865*. Baton Rouge: Louisiana State University Press, 2004.

Daniel, Pete. *Lost Revolutions: The South in the 1950s*. Chapel Hill: University of North Carolina Press for the Smithsonian National Museum of American History, 2000.

Davis, William C. *An Honorable Defeat: The Last Days of the Confederate Government*. New York: Harcourt, 2001.

———. *Breckinridge: Statesman, Soldier, Symbol*. Baton Rouge: Louisiana State University Press, 1974.

———. *Look Away: A History of the Confederate States of America*. New York: Free Press, 2002.

DeLozier, Mary Jean. *Putnam County, Tennessee, 1850–1970*. Cookeville, TN: The County, 1979.

Dickenson, W. Calvin, and Larry H. Whiteaker. *Tennessee: State of the Nation.* 2d ed. New York: American Heritage, 1994.

Dictionary of American Biography. New York: Charles Scribner's Sons, 1928–1937.

Dollar, Kent T., Larry H. Whiteaker, and W. Calvin Dickinson, eds. *Sister States, Enemy States: The Civil War in Kentucky and Tennessee*. Lexington: University Press of Kentucky, 2009.

Donald, David Herbert. *Lincoln*. London, UK: Jonathan Cape, 1995.

Drake, Richard B. *A History of Appalachia*. Lexington: University Press of Kentucky, 2001.

DuBose, John Witherspoon. *General Joseph Wheeler and the Army of Tennessee*. New York: Neale, 1912.

Dumond, Dwight Lowell. *The Secession Movement, 1860–1861*. New York: Octagon, 1963.

Dunaway, Wilma A. *Slavery in the American Mountain South*. Studies in Modern Capitalism. Cambridge, UK: Cambridge University Press, 2003.

Duncan, Richard R. *Beleaguered Winchester: A Virginia Community at War, 1861–1865*. Baton Rouge: Louisiana State University Press, 2007.

Durham, Walter T. *Josephus Conn Guild and Rose Mont: Politics and Plantation in Nineteenth Century Tennessee*. Franklin, TN: Hillsboro Press, 2002.

Dyer, John P. *From Shiloh to San Juan: The Life of "Fightin Joe" Wheeler*. Baton Rouge: Louisiana State University Press, 1989.

Echoes from the Foothills. Nashville: A. L. Young, 1952.

Eldridge, Robert L. and Mary Eldridge. *Bicentennial Echoes of the History of Overton County, Tennessee, 1776–1976.* Livingston, TN: Enterprise, 1976.

Engle, Stephen D. *Don Carlos Buell: Most Promising of All.* Chapel Hill: University of North Carolina Press, 1999.

Eskew, Glenn T. *But for Birmingham: The Local and State Movements in the Civil Rights Struggle.* Chapel Hill: University of North Carolina Press, 1997.

Evans, Clement A., Jr. *Confederate Military History.* Atlanta, GA, 1899.

Faragher, John Mack. *Sugar Creek: Life on the Illinois Prairie.* New Haven: Yale University Press, 1986.

Fehrenbach, T. R. *Lone Star: A History of Texas and the Texans.* Toronto, Ontario, Canada: Macmillan, 1968.

Fellman, Michael. *Inside War: The Guerrilla Conflict in Missouri During the American Civil War.* New York: Oxford University Press, 1989.

Fentress County, Tennessee Pictorial History. Vol. 1. Jamestown, TN: Fentress County Historical Society, 1998.

Ferguson, Jack. *Early Times in Clinton County.* 3 vols. Albany, KY: J. Ferguson, 1986–2003.

Fisher, John E. *They Rode with Forrest and Wheeler: A Chronicle of Five Tennessee Brothers' Service in the Confederate Western Cavalry.* Jefferson, NC: McFarland, 1995.

Fisher, Noel C. *War at Every Door: Partisan Politics and Guerrilla Violence in East Tennessee, 1860–1869.* Chapel Hill: University of North Carolina Press, 1997.

Fox, John, Jr. *The Little Shepherd of Kingdom Come.* New York: Charles Scribner's Sons, 1903. Reprint, Lexington: University Press of Kentucky, 1987.

Gienapp, William E. *The Origins of the Republican Party, 1852–1856.* New York: Oxford University Press, 1987.

Glatthaar, Joseph T. *The March to the Sea and Beyond: Sherman's Troops in the Savannah and Carolinas Campaigns.* Baton Rouge: Louisiana State University Press, 1985.

Goodrich, Thomas. *Black Flag: Guerrilla Warfare on the Western Border, 1861–1865.* Bloomington: Indiana University Press, 1995.

Gorin, Betty J. *"Morgan Is Coming!" Confederate Raiders in the Heartland of Kentucky.* Louisville, KY: Harmony House, 2006.

Green, Harold Everett. *Towering Pines: The Life of John Fox, Jr.* Boston: Meador, 1943.

Grimsley, Mark. *The Hard Hand of War: Union Military Policy Toward Southern Civilians, 1861–1865.* Cambridge, UK: Cambridge University Press, 1995.

Groce, W. Todd. *Mountain Rebels: East Tennessee Confederates and the Civil War, 1860–1870.* Knoxville: University of Tennessee Press, 1999.

Guild, George B. *A Brief Narrative of the Fourth Tennessee Cavalry Regiment: Wheeler's Corps, Army of Tennessee.* Nashville: Unknown, 1913.

Hafendorfer, Kenneth A. *Mill Springs: Campaign and Battle of Mill Springs, Kentucky.* Louisville, KY: KH Press, 2001.

Hahn, Steven. *The Roots of Southern Populism: Yeoman Farmers and the Transformation of the Georgia Upcountry, 1850–1890.* New York: Oxford University Press, 1983.

Hall, Alexander Wilford. *The Christian Register: Containing a Statistical Report of the Christian Churches in Europe and America.* Lexington, KY: Lexington Theological Seminary, 1979.

Hall, Stephen, and Jonathan Prude, eds. *The Countryside in the Age of Capitalist Transformation: Essays in the Social History of Rural America.* Chapel Hill: University of North Carolina Press, 1985.

Hallock, Judith Lee. *Braxton Bragg and Confederate Defeat.* Vol. II. Tuscaloosa: University of Alabama Press, 1991.

Harrison, Lowell H., ed. *Kentucky's Governors, 1792–1985.* Lexington: University Press of Kentucky, 1985.

———. *The Civil War in Kentucky.* The Kentucky Bicentennial Bookshelf. Lexington: University Press of Kentucky, 1975.

Haynes, Sam W. *Soldiers of Misfortune: The Somervell and Mier Expeditions.* Austin: University of Texas Press, 1990.

Heidler, David S., and Jeanne T. Heidler, eds. *Encyclopedia of the American Civil War: A Political, Social, and Military History.* Santa Barbara, CA: ABC-CLIO, 2000.

Hess, Earl J. *Banners to the Breeze: The Kentucky Campaign, Corinth, and Stones River.* Lincoln: University of Nebraska Press, 2000.

Hill, Samuel S., ed. *Encyclopedia of Religion in the South.* Macon, GA: Mercer University Press, 1984.

Hinton, Harold B. *Cordell Hull: A Biography.* Garden City, NY: Doubleday, Doran, 1942.

History Committee of the Stoddard Historical Society. *The History of the Town of Stoddard, New Hampshire.* Stoddard, NH: N. P., 1974.

Hogue, Albert R. *History of Fentress County, Tennessee.* Baltimore: Regional, 1975.

———. *Mark Twain's Obedstown and Knobs of Tennessee: A History of Jamestown and Fentress County, Tennessee.* Jamestown, TN: Cumberland Print, 1950.

———. *One Hundred Years in the Cumberland Mountains Along the Continental Line.* McMinnville, TN: Standard Printing, 1933.

Holifield, E. Brooks. *Theology in America: Christian Thought from the Age of the Puritans to the Civil War.* New Haven, CT: Yale University Press, 2003.

Holt, Michael F. *The Political Crisis of the 1850s.* New York: John Wiley and Sons, 1978.

———. *The Rise and Fall of the American Whig Party: Jacksonian Politics and the Onset of the Civil War.* New York: Oxford University Press, 1999.

Honninghausen, Lothar, and Valeria Gennaro Lerda, eds. *Rewriting the South: History and Fiction.* Transatlantic Perspectives. Tubingen, GE: A. Francke Verlag, 1993.

Hopson, Mary. *Siftings from Putnam County, Tennessee: Towns, Communities, People.* Unknown: Diversified Graphics, 1991.

Horton, Louise. *Samuel Bell Maxey: A Biography.* Austin: University of Texas Press, 1974.

Huddleston, Tim. *History of Pickett County, Tennessee.* Collegedale, TN: College Press, 1973.

Inscoe, John C. *Race, War, and Remembrance in the Appalachian South.* Lexington: University Press of Kentucky, 2008.

Inscoe, John C., and Robert C. Kenzer. *Enemies of the Country: New Perspectives on Unionists in the Civil War South.* Athens, GA: University of Georgia Press, 2001.

Joes, Anthony James. *America and Guerrilla Warfare.* Lexington: University Press of Kentucky, 2000.

———. *Resisting Rebellion: The History and Politics of Counterinsurgency.* Lexington: University Press of Kentucky, 2004.

Johannsen, Robert W. *Stephen A. Douglas.* New York: Oxford University Press, 1973.

Johnson, Adam Rankin. *The Partisan Rangers of the Confederate States Army.* Austin, TX: State House Press, 1995.

Johnson, Augusta Phillips. *A Century of Wayne County, Kentucky, 1800–1900.* Louisville, KY: Standard Printing, 1939.

Johnson, Mark W. *That Body of Brave Men: The U.S. Regular Infantry and the Civil War in the West.* New York: Da Capo, 2003.

Jones, Virgil Carrington. *Gray Ghosts and Rebel Raiders: The Daring Exploits of the Confederate Guerillas.* New York: Galahad, 1956.

Jordan, Thomas, and J. P. Pryor. *The Campaigns of Lieut.-Gen. N. B. Forrest and of Forrest's Cavalry.* Dayton, OH: Press of Morningside Bookshop, 1973.

Kent, William B. *A History of Saltville, Virginia.* Johnson City: East Tennessee State College, 1955.

Kirby, Jack Temple. *Media-Made Dixie: The South in the American Imagination.* Baton Rouge: Louisiana State University Press, 1978.

Kirwan, Albert D. *John J. Crittenden: The Struggle for the Union.* Lexington: University Press of Kentucky, 1962.

Klebenow, Anne. *200 Years through 200 Stories: A Tennessee Bicentennial Collection.* Knoxville: University of Tennessee Press, 1996.

Kleber, John E., ed. *The Kentucky Encyclopedia.* Lexington: University Press of Kentucky, 1992.

Kolchin, Peter. *American Slavery, 1619–1877.* New York: Hill and Wang, 1993.

Lamers, William M. *The Edge of Glory: A Biography of General William S. Rosecrans, U.S.A.* Baton Rouge: Louisiana State University Press, 1961.

Lawson, Lewis A. *Wheeler's Last Raid.* Greenwood, FL: Penkevill, 1986.

Leonard, Elizabeth D. *Lincoln's Avengers: Justice, Revenge, and Reunion after the Civil War.* New York: W. W. Norton, 2004.

Lindsley, John Berrien, ed. *The Military Annals of Tennessee: Confederate.* Nashville: J. M. Lindsley, 1886.

Long, E. B. *The Civil War Day By Day: An Almanac, 1861–1865.* New York: Da Capo, 1971.

Mackey, Robert R. *The Uncivil War: Irregular Warfare in the Upper South, 1861–1865.* Norman: University of Oklahoma Press, 2004.

Malone, Dumas, ed. *Dictionary of American Biography.* Vol. 20. New York: Charles Scribner's Sons, 1936.

Marszalek, John F. *Sherman: A Soldier's Passion for Order.* New York: Free Press, 1993.

Martis, Kenneth C. *The Historical Atlas of the Congresses of the Confederate States of America: 1861–1865.* New York: Simon and Schuster, 1994.

———. *The Historical Atlas of United States Congressional Districts, 1789–1983.* New York: Free Press, 1982.

Marvel, William. *Burnside.* Chapel Hill: University of North Carolina Press, 1991.

———. *The Battles for Saltville: Southwest Virginia in the Civil War.* Lynchburg, VA: H. E. Howard, 1992.

Maslowski, Peter. *Treason Must Be Made Odious: Military Occupation and Wartime Reconstruction in Nashville, Tennessee, 1862–65.* KTO Studies in American History. Ed. Harold M. Hyman. Millwood, NY: KTO Press, 1978.

Mason, Robert L. *Cannon County.* Memphis: Memphis State University Press, 1982.

———. *History of Cannon County, Tennessee.* Woodbury, TN: Cannon County Historical Society, 1984.

Matthews, Gary Robert. *Basil Wilson Duke, C.S.A.: The Right Man in the Right Place.* Lexington: University Press of Kentucky, 2005.

Mays, Thomas D. *Cumberland Blood: Champ Ferguson's Civil War.* Carbondale: Southern Illinois University Press, 2008.

———. *The Saltville Massacre.* Abilene, TX: McWhiney Foundation Press, 1998.

McCurry, Stephanie. *Masters of Small Worlds: Yeoman Households, Gender Relations, and the Political Culture of the Antebellum South Carolina Low Country.* New York: Oxford University Press, 1995.

McDonough, James Lee. *War in Kentucky: From Shiloh to Perryville.* Knoxville: University of Tennessee Press, 1994.

McKinney, Francis F. *Education in Violence: The Life of George H. Thomas and the History of the Army of the Cumberland.* Detroit, MI: Wayne State University Press, 1961.

McKnight, Brian D. *Contested Borderland: The Civil War in Appalachian Kentucky and Virginia.* Lexington: University Press of Kentucky, 2006.

McMurry, Richard M. *John Bell Hood and the War for Southern Independence.* Lexington: University Press of Kentucky, 1982.

———. *Two Great Rebel Armies: An Essay in Confederate Military History.* Chapel Hill: University of North Carolina Press, 1989.

McPherson, James M. *Battle Cry of Freedom: The Civil War Era.* New York: Oxford University Press, 1988.

———. *Ordeal by Fire: The Civil War and Reconstruction.* 3d ed. Boston: McGraw-Hill, 1982.

McWhiney, Grady. *Braxton Bragg and Confederate Defeat.* Vol. I. Field Command. New York: Columbia University Press, 1969.

———. *Cracker Culture: Celtic Ways in the Old South.* Tuscaloosa: University of Alabama Press, 1988.

Melton, J. Gordon. *The Encyclopedia of American Religions.* Wilmington, NC: McGrath, 1978.

Miller, Francis Trevelyan, ed. *The Photographic History of the Civil War.* 10 volumes. New York: The Review of Reviews Company, 1912.

Miller, Gregory K. *The Civil War and Campbell County, Tennessee.* Jacksboro, TN: Action, 1992.

Montell, William Lynwood. *Don't Go Up Kettle Creek: Verbal Legacy of the Upper Cumberland.* Knoxville: University of Tennessee Press, 1983.

———. *Killings: Folk Justice in the Upper South.* Lexington: University Press of Kentucky, 1986.

———. *Monroe County History, 1820–1970.* Tompkinsville, KY: Tompkinsville Lions Club, 1970.

Mountcastle, Clay. *Punitive War: Confederate Guerrillas and Union Reprisals.* Lawrence: University Press of Kansas, 2009.

Myers, Barton A. *Executing Daniel Bright: Race, Loyalty, and Guerrilla Violence in a Coastal Carolina Community, 1861–1865.* Baton Rouge: Louisiana State University Press, 2009.

Myers, Raymond E. *The Zollie Tree.* Louisville, KY: Filson Club Press, 1964.

New Handbook of Texas. 6 volumes. Austin: Texas State Historical Association, 1996.

Noe, Kenneth W. *Perryville: This Grand Havoc of Battle.* Lexington: University Press of Kentucky, 2001.

———. *Southwest Virginia's Railroad: Modernization and the Sectional Crisis.* Urbana: University of Illinois Press, 1994.

Noe, Kenneth W., and Shannon H. Wilson, eds. *The Civil War in Appalachia.* Knoxville: University of Tennessee Press, 1997.

Noll, Mark A. *A History of Christianity in the United States and Canada.* Grand Rapids, MI: Eerdmans, 1992.

Norris, Gary Denton. *Champ Ferguson's Scouts.* Albany, KY: Author, 2002.

Nosworthy, Brent. *The Bloody Crucible of Courage: Fighting Methods and Combat Experience of the Civil War.* New York: Carroll and Graf, 2003.

Nunn, W. C., ed. *Ten More Texans in Gray.* Hillsboro, TX: Hill Junior College Press, 1980.

O'Brien, Sean Michael. *Mountain Partisans: Guerrilla Warfare in the Southern Appalachians, 1861–1865*. Westport, CT: Praeger, 1999.

Paludan, Phillip Shaw. *Victims: A True Story of the Civil War*. Knoxville: University of Tennessee Press, 1981.

Palumbo, Frank A. *George Henry Thomas: The Dependable General*. Dayton, OH: Morningside House, 1983.

Parks, Joseph Howard. *General Edmund Kirby Smith, C.S.A.* Baton Rouge: Louisiana State University Press, 1954.

———. *John Bell of Tennessee*. Baton Rouge: Louisiana State University Press, 1950.

Peavyhouse, Will C., and Merle Tipton Peavyhouse. *A History of Buffalo Cove, Fentress County, Tennessee*. Unknown, 1969.

Poole, John Randolph. *Cracker Cavaliers: The 2nd Georgia Cavalry under Wheeler Forrest*. Macon, GA: Mercer University Press, 2000.

Potter, David M. *The Impending Crisis, 1848–1861*, ed. Don E. Fehrenbacher. New York: Harper and Row, 1976.

Price, R. N. *Holston Methodism: From Its Origin to the Present Time*. Nashville: Publishing House of the Methodist Episcopal Church, South, 1913.

Prokopowicz, Gerald J. *All for the Regiment: The Army of the Ohio, 1861–1862*. Ed. Gary W. Gallagher. Chapel Hill: University of North Carolina Press, 2001.

Ramage, James A. *Rebel Raider: The Life of General John Hunt Morgan*. Lexington: University Press of Kentucky, 1986.

Reid, Richard J. *The Rock Riseth: George H. Thomas at Logan's Crossroads*. Central City: Western Kentucky Printing and Office Supply, 1988.

Rennick, Robert M. *Kentucky Place Names*. Lexington: University Press of Kentucky, 1984.

Ridley, Bromfield L. *Battles and Sketches of the Army of Tennessee*. Mexico, MO: Missouri Printing and Publishing, 1906.

Robertson, Jno., ed. *Michigan in the War*. Lansing, MI: W. S. George, 1882.

Rogers, E. G. *Memorable Historical Accounts of White County and Area*. Collegedale, TN: The College Press, 1972.

Rowell, John W. *Yankee Cavalrymen: Through the Civil War with the Ninth Pennsylvania Cavalry*. Knoxville: University of Tennessee Press, 1971.

Rowland, Charles P. *Albert Sidney Johnston: Soldier of Three Republics*. Lexington: University Press of Kentucky, 2001.

Roy, Paul. *Scott County in the Civil War*. Huntsville, TN: Scott County Historical Society, 2001.

Sanderson, Esther Sharp. *County Scott and Its Mountain Folk*. Huntsville, TN: Esther Sharp Sanderson, 1958.

Sarris, Jonathan D. *A Separate Civil War: Communities in Conflict in the Mountain South*. Charlottesville: University of Virginia Press, 2007.

Seals, Monroe. *History of White County, Tennessee.* Spartanburg, SC: The Reprint Company, 1982.

Sensing, Thurman. *Champ Ferguson: Confederate Guerilla.* Nashville: Vanderbilt University Press, 1942.

Sickles, John. *The Legends of Sue Mundy and One Armed Berry: Confederate Guerrillas in Kentucky.* Merrillville, IN: Heritage Press, 1999.

Smith, H. Clay. *Dusty Bits of the Forgotten Past.* Oneida, TN: Scott County Historical Society, 1984–85.

Smith, John David, ed. *Black Soldiers in Blue: African American Troops in the Civil War Era.* Chapel Hill: University of North Carolina Press, 2002.

Smith, John Wesley. *The Mountaineers, or, Bottled Sunshine for Blue Mondays.* Nashville: Publishing House for the Methodist Episcopal Church, South, 1902.

Speed, Thomas. *The Union Cause in Kentucky, 1860–1865.* New York: G. P. Putnam's Sons, 1907.

Speer, Lonnie R. *Portals to Hell: Military Prisons of the Civil War.* Mechanicsburg, PA: Stackpole, 1997.

Stampp, Kenneth M. *The Peculiar Institution: Slavery in the Ante-Bellum South.* New York: Vintage, 1956.

Stiles, T. J. *Jesse James: Last Rebel of the Civil War.* New York: Knopf, 2002.

Strickler, Theodore E., compiler. *When and Where We Met Each Other on Shore and Afloat: Battles, Engagements, Actions, Skirmishes, and Expeditions During the Civil War, 1861–1866.* Washington, D.C.: National Tribune, 1899.

Summers, Lewis Preston. *History of Southwest Virginia, 1746–1786, Washington County, 1777–1870.* Johnson City, TN: Overmountain Press, 1989.

Sutherland, Daniel E. *Guerrillas, Partisans, and Bushwhackers: Revisiting the American Civil War.* Chapel Hill: University of North Carolina Press, 2009.

———. *A Savage Conflict: The Decisive Role of Guerrillas in the American Civil War.* Chapel Hill: University of North Carolina Press, 2009.

Sutherland, Daniel E., ed. *Guerrillas, Unionists, and Violence on the Confederate Home Front.* Fayetteville: University of Arkansas Press, 1999.

Swiggett, Howard. *The Rebel Raider: A Life of John Hunt Morgan.* Indianapolis, IN: Bobbs-Merrill, 1934.

Symonds, Craig L. *Joseph E. Johnston: A Biography.* New York: W. W. Norton, 1992.

———. *Stonewall of the West: Patrick Cleburne and the Civil War.* Lawrence: University Press of Kansas, 1997.

Taylor, Amy Murrell. *The Divided Family in Civil War America.* Chapel Hill: University of North Carolina Press, 2005.

Tennesseans in the Civil War: A Military History of Confederate and Union Units with Available Rosters of Personnel. 2 vols. Nashville: Civil War Centennial Commission, 1964.

Thomas, Benjamin P., and Harold M. Hyman. *Stanton: The Life and Times of Lincoln's Secretary of War.* New York: Knopf, 1962.

Thomas, Emory M. *The Confederate Nation, 1861–1865.* New York: Harper and Row, 1979.

Thomas, Lately. *The First President Johnson: The Three Lives of the Seventeenth President of the United States of America.* New York: William Morrow, 1968.

Thomas, Wilbur. *General George H. Thomas: The Indomitable Warrior.* New York: Exposition Press, 1964.

Titus, Warren I. *John Fox, Jr.* New York: Twayne, 1971.

The Union Army: A History of Military Affairs in the Loyal States, 1861–65. 9 vols. Wilmington, NC: Broadfoot, 1997–98.

Urwin, Gregory J. W., ed. *Black Flag Over Dixie: Racial Atrocities and Reprisals in the Civil War.* Carbondale: Southern Illinois University Press, 2004.

Waller, Altina L. *Feud: Hatfields, McCoys, and Social Change in Appalachia, 1860–1900.* Chapel Hill: University of North Carolina Press, 1988.

Warner, Ezra J. *Generals in Blue: Lives of the Union Commanders.* Baton Rouge: Louisiana State University Press, 1964.

———. *Generals in Gray: Lives of the Confederate Commanders.* Baton Rouge: Louisiana State University Press, 1959.

Waugh, John C. *The Class of 1846: From West Point to Appomattox: Stonewall Jackson, George McClellan, and Their Brothers.* New York: Warner, 1994.

Welcher, Frank J. *The Union Army, 1861–1865.* 2 vols. *The Western Theater.* Bloomington: Indiana University Press, 1993.

Wells, J. W. *History of Cumberland County.* Louisville, KY: Standard Printing, 1947.

West, Carroll Van. *The Tennessee Encyclopedia of History and Culture.* Nashville: Rutledge Hill Press, 1998.

West, William Garrett. *Barton Warren Stone: Early American Advocate of Christian Unity.* Nashville: The Disciples of Christ Historical Society, 1954.

Whiteaker, Larry H., and W. Calvin Dickenson, eds. *Tennessee in American History.* Needham, MA: Ginn, 1989.

Whiteaker, Larry H., W. Calvin Dickenson, Leo McGee, and Homer Kemp, eds. *Lend an Ear: Heritage of the Tennessee Upper Cumberland.* Lanham, MD: University Press of America, 1983.

Whitsitt, William H. *Origin of the Disciples of Christ (Campbellites).* New York: A. C. Armstrong and Son, 1888.

Wiley, Bell Irvin. *The Plain People of the Confederacy.* Gloucester, MA: Peter Smith, 1971.

Williams, David. *A People's History of the Civil War: Struggles for the Meaning of Freedom.* New York: New Press, 2005.

Williams, John Alexander. *Appalachia: A History.* Chapel Hill: University of North Carolina Press, 2002.

Wills, Brian Steel. *A Battle from the Start: The Life of Nathan Bedford Forrest.* New York: HarperPerennial, 1992.

———. *Gone With the Glory: The Civil War in Cinema.* Lanham, MD: Rowman & Littlefield, 2006.

———. *The War Hits Home: The Civil War in Southeastern Virginia.* A Nation Divided: New Studies in Civil War History. Ed. James I. Robertson, Jr. Charlottesville: University Press of Virginia, 2001.

Wilson, Goodridge. *Smyth County History and Traditions.* Centennial Celebration of Smyth County, Virginia, 1932.

Winik, Jay. *April 1865: The Month That Saved America.* New York: HarperCollins, 2001.

Winston, Robert W. *Andrew Johnson: Plebeian and Patriot.* New York: Barnes and Noble, 1969.

Wise, John S. *The End of an Era.* Boston: Houghton, Mifflin, 1899.

Wittenberg, Eric J. *The Battle of Monroe's Crossroads and the Civil War's Final Campaign.* New York: Savas Beatie, 2006.

Woodworth, Steven E. *Jefferson Davis and His Generals: The Failure of Confederate Command in the West.* Modern War Studies. Ed. Theodore A. Wilson. Lawrence: University Press of Kansas, 1990.

Wooster, Ralph A. *Lone Star Generals in Gray.* Austin, TX: Eakin, 2000.

Wright, Marcus J. *Texas in the War, 1861–1865.* Compiled by Harold B. Simpson. Hillsboro, TX: Hill Junior College Press, 1965.

Articles and Chapters

Ash, Stephen V. "A Community at War: Montgomery County, 1861–65." *Tennessee Historical Quarterly* 36 (1977): 30–43.

———. "Sharks in an Angry Sea: Civilian Resistance and Guerrilla Warfare in Occupied Middle Tennessee, 1862–1865." *Tennessee Historical Quarterly* 45 (1986): 217–29.

Bailey, Fred A. "The Poor, Plain Folk, and Planters: A Social Analysis of Middle Tennessee Respondents to the Civil War Veterans' Questionnaires." *West Tennessee Historical Society Papers* 36 (October 1982): 5–24.

Barra, Allen. "The Education of Little Fraud: How Did a Racist Speechwriter for George Wallace Turn into a 'Cherokee' Sage and Author of a Revered Multicultural Text? The Weird Tale of Asa ('Forrest') Carter." *Salon,* 20 December 2001.

Carter, Dan T. "Southern History, American Fiction: The Secret Life of Southwestern Novelist Forrest Carter." In Lothar Honninghausen and Valeria Gennaro Lerda, eds., *Rewriting the South: History and Fiction.* Tubingen, GE: A. Francke Verlag, 1993, 286–304.

Colgin, James H., ed. "The Life Story of Brig. Gen. Felix Robertson." *Texana* (1970): 154–82.

Copeland, James E. "Where Were the Kentucky Unionists and Secessionists?" *Register of the Kentucky Historical Society* 71 (1973): 344–63.

Dalton, C. David. "Zollicoffer, Crittenden, and the Mill Springs Campaign: Some Persistent Questions." *Filson Club History Quarterly* 60 (October 1986): 463–71.

Daniel, W. Harrison. "Protestant Clergy and Union Sentiment in the Confederacy." *Tennessee Historical Quarterly* 23 (1965): 284–90.

Davis, William C. "The Massacre at Saltville." *Civil War Times Illustrated* (February 1971): 4–11, 43–48.

De Falaise, Louis. "General Stephen Gano Burbridge's Command in Kentucky." *Register of the Kentucky Historical Society* 69 (April 1971): 101–127.

Deimling, Paula. "Family Stories of the Civil War." *Kentucky Living* (August 2006): 32–38; 44–45.

DeLozier, Mary Jean. "The Civil War and Its Aftermath in Putnam County." *Tennessee Historical Quarterly* 38 (Winter 1979): 436–61.

Doran, Paul E. "The Legend and History of a Man Who Was Feared and Hated." *Kentucky Explorer* (October 2002): 48–50.

Dues, Michael T. "The Pro-Secessionist Governor of Kentucky: Beriah Magoffin's Credibility Gap." *Register of the Kentucky Historical Society* 67 (1969): 221–31.

Dyer, Brainerd. "The Treatment of Colored Union Troops by the Confederates, 1861–1865." *Journal of Negro History* 20 (July 1935): 273–86.

Gildrie, Richard P. "Guerrilla Warfare in the Lower Cumberland River Valley, 1862–1865." *Tennessee Historical Quarterly* 49 (1990): 161–76.

Harrison, Lowell H. "General Basil W. Duke, C.S.A." *Filson Club History Quarterly* 54:1 (January 1980): 5–36.

———. "Governor Magoffin and the Secession Crisis." *Register of the Kentucky Historical Society* 72 (1974): 91–110.

"Irregular Warfare, 1861–1865." *North & South.* Volume 11, Number 3 (June 2009): 17–29.

Jones, William S. "The Civil War in Van Buren County, 1861–1865." *Tennessee Historical Quarterly* 67 (Spring 2008): 56–64.

Leland, John, and Marc Peyser. "New Age Fable from an Old School Bigot? The Murky History of the Best-Selling 'Little Tree.'" *Newsweek,* October 14, 1991.

Lucas, Scott J. "'Indignities, Wrongs, and Outrages': Military and Guerrilla Incursions on Kentucky's Civil War Home Front." *Filson Club History Quarterly* 73 (1999): 355–76.

Lufkin, Charles L. "Secession and Coercion in Tennessee, the Spring of 1861." *Tennessee Historical Quarterly* 50 (1991): 98–109.

Marvel, William. "The Battle of Saltville: Massacre or Myth?" *Blue and Gray Magazine* 8:6 (August 1991): 11–19, 46–60.

McDade, Arthur. "The Civil War: Champ Ferguson, Guerrilla of the Upper Cumberland Plateau." *Tennessee Conservationist* 63:5 (September/October 1997): 12–16.

McKnight, Brian D. "The Winnowing of Saltville: Remembering a Civil War Atrocity." *Journal for the Liberal Arts and Sciences* 14 (Fall 2009): 34–51.

Noe, Kenneth W. "Who Were the Bushwhackers? Age, Class, Kin, and Western Virginia's Confederate Guerrillas, 1861–1862." *Civil War History* 49: 1 (2003): 5–31.

Pearson, Alden B., Jr. "A Middle-Class, Border-State Family During the Civil War." *Civil War History* 22 (December 1976): 318–36.

Pritchard, James M. "Champion of the Union: George D. Prentice and the Secession Crisis in Kentucky." *Cincinnati Historical Society Bulletin* 39 (1981): 113–25.

Quisenberry, Anderson Chenault. "The Eleventh Kentucky Cavalry, C.S.A." *Southern Historical Society Papers* 35 (1907): 259–89.

Rachal, William M. E. "Salt the South Could Not Savor." *Virginia Cavalcade* (Autumn 1953): 4–7.

Rubin, Dana. "The Real *Education* of *Little Tree*." *Texas Monthly* 20, no. 2, February 1992. 79–81, 93–96.

Sanderson, Esther Sharp. "Guerrilla Warfare During the Civil War." *Tennessee Valley Historical Review* 1 (1972): 25–33.

Schroeder, Albert W., Jr. "Writings of a Tennessee Unionist." *Tennessee Historical Quarterly* 9 (September 1950): 244–72.

Siburt, James T. "Colonel John M. Hughs: Brigade Commander and Confederate Guerrilla." *Tennessee Historical Quarterly* 51:2 (Summer 1992): 87–95.

Smith, Madelon, ed. "The John Hale Family of Smith County During the Civil War." *Smith County Historical and Genealogical Society Newsletter* 6:4 (Fall 1994): 143–47.

Smith, Troy D. "Don't You Beg, and Don't You Dodge." *Civil War Times Illustrated* (December 2001): 40–46, 72–73.

Sutherland, Daniel E. "Guerrilla Warfare, Democracy, and the Fate of the Confederacy." *Journal of Southern History* 68 (May 2002): 259–92.

Tapp, Hambleton. "Incidents in the Life of Frank Wolford, Colonel of the First Kentucky Union Cavalry." *Filson Club History Quarterly* 10 (April 1936): 82–100.

Turner, Wallace B. "The Secession Movement in Kentucky." *Register of the Kentucky Historical Society* 66 (1968): 259–78.

Valentine, L. L. "Sue Mundy of Kentucky." *Register of the Kentucky Historical Society* 62 (July 1964): 175–205.

———. "Sue Mundy of Kentucky, Part II." *Register of the Kentucky Historical Society* 62 (October 1964): 278–306.

White, Linda C. "Champ Ferguson: A Legacy of Blood." *Tennessee Folklore Society Bulletin* 44 (June 1978): 66–70.

Theses and Dissertations

Bollman, Amy Kallio. "Dangerous Eloquence: Hate Speech Tactics in the Discourse of Asa/Forrest Carter from 1954–74." Ph.D. diss., University of Oklahoma, 2004.

Daniel, John S., Jr. "Special Warfare in Middle Tennessee and Surrounding Areas, 1861–62." M.A. thesis, University of Tennessee, 1971.

Dudney, Betty Jane. "Civil War in White County, Tennessee, 1861–1865." M.A. thesis, Tennessee Technological University, 1985.

Finck, James W. "Cling to the Olive Branch While Holding to the Sword: Kentucky's Struggle for Armed Neutrality, 1860–1861." Ph.D. diss., University of Arkansas, 2008.

Gossett, Larry D. "The Keepers and the Kept: The First Hundred Years of the Tennessee State Prison System, 1830–1930." Volume 1. Ph.D. diss., Louisiana State University and Agricultural and Mechanical College, 1992.

Kruger, Arthur Newman. "The Life and Works of John Fox, Jr." Ph.D. diss., Louisiana State University and Agricultural and Mechanical College, 1941.

Mays, Thomas Davidson. "Cumberland Blood: Champ Ferguson's Civil War." Ph.D. diss., Texas Christian University, 1996.

Miles, Nicholas Stayton. "I Do Not Want to Be Buried in Such Soil as This: The Life and Times of Confederate Guerrilla Champ Ferguson." M.A. thesis, University of Kentucky, 2005.

Williams, Gladys Inez. "The Life of Horace Maynard." M.A. thesis, University of Tennessee, 1931.

Newspapers and Magazines

Abingdon Virginian
Clinton County (KY) *News*
Columbus (OH) *Gazette*
Commercial Appeal (Memphis, TN)
Confederate Veteran
Daily Dispatch (Richmond, VA)
Daily Nashville Union
Daily Picayune (New Orleans, LA)
Daily Press (Nashville, TN)
Daily Press and Times (Nashville, TN)
Fentress (TN) *Courier*
Frank Leslie's Illustrated Newspaper
Harper's Weekly
Herald-Citizen (Cookeville, TN)

Louisville (KY) Courier Journal
Louisville (KY) Daily Democrat
Louisville (KY) Journal
Lynchburg Daily Virginian
Memphis Daily Appeal
Nashville Banner
Nashville Daily Press
Nashville Daily Press and Times
Nashville Dispatch
Nashville Patriot
Nashville Tennessean
Nashville Union
Nashville Union and American
New York Herald
The New York Times
Pickett County (TN) Press
Richmond (VA) Daily Dispatch
Richmond (VA) Enquirer
Republican Banner (Nashville, TN)
Sparta (TN) Expositor
Weekly Press and Times (Nashville, TN)

Other

The Outlaw Josey Wales. Videocassette. Produced by Robert Daley, directed by Clint
    Eastwood. 136 min. Warner Brothers, 1976.

INDEX